PLANNING THE CAPITALIST CITY

PLANNING
THE CAPITALIST CITY

The Colonial Era to the 1920s

—— BY ——

RICHARD E. FOGLESONG

PRINCETON UNIVERSITY PRESS
PRINCETON, NEW JERSEY

Published by Princeton University Press, 41 William Street,
Princeton, New Jersey 08540
In the United Kingdom: Princeton University Press, Guildford, Surrey

Library of Congress Cataloging in Publication Data will be
found on the last printed page of this book

ISBN 0-691-07705-3

This book has been composed in Linotron Trump

Clothbound editions of Princeton University Press books
are printed on acid-free paper, and binding materials are
chosen for strength and durability

Printed in the United States of America by Princeton University Press
Princeton, New Jersey

For Carol, Eric, and Christopher

CONTENTS

PREFACE

THIS IS A WORK of political science, urban history, political economy, and planning theory. Although I hope its contribution will be recognized in each of these areas, it will no doubt disappoint some for failing to take account of all the analytical concerns and relevant literature in each of these fields; that is perhaps the risk of attempting to write a multidisciplinary work. More than that, I have attempted to write a theoretically informed history, one that goes beyond the marshaling of facts around narrow historical questions or theorizing without historical reference. The danger of course is that neither side will appreciate my attempt to synthesize theory and history. I ask only to be judged in terms of my own project, and in comparison with what others have written about urban planning.

Inasmuch as this book originated as a dissertation, my debts of gratitude are numerous. Among my professors in political science at the University of Chicago, I wish to thank Paul Peterson for stimulating my interest in urban planning at an early stage; Adam Przeworski for nurturing my interest in marxist structuralism; David Greenstone and Lloyd Rudolph for their thoughtful commentary on my dissertation; and especially Ira Katznelson, who helped me explore the connection between theory and history, and who has continued to provide support and good example.

Various friends and colleagues read and commented on my manuscript along the way, some with more involvement than others, but all with insight. Jan Dizard, at Amherst College, was especially helpful. I also wish to thank, from the same institution, Barry O'Connell, Hugh Hawkins, and Robert Gross. I also benefited from the comments of John Brigham, of the University of Massachusetts, and from those of my colleagues in history at Rollins College, Jack Lane and Gary Williams.

In a special category, I must express my debt to Amy Bridges, who made many thoughtful contributions and helped me to understand my own argument in the course of her several readings of the manuscript. I am also grateful to my reviewer, Thomas Bender, for his insightful comments on the manuscript; to my Princeton University Press editor, Gail Ullman, for her unfailing support and wisdom; and to my copyeditor, Janet Stern, for her thoroughness and skill in uncovering inconsistencies and improving my prose. There are also those former colleagues who might have sought to assist me and did not do so; this book is probably better because they did not try.

I owe thanks as well to a number of institutions. The University of Chicago introduced me to the world of ideas and gave me a sense of intellectual purpose. Amherst College provided partial support for a sabbatical leave and excellent library resources, including the invaluable reference assistance of Floyd Merritt, Margaret Groesbeck, and Michael Kasper. Rollins College has provided supportive colleagues, as well as assistance in preparing my manuscript. I also benefited from access to the Harvard Graduate School of Design Library. And in the present political climate, it is appropriate to mention that, were it not for the Ford Foundation and the federal student loan program, I might not have advanced to the stage of writing this book.

In addition to those named above, a number of friends and professional colleagues provided moral support and good cheer during the course of this long project. I wish to thank in particular David Abraham, Amrita Basu, Midge Bowser, Deborah Gewertz, Jim Greer, Richard Kronick, Carol Nackenoff, Mark Petracca, Judson Starr, Mike Underhill, Joel Wolfe, and, in her own category, B. L. Retriever. Expert typing (or, more accurately, word processing) was provided by Dianne Kaplan, Lurline Dowell, and Sandra Davis, who showed more dedication to this project than I had a right to expect in the course of my almost endless revision and editing of the text. If word processing saved my time, it did not so clearly save theirs. In addition, Jim Warden of the Rollins College Computer Center assisted me numerous times in gaining computer access to my files, for which I am thankful.

Finally, I wish to express my gratitude to my parents; to my wife, Carol, for her love and understanding; and to my sons, Eric and Christopher, who had less quality time with their father because of this project, but who nevertheless made it possible for me to escape from time to time and be a child with them. Yet this is very much my book, and I alone am responsible for any errors or shortcomings.

PLANNING THE CAPITALIST CITY

Things economic and social move by their own momentum and the ensuing situations compel individuals and groups to behave in certain ways whatever they may wish to do—not indeed by destroying their freedom of choice but by shaping the choosing mentalities and by narrowing the list of possibilities from which to choose.

JOSEPH A. SCHUMPETER
Capitalism, Socialism and Democracy

It may be ruled out that immediate economic crises of themselves produce fundamental historical events; they can simply create a terrain more favourable to the dissemination of certain modes of thought, and certain ways of posing and resolving questions involving the entire subsequent development of national life.

ANTONIO GRAMSCI
Selections from the Prison Notebooks

ONE

The Problem of Planning

In 1909, the first national conference on city planning was held in Washington, D.C., bringing together the disparate groups and individuals working in this embryonic field of urban reform. At this gathering and at the conferences that followed, these early planners complained that the process of city building was being determined by real estate speculation rather than by public policies based on the long-term interests of the community. They objected to this excessive reliance on the market system on the grounds that it stymied the development of collective facilities of general benefit to the community, and that it allowed private developers to ride roughshod over the interests of the public, as reflected in the sordid housing, chaotic street systems, and drab urban environments of the day. Although there was general agreement that some form of government intervention was necessary to correct these abuses, there was a lack of consensus on what form that intervention should take.

These concerns were best expressed by Frederick Law Olmsted, Jr. As the son of the famous co-designer of New York City's Central Park, Olmsted was a successor to the tradition of park planning and civic adornment, a tradition whose financial and political support had come from downtown merchants and the well-to-do. Yet Olmsted was no apologist for the market system. In his opening speech at the 1910 planning conference, he pinned the blame for the city's problems—poor housing, inadequate sanitation, narrow and crowded streets, and the dearth of parks and open space—on the policy of laissez-faire in matters of land use and housing. The task of city planning was encumbered, he said, by a "pious, stand-pat attitude" that population congestion was "self-limiting": it was assumed that a "natural equilibrium" would be achieved in which the advantages of urban living would be offset by the misery of town life and the increasing death rate in the city. Yet, echoing the view of early socialists, Olmsted proclaimed that "mankind will not be content with such an attitude after the imagination has grasped the larger possibility of control."[1]

[1] Olmsted, Jr., "Introductory Address on City Planning," pp. 16-17.

Nor did Olmsted believe that the evils of urban life should be attacked separately. In order to control the destiny of cities, it would be necessary to untangle the "complex interwoven web of cause and effect" producing those evils. "As intelligent human beings," he said, "we cannot fail to pluck at the web and try as best we can to untangle it, and begin to ask, each one of us in his own corner, 'Will my cutting away of old threads and my building up of new, burden or help my brother who is working at some other tangle in his part of the field?' "[2]

With these words, Frederick Olmsted, Jr., set forth the agenda of this first generation of American city planners. That there was fairly wide agreement on this agenda is significant in light of the many differences among these early planners. Representing professions as diverse as architecture, engineering, and social work, they were motivated by different substantive concerns, ranging from housing and tenement reform, to park planning and civic adornment, to rationalizing the system of land use and transportation. And these concerns corresponded with the interests of different social groups: housing reform benefited workers and their employers, park planning and civic adornment were a boon to downtown property holders, and a more efficient system of land use and transportation was a concern principally of commercial and manufacturing groups. However, in spite of these differences, there was a generally shared view that the practice of laissez-faire in matters of housing and land use was not only a cause of the burgeoning problems of the city, but also a hindrance to their solution. Furthermore, there was general agreement that the control of urban development could not be left solely to the market system. Part of the agenda, therefore, was to promote restrictions on the market and thus widen the scope of government action. Yet these early planners also recognized that some new form of coordination, operating under the aegis of the state, was necessary to guide urban development toward the achievement of conscious objectives that would be of general benefit to the community. Thus, the problem was not just the market; some new form of government decision making was also necessary. These planners were searching for a directive system, a method of decision making—a system they called "planning" without knowing precisely what they meant by the term—that was different from the existing method of government policy formulation.

[2] Ibid., p. 18.

Planning the Capitalist City shows how this loose assemblage of groups and individuals sought to define this directive system, give it a substantive purpose, and move toward its creation. Starting with the colonial era of planning, and focusing particularly on the period from 1860 to the 1920s, this study will illustrate that American urban planning developed in two senses: as a form of state intervention and as a particular method of policy formulation. It will examine the origins of urban planning, how it came to be organized as it did, and how its development has been shaped by and reflects features of American capitalist democracy. Attention also will be given to the role of planners and planning advocates in the development of planning, as we examine who these people were, whose interests they represented, and how their efforts contributed to the maintenance of the existing political economy.

The objective of this analysis is not only to explain and understand but also to criticize. While seeking to explain and understand the development of urban planning and the role of planners and planning advocates in that historical process, this book also maintains a critical outlook on the course of development of planning and the aims and activities of planners. The framework for understanding and criticism is adopted from marxist theories of state and society. I refer in particular to recent marxist analyses of the "state," especially the work of Nicos Poulantzas and Claus Offe, and to the developing marxist urban literature, notably the work of Manuel Castells and David Harvey.[3] This book is therefore written from a specific point of view, which will be described more fully in due course. The task is both to use this Marxian point of view to try to elucidate the meaning and importance of the role of planning and planners and, conversely, to discover what the early planning experience in the United States teaches about the adequacy of this theoretical approach.

Corresponding with these objectives, the argument of the book proceeds on two levels, one macro-theoretical, the other more concrete and historical. The first seeks to show that the development of urban planning cannot be understood either in its own

---

[3] On the subject of the "state," see, e.g., Poulantzas, *Political Power and Social Classes*; Offe, "The Theory of the Capitalist State and the Problem of Policy Formation," pp. 125-44; and also Offe's "Structural Problems of the Capitalist State," pp. 31-57. On the subject of urban conflict and urban planning, the most important book-length works in the marxist literature are Harvey, *Social Justice and the City*, and Castells, *The Urban Question*.

5

terms, that is, in terms of the progressive development of the "planning idea," or in terms of the pluralist-liberal paradigm used by most political scientists who have written about planning. Rather, urban planning and urban planners are best understood in terms of the structures and contradictions of American capitalist democracy; or to say much the same, they are best seen through the lens of marxist theories of state and society. At a second level, the argument of the book concerns the relationship between planners, class interests, and the state.[4] The key questions here are how and whether the interests of capital are incorporated into planning policy and what role planners play in that process. It will be argued that although urban planning has indeed had a pro-capitalist bias, the planning idea came from neither businessmen themselves nor from members of the apparatus of the state, but from new actors on the political scene—from persons who came to be called "planners"—and that these planners served to identify, organize, and legitimate the interests of capital in the sphere of urban development. To complicate but also enrich the analysis, it will be argued that these planners possessed a significant degree of autonomy from capital.

ENGAGEMENTS

This study relates to a number of currents of analysis and debate. One of the most important is the ongoing debate in policy and academic circles in the United States over what role the state should play in a capitalist economy and society, and what role it does play currently and why. These questions have become more timely in light of recent efforts to formulate an "industrial policy" for the United States; legislative proposals in this area raise the issue of national economic planning in a serious way for the first time since the 1930s. More analytically, these proposals raise the issue of the relationship of planning to both capitalism and democracy. On the relationship between capitalism and state intervention (which for many is synonymous with planning), there is in the United States a widely held view, reflected in and galvanized by the election of Ronald Reagan, that the growth of the modern state is the work of anti-capitalist or otherwise misguided politicians, aided by labor unionists, civil rights organizations, and other rep-

[4] The term *state* will be used throughout to refer to the total orbit of government at all levels, except when the meaning "state government" (referring to one of the fifty states) is clearly indicated by the context.

resentatives of the disadvantaged.[5] Indeed, the history of urban planning reveals that urban planning did develop, at least initially, in response to criticism of the market system as a method for guiding urban development. It should not be inferred from this, however, that urban planning was anti-capitalist in either its origins or its effects. While the demand for urban planning arose in response to forces that were endogenous to capitalism, planning interventions served to shape the process of urban development and to mitigate the effects of the market system in ways that contributed to the maintenance of the capitalist system. Moreover, the early city planning movement—actually a confluence of the housing reform, park planning, and City Beautiful movements—was hardly a lower-class movement. As will be shown, members of the business community were in the forefront in demanding a larger government role in guiding urban development.

This analysis is also relevant to understanding the relationship between planning and democracy, the subject of much debate and misunderstanding. Complicating the debate over this relationship has been the failure to distinguish adequately between planning as state intervention and planning as a method of policy formulation. Consequently, the participants in this debate have often spoken past one another. The idea of decision making by intellectual problem solving (or what Charles Lindblom calls "synoptic planning"), which involves identifying overarching goals and selecting the policy means that most efficiently correspond with those goals, has been criticized for being inconsistent with the notion of democracy, since it substitutes expertise for participation.[6] Friedrich Hayek, writing in 1944, argued that the urge to plan carried with

---

[5] Indicative of this viewpoint is the statement of Ronald Reagan's Secretary of Interior, James Watt: "[For government] to tell people how to manage their own land—that's despicable in America." To lionize capitalism as Watt does, while attributing government intervention to forces external to capitalism, is to fail to understand the capitalist system. The quotation is from "James Watt's Land Rush," p. 30.

[6] The classic critique of the "tyranny" of government planning is, of course, Hayek, The Road to Serfdom, especially chaps. 5-6. A less bombastic statement of the anti-planning position can be found in the early work of Charles Lindblom; see "The Science of Muddling Through," pp. 79-88; The Intelligence of Democracy; and Lindblom and Braybrooke, A Strategy of Decision. In Politics and Markets, Lindblom modifies his view of planning, accepting the need for some form of national economic planning as a condition for securing democracy (see p. 168 and chaps. 12-14 and 23-25). The term "synoptic planning" is developed by Lindblom in the same volume (chap. 23).

it a logic favoring reliance on expertise and technically correct decision making, which he believed was subversive of both liberty and democracy.[7] Yet in the early planning movement, urban planning was seen as an expansion of the scope of local democracy inasmuch as it opened urban development to public control. Typifying this view, planning historians Theodora and Henry Hubbard referred in a 1929 text to the "great democratic experiment in city planning."[8] Here, they presented planning as a form of state intervention, since city planning entailed an expansion of the government role in urban development—as reflected in the establishment of housing standards, coherent street systems, land use zoning, and attempts to promote "civic beauty." Yet, if this expansion of the scope of government limited or otherwise mitigated the effects of the market system, it seldom provided for greater popular control of urban development. In Roy Lubove's apt phrase, it was more often a case of the "discipline of the expert" replacing the discipline of the market.[9] Thus, whether planning is or can be made democratic depends on the method of decision making involved, as well as on the type and extent of state intervention. While this important conceptual distinction and the tension between these two essences of planning are discussed later in this chapter, it is important to note at this point that the separation of American urban planning from institutions of popular control is not an inevitable concomitant of planning, but rather the result of efforts by economically dominant groups to institutionalize their control of planning.

As we consider these issues, we should recognize that the history of urban planning is not separate from that of other forms of state planning. In the United States, as in most other advanced industrialized societies, urban planning was the first form of state planning. As such, it served as the foundation, the source of training and experience, and the model of the planning process for broader planning efforts, including the movement for national economic and social planning. The interest in national planning grew out of the experience in urban planning, when, during the depression of the 1930s, a group of urban and regional planners and reform-minded social scientists, led by Charles Merriam, became aware that the problems of cities were national in origin and scope

[7] Hayek, chaps. 4-5.
[8] Hubbard and Hubbard, *Our Cities To-Day and To-Morrow*, p. 5.
[9] "The Roots of Urban Planning," p. 327.

and required nationally administered solutions. This recognition led to the formation of Franklin Roosevelt's National Resources Planning Board (NRPB).[10] In the history of urban planning, therefore, we have an opportunity to examine the development of the planning apparatus of the modern state.

The present study is relatively unique because it focuses on the early history of urban planning. This early period was "formative" in the sense that the ideas, practices, and routines worked out then have had a lasting effect upon the development of planning. Thus, an analysis of this period will enable us to understand the origins of urban planning and how it came to be organized as it did. By contrast, most contemporary analyses of planning have centered on the post–World War II era, a period in which the basic form and procedures of planning already were established.[11]

This study is also unique in its theoretical point of departure. Planning histories written by persons within the field of planning have typically adopted a historical idealist point of view, presenting the history of planning as the progressive development of the "planning idea."[12] Such histories have made little allowance for the ways in which material forces and even social history have

[10] For the contribution of the NRPB to the creation of a national planning apparatus, as well as the role of municipal reformers and reform-minded social scientists in that process, see Karl, *Charles E. Merriam and the Study of Politics*; Merriam, "The National Resources Planning Board; A Chapter in the American Planning Experience," pp. 1075-88; and Fox, *Better City Government*.

[11] Noteworthy examples are Meyerson and Banfield, *Politics, Planning and the Public Interest*, which examines the conflict surrounding public housing in Chicago between 1949 and 1951; Altshuler, *The City Planning Process*, which focuses on four planning controversies in Minneapolis and St. Paul between 1959 and 1960; and Rabinovitz, *City Politics and Planning*, which is based upon case studies of planning decisions in six New Jersey cities in the 1950s and 1960s.

[12] This is true of the two basic histories of American urban planning, Reps, *The Making of Urban America*, and Scott, *American City Planning Since 1890*. The latter is a semiofficial history, written in commemoration of the fiftieth anniversary of the American Institute of Planners. These two texts are rich in detail and prodigiously researched, but they fail to relate the history of planning to the organizing structure of American society and, consequently, do not provide an adequate explanation for the development of planning.

More recent contributions to this historical literature include the two collections of essays edited by Krueckeberg, *Introduction to Planning History in the United States* and *The American Planner*, and, on the comparison between planning in Europe and North America, Sutcliffe, *Toward the Planned City: Germany, Britain, the United States and France, 1780-1914*, and Sutcliffe, ed., *The Rise of Modern Urban Planning, 1800-1914*.

shaped the development of planning.[13] Most political scientists who have written about planning have viewed the subject from the perspective of the pluralist-liberal paradigm. While their analyses have demonstrated accurately how the local planning process is insulated from popular participation, they have failed to explain the patterned bias that produces this result.[14] Moreover, in viewing planners as a discrete set of actors motivated by their own professional and occupational interests, pluralists have failed to observe how planners serve to organize and legitimate the interests of other groups in society.[15] In contrast to the pluralist analysis of planning is the recent marxist literature on urban conflict and urban planning.[16] Focusing on the development of planning in Europe, particularly in France, where planning is far more extensive than in the United States, this literature has been strongly influenced by developments in European marxism, especially marxist structuralism. Indicative of this literature's perspective is the characterization of planning offered by Manuel Castells and François Godard, based on their study of urban planning in France's Dunkirk region. They write that urban planning serves two very important purposes in a class society: on the political plane, it

[13] A variation on this theme is Boyer, *Dreaming the Rational City: The Myth of American City Planning*, which uses the ideas of Michel Foucault to examine the "genealogy" of efforts to control urban population and urban development. In self-consciously excluding the issues of who planners were, what their relationship was to those who hired them, and what she terms "functional causal explanation," Boyer ends up making a fetish of the study of "planning discourse," implicitly attributing to discourse the same self-actualizing properties that more mainstream historians have imputed to the planning idea. What is frustratingly unclear in her impressively researched history is who is "doing" the discourse, what their aims are, and how their efforts correspond with the organizing structure of society.

[14] See, e.g., Banfield and Wilson, *City Politics*, p. 192; Allensworth, *The Political Realities of Urban Planning*, pp. 58-59, 119; and Altshuler, p. 323 and chap. 7.

[15] The pluralist literature recognizes that planners play a coordinative role in the process of coalition building, but it fails to take account of which groups benefit from this role, even though pluralist case studies suggest that businessmen have been the principal beneficiaries. See, e.g., Altshuler, *City Planning Process*, p. 310 n.6 and chap. 4; Meyerson and Banfield, *Politics*, p. 191; and Rabinovitz, *City Politics and Planning*, p. 149.

[16] In addition to the texts by Harvey and Castells, there are three important collections of essays in this literature: Pickvance, ed., *Urban Sociology: Critical Essays*; Harloe, ed., *Captive Cities: Studies of the Political Economy of Cities and Regions*; and Dear and Scott, eds., *Urbanization and Urban Planning in Capitalist Society*. In addition, the *International Journal of Urban and Regional Research* was founded in 1977 to bring together contributors to this literature from Europe and the United States.

serves as an instrument for mediating and organizing dominant class interests in relation to the pressures and claims of dominated classes; on the ideological plane, it rationalizes and legitimates this ensemble of dominant class interests in terms of an ideological conception of the common good.[17] Without embracing this characterization as a description of urban planning in the United States, the present study adopts the broad perspective, problem-focus, and much of the conceptual apparatus of the marxist urban literature. This book is therefore relatively unusual in its application of a Marxian analysis, moreover an analysis derived largely from the European intellectual and historical experience, to the study of urban planning in the United States. As persons familiar with this literature will recognize, the present study is also somewhat unusual because it relies upon concrete historical research, whereas the marxist urban literature (like much of the marxist literature on the state) suffers from an abstract formalism that has deterred empirical research.

PLANNING AND THE STATE

Our questions are never innocent, as Louis Althusser reminds us.[18] Our theoretical presuppositions influence not only the questions we ask, but also the way we define our subject of investigation. Therefore, it is appropriate to begin this study by briefly indicating the view of the state and of state-society relations that underlies my analytical approach.

My inquiry begins with the concept of the state provided by the late Nicos Poulantzas, a leading contributor to the French school of marxist structuralism. I begin with Poulantzas's view of the state not because it is accepted as an adequate theorization of the state—indeed, the opposite evaluation is made—but because, in my own view, our understanding of the liberal-capitalist state cannot proceed until it resolves questions left unanswered by Poulantzas, and because the questions raised by Poulantzas are particularly relevant to planning and planners.

In his book *Political Power and Social Classes*, Poulantzas conceptualizes the state as the "factor of cohesion" of the social formulation.[19] In essence, he conceives of the state as a "giant planner" (my term): it soothes, or represses, outbreaks of social

---

[17] *Monopoville*, pp. 451-52.
[18] "From 'Capital' to Marx's Philosophy," pp. 11-69.
[19] P. 44.

11

discontent and synchronizes the various elements of society so as to ensure the continued functioning of the underlying capitalist structure. This view of the state contrasts with the pluralist-liberal view, in which the state is seen as a more or less neutral umpire that protects the rules of the game and ratifies the outcome of a group bargaining process that is regarded as basically fair.[20] It also contrasts with the "instrumentalist" view of the state that is associated with the work of Ralph Miliband.[21] In the instrumentalist view, the state is regarded as an instrument of the capitalist class: it is held that the state is directly dominated by capitalists or their agents, and that this domination is the source of the state's capitalist bias.

The value of Poulantzas's concept of the state is that it recognizes, as the instrumentalist concept does not, that capitalists more often act as individuals than as members of a class. Poulantzas argues that capitalists are prevented by their practice as capitalists, that is, by their market-imposed competition with other capitalists, from comprehending and acting on their collective class interests.[22] It should be noted that this view of capital as an internally divided class is a central element of the pluralist-liberal view of the state; as the statement goes, it is something pluralists have "always known." Yet the pluralist-liberal school fails to recognize the systematic way in which state actions serve to maintain and reproduce a distinctly *capitalist* society, despite capitalists' inability to act on their collective interests. This is the problem that Poulantzas poses, and it is because we are unable to satisfactorily resolve this problem that we are prevented from going beyond his analysis of the state.

For many of those on the left, Poulantzas's concept of the state is a fairly accurate assessment of the way things *appear* in a capitalist-democracy such as the United States. That is, everything happens *as if* the state were the "factor of cohesion" or "giant planner" for the social formation, a unitary actor bent on the reproduction of the capitalist system.[23] However, Poulantzas solves

[20] The best statement of the pluralist-liberal view is found in the two works by Dahl, *Who Governs?* and *Preface to Democratic Theory.*

[21] See Miliband, *The State in Capitalist Society.*

[22] Poulantzas, *Political Power,* pp. 275-89.

[23] This concept corresponds with E. P. Thompson's characterization of marxist structuralism as the "illusion of this epoch," in his remarkable essay "The Poverty of Theory"; see his *The Poverty of Theory and Other Essays,* p. 71. To say, as I have done, that Poulantzas's concept of the state is based on the way things appear, is to

the problem of how-the-state-serves-capital-despite-capital's-ignorance-of-its-own-needs by merely transposing the problem to another level. He denies capital the capacity to organize its own rule but presumes the state can somehow, as if by magic, do that which capital cannot. The result is an anthropomorphic view of the state in which the state is accorded a consciousness and will all its own.[24] As Fred Block has pointed out, Poulantzas's formulation is inadequate for understanding the source of either the bias of the state or the state's capitalist rationality.[25]

Two questions raised by Poulantzas's globalist concept of the state are pertinent to this inquiry. The first concerns capital's interpersonal linkage with the state; that is, we need to know how the state comes to represent the interests of capital if the capitalist class is ignorant of its own needs. The answer presented here— overstated—is that "planners do it": if capitalists are prevented by their practice as capitalists from being cognizant of and articulating their collective class interests, there are others whose practice as "planners," "intellectuals," and the like enables them to perform this function for capital.[26] To use the scientific language of positivist political science, this study will hypothesize that urban planners have served to identify, organize, and legitimate the interests of capital in the field of urban development, providing a critical mediating link between capital and the state. It is not argued, however, that planners have served as the agents or self-conscious representatives of capital. Typically, they have acted for what could be called "their own reasons." Moreover, in the period we are examining, planners were generally semi-independent of direct capitalist control, and this independence was a condition of their ability to serve the broader class interests of capital.

The second question raised by Poulantzas's view of the state as a "giant planner" concerns the state's internal processes or methods of policy formulation. As Claus Offe, a German sociologist

---

turn his analysis on its head. In his view, everything happens "as if" the state were the "representative of the people nation" (*Political Power*, p. 135), whereas, in fact (he writes), the state is the "factor of cohesion" of a society predicated upon the existence of classes (p. 44).

[24] On this point, see the excellent critique of Poulantzas by Amy Bridges, "Nicos Poulantzas and the Marxist Theory of the State," pp. 161-90.

[25] "The Ruling Class Does Not Rule: Notes on the Marxist Theory of the State," pp. 6-28.

[26] This analysis derives in part from Antonio Gramsci's thoughts on the role of "intellectuals" in raising class interests to the "political level"; see Gramsci, *Selections from the Prison Notebooks*, pp. 3-24, 175-84.

and leading contributor to marxist state theory, has asked: "What structural features put the state in a position to formulate and express class-interests more appropriately and circumspectly than can be done by the members of the [capitalist] class, namely the isolated and competing individual accumulating units?"[27] If it is acknowledged, as it has been by Poulantzas and others, that the capitalist class is incapable of organizing its own rule, why assume that the state *can* perform this function for capital, let alone that it *would* do so? What structural features of the state put it in touch with the reproductive requirements of the capitalist system? The same questions can be raised with respect to the problem of "market breakdown" and the asserted ability of the state to take over from the market system the steering and control functions of society.[28] Following Offe, then, we are led to ask: What are the internal processes of the state, the methods of policy production, that enable the state to produce decisions corresponding with the requirements for maintaining the capitalist system? Among state theorists, Offe has done the most to illuminate the internal structure of the state. A brief excursion into his analysis is therefore appropriate.

Offe argues that there is a disjunction between the demands placed upon the state and what the internal structure of the state will permit it to do.[29] Assuming a formally democratic state, he argues that the state in capitalist society is confronted with two potentially contradictory objectives: facilitating capital accumulation, the sine qua non of the capitalist system, and maintaining democratic legitimacy, necessitated by the formally democratic character of the state. In Offe's view, however, there exists no method of policy formulation that would enable the state to satisfactorily carry out these objectives in the long term. In developing this argument, he distinguishes three methods of policy formulation: (1) policy making by bureaucracy (corresponding with the structures and processes in Weber's ideal-type), (2) policy making by interest group conflict or political bargaining, and (3) policy making by purposive rationality or planning. Of these, planning, in his view, is best able to produce decisions facilitating capital ac-

[27] "Structural Problems of the Capitalist State," p. 37.

[28] Scholars as diverse as Theodore Lowi and Jurgen Habermas have related the growth of the capitalist state to the problem of "market breakdown" and the take-over by the state of the directive functions of society. See Lowi, *The End of Liberalism*, chaps. 1-3, and Habermas, *Legitimation Crisis*, chap. 4.

[29] The following discussion is drawn from Offe's "The Theory of the Capitalist State and the Problem of Policy Formation."

cumulation. This is because the criterion for decision making in planning is the production of a designated end result, such as a particular pattern of land use or a specified level of economic growth. This focus of planning on the achievement of end states in the external environment is what distinguishes planning from decision making by bureaucracy (the application of fixed rules to cases) or by interest group competition, neither of which are as adaptable to the purposes of capital. Bureaucracy in the classic sense is described by Offe as too procedure-bound, whereas decision making by interest group competition invites the representation of too many points of view, producing chaos and disorder and impeding rational decision making. In addition, planning is better able to anticipate threats to the system.

On the negative side, the planning method of decision making, because of its technocratic nature, does not correspond with beliefs about how "democratic" decisions should be made; thus, it has a low capacity for maintaining the state's democratic legitimacy. Nevertheless, Offe sees a gravitation toward planning as the preferred method of policy formulation, based on the theory that facilitating capital accumulation takes priority over maintaining democratic legitimacy in the definition of "good" public policy. Yet Offe argues that planning can never be successful in simultaneously facilitating capital accumulation and maintaining democratic legitimacy. In part, this is because effective planning requires effective control over individual accumulating units—something that is denied capitalist state planners. But more fundamentally it is because the requirements for maintaining capital accumulation are objectively in conflict with the requirements for maintaining democratic legitimacy. In Offe's view (and my own), there exists no internal structure of the state, no set of policy formulation processes, that would enable the state to smoothly carry out these contradictory objectives in the long term. Thus, planning in a democratic-capitalist society is seen as both necessary and impossible.

Offe's analysis makes possible a twofold conception of planning, one that helps to bridge the gap between pluralist and marxist analyses of planning. In the pluralist literature, planning is seen as a particular *method of policy formulation* characterized by the attempt to coordinate means-ends relations toward the achievement of some core objective(s).[30] Planning, then, is conceived of as

[30] The most precise statement of this view can be found in Meyerson and Ban-

instrumental rationality institutionalized. This concept is the product of the pluralist focus on the democratic character of "polyarchy," that is, the "pluralist bargaining order"—terms that refer to an idealized system of political decision making, based upon plural sources of power, plural points of access to government, and plural, competing interests.[31] Given this problem-focus, pluralists have defined planning in opposition to decision making by pluralist bargaining and have sought to show how "politics" (meaning the pluralist bargaining process) triumphs over attempts to impose "planning" decision making; they interpret this triumph as evidence of the superiority of "politics"/pluralist bargaining as a method of social choice.[32]

In contrast to the pluralist view, the marxist literature typically has conceptualized planning as a *form of state intervention* in the market. While pluralist writers have contrasted planning with decision making by pluralist bargaining, the marxist approach has related planning to the workings of the market. Like the pluralist concept, the marxist view of planning as state intervention grows out of a particular theoretical problem-focus. In marxist analyses of planning, the growth of planning (meaning the growth of state intervention) typically is taken to indicate the shortcomings of the market as a means of organizing the reproduction of capitalism. As we shall see shortly, the position is not simply that the market fails to meet the needs of workers or particular sectors of capital, but that it fails to meet the needs of the capitalist system as a whole, and that capitalists therefore turn to the state to regulate, replace, or mitigate the effects of the market system. This analysis is part of contemporary marxism's larger effort to understand how the state forestalls, without (it is presumed) eradicating, the inter-

---

field, *Politics, Planning and the Public Interest;* see Banfield's "Supplement: Note on Conceptual Scheme," pp. 303-30.

[31] "Polyarchy" is the term used by Robert Dahl, and later by other pluralist writers, to refer to a quasi-democratic political system characterized by multiple, competing sources of political influence; see, *Preface to Democratic Theory,* p. 84. "Pluralist bargaining order" is used, e.g., by Greenstone and Peterson, *Race and Authority in Urban Politics,* pp. 102-4.

[32] For example, Meyerson and Banfield sympathetically observe in their study of public housing controversies in Chicago that "the principle of decision by political power [takes] precedence over decision by planning" (Meyerson and Banfield, *Politics,* p. 239). A complementary analysis that nicely demonstrates the association between the greater "success" of urban planning in contemporary London and the more centralized, unfragmented, and less pluralistic politics of that city is Elkin, *Politics and Land Use Planning: The London Experience.*

nal contradictions that Marx thought would lead to the self-destruction of capitalism.

As already noted, Offe's analysis provides a bridge between pluralist and marxist analyses of planning. He makes it possible to relate questions concerning the choice and "adequacy" of a method of policy formulation (questions that pluralists have addressed) to the question of the capacity of the democratic-capitalist state to cope with the contradictory demands placed upon it (a question raised by marxists). He offers an explanation for why no method of policy formulation can be entirely successful in meeting these demands over the long run, while recognizing that some methods of policy formulation are able to meet these demands better than others. His analysis thus helps to explain the conflict surrounding the choice or establishment of a particular method of policy formulation, as well as why there might be a gravitation from one method to another. Accordingly, both concepts of planning will be applied here. We will examine how urban planning has developed both as a form of state intervention, in response to dissatisfaction with the system of laissez-faire in land use and housing, *and* as a particular method of policy formulation, in response to efforts to determine the use and control of state interventions in this field.

This section began with Nicos Poulantzas's globalist concept of the state ("the state as planner") and raised two questions. First, how does the state come to represent the interests of capital if capitalists are incapable of organizing their own rule and if the state is "relatively autonomous" from the capitalist class? This question led us to consider the role of planners in identifying, organizing, and legitimating the interests of capital. Second, what are the internal processes of the state that enable it to produce decisions corresponding with the collective interests of capital? It is this second question that prompts our interest in planning as a method of policy formulation. Yet state theory is applicable to only part of the problem of understanding the development of urban planning. It speaks to the questions of how and whether the interests of capital get translated into state policy, but it does not address the questions of where demands for urban planning come from, what their history is, and how and whether these demands correspond to the logic of development and structural contradictions of capitalism. The latter questions must also be addressed if we are to account for the development of planning and demonstrate the adequacy of the theoretical approach adopted here. To consider these questions, we will turn to the marxist urban literature, in which we find an attempt to theorize about the connection between urban conflict, urban planning, and the reproduction processes of capitalist society.

CAPITALISM AND URBAN PLANNING

David Harvey, a marxist social geographer, has conceptualized urban conflict as a conflict over the "production, management and use of the urban built environment."[33] Harvey uses the term "built environment" to refer to physical entities such as roads, sewerage networks, parks, railroads, and even private housing—facilities that are collectively owned and consumed or, as in the case of private housing, whose character and location the state somehow regulates. These facilities have become politicized because of conflict arising out of their being collectively owned and controlled, or because of the "externality effects" of private decisions concerning their use. At issue is how these facilities should be produced—whether by the market or by the state; how they should be managed and by whom; and how they should be used—for what purposes and by what groups, races, classes, and neighborhoods. Following Harvey, the development of American urban planning is seen as the result of conflict over the production, management, and use of the urban built environment.

The development of this analysis depends on the recognition that capitalism both engenders and constrains demands for state intervention in the sphere of the built environment. First, let us consider some of the theories about how capitalism engenders demands for state intervention.

Sources of Urban Planning

Within the developing marxist urban literature, there has been a variety of attempts to link urban conflict and demands for state intervention to the reproduction processes of capitalist society. Manuel Castells, one of the leading contributors to this literature, emphasizes the connection between state intervention in the urban development process and the reproduction of *labor power*.[34]

[33] "Labor, Capital, and Class Struggle around the Built Environment in Advanced Capitalist Societies," p. 265.

[34] *Urban Question*, pp. 460-61. Castells modifies his view in his most recent book, *The City and the Grass Roots*, which appeared after the manuscript of *Planning the Capitalist City* was essentially written. In this new book, Castells seeks

The market system cannot meet the consumption needs of the working class in a manner capable of maintaining capitalism; this, according to Castells, is the reason for the growth of urban planning/state intervention. To the extent that the state picks up the slack and assumes this responsibility, there occurs a transformation of the process of consumption, from individualized consumption through the market to collective consumption organized through the state. This transformation entails not only an expansion of the role of the state, which is seen in the growth of urban planning, but also a politicization of the process of consumption, which Castells sees as the underlying dynamic of urban political conflict.

By contrast, David Harvey and Edmond Preteceille, writing separately, have related state intervention in the urban development process to the inability of the market system to provide for the maintenance and reproduction of the immobilized fixed capital investments (for example, bridges, streets, sewerage networks) used by capital as *means of production*.[35] The task of the state is not only to maintain this system of what Preteceille calls "urban use values," but also to provide for the coordination of these use values in space (for example, the coordination of streets and sewer lines), creating what he terms "new, complex use values."[36] François Lamarche, on the other hand, relates the whole question of urban planning/state intervention to the *sphere of circulation* and the need to produce a "spatial organization which facilitates the

---

to avoid the "excesses of theoretical formalism" that marked some of his earlier work (p. xvii). He also asserts that "although class relationships and class struggle are fundamental in understanding the process of urban conflict, they are by no means the only or even the primary source of urban social change" (p. xviii). My critical evaluation of Castells's earlier work is still valid and useful, however, since it lends emphasis and historical reference to some of Castells's own criticisms. Furthermore, my criticisms apply to a literature and a theoretical orientation that encompasses, as I point out, more than Castells's work.

[35] Harvey, "The Political Economy of Urbanization in Advanced Capitalist Societies: The Case of the United States," p. 120; Preteceille, "Urban Planning: The Contradictions of Capitalist Urbanization," pp. 69-76. For Harvey, the need for a built environment usable as a collective means of production is only one of the connections between urban planning and capitalist development; he also recognizes the need for facilities for collective consumption to aid in reproducing labor power. See, e.g., his "Labor, Capital, and Class Struggle around the Built Environment."

[36] Preteceille, "Urban Planning," p. 70.

circulation of capital, commodities, information, etc."[37] In his view, capitalism has spawned a particular fraction of capital, termed "property capital," which is responsible for organizing the system of land use and transportation; and urban planning is a complement and extension of the aims and activities of this group. In addition, and somewhat distinct from these attempts to relate urban planning to the reproduction processes of capitalist society, David Harvey has linked urban planning to the problems arising from the *uniqueness of land as a commodity*, namely the fact that land is not transportable, which makes it inherently subject to externality effects.[38]

The theories discussed above demonstrate that there are a variety of problems arising from relying upon the market system to guide urban development. At various times, urban planning in the United States has been a response to each of these problems. Yet these problems have different histories. They have not had equal importance throughout the development of planning. Moreover, no one of these problems is sufficient in itself to explain the logic of development of planning.

Constraints on Urban Planning

If the problems noted above arise from the workings of the market system, so that capitalism can be said to engender demands for state intervention in response to these problems, the capitalist system also constrains the realization of these demands. The operative constraint in this connection is the institution of private property. It is here that we confront what might be termed the central contradiction of capitalist urbanization: the contradiction between the social character of land and its private ownership and control. Government intervention in the ordering of the urban built environment—that is, urban planning—can be seen as a response to the social character of land, to the fact that land is not only a commodity but also a collective good, a social resource as well as a private right. Indeed, as the marxist urban literature has sought to demonstrate, the treatment of land as a commodity fails to satisfy the social needs of either capital or labor. Capital has an objective interest in socializing the control of land in order to (1) cope with the externality problems that arise from treating land as

[37] "Property Development and the Economic Foundations of the Urban Question," p. 86.

[38] *Social Justice*, chap. 5.

a commodity; (2) create the housing and other environmental amenities needed for the reproduction of labor power; (3) provide for the building and maintenance of the bridges, harbors, streets, and transit systems used by capital as means of production; and (4) ensure the spatial coordination of these infrastructural facilities for purposes of efficient circulation. Yet the institution of private property stands as an impediment to attempts to socialize the control of land in order to meet these collective needs. Thus, if urban planning is necessary for the reproduction of the capitalist system on the one hand, it threatens and is restrained by the capitalist system on the other; and it is in terms of this Janus-faced reality that the development of urban planning is to be understood. Moreover, this contradiction is intrinsic to capitalist urbanization, for the impulse to socialize the control of urban space is as much a part of capitalism as is the institution of private property. Each serves to limit the extension of the other; thus, they are in "contradiction."[39] This contradiction, which will be termed the "property contradiction," is one of two that have structured the development of planning.[40]

THE "PROPERTY CONTRADICTION"   To state that capitalist urbanization has an inherent contradiction is *not* to predict the inevitable downfall of capitalism (although it does indicate a weak-

[39] For a discussion of this use of *contradiction*, see Godelier, "Structure and Contradiction in *Capital*," pp. 334-68.

[40] Cf. Michael Dear and Allen Scott's assertion that the "urban question" (a reference to the work of Castells) is "structured around the particular and indissoluble geographical and land-contingent phenomena that come into existence as capitalist social and property relations are mediated through the dimension of urban space." They also write that planning is "a historically-specific and socially-necessary response to the self-disorganizing tendencies of *privatized* capitalist social and property relations as these appear in urban space" ("Towards a Framework for Analysis," pp. 6, 13). Cf. also, in the same volume, Shoukry Roweis's statement that "[u]rban planning in capitalism, both in theory and in practice, and whether intentionally or unknowingly, attempts to grapple with a basic question: how can *collective action* (pertinent to decisions concerning the social utilization of urban land) be made possible under capitalism?" ("Urban Planning in Early and Late Capitalist Societies," p. 170). These two theoretical analyses relate urban planning under capitalism to the problem of "collective control"—how to organize socially necessary forms of collective consumption and control in a society based upon private ownership—but they do not take note of the contradiction between capital's need for collective control in its own interest and the limits imposed by the internal structure of the *state*. This is the issue raised by Offe and which I capture in my concept of the "capitalist-democracy contradiction" (below).

ness in the capitalist structure of society that oppositional forces could conceivably exploit). Rather, it is assumed that capitalism is capable of coping with this contradiction, within limits, but that it is a continuing source of tension and a breeding ground of political conflict. Thus, our analytical interest is in the institutional means that have been devised to keep this contradiction from exploding into a system-threatening crisis. In recognizing this contradiction, we therefore gain a better appreciation of the importance, both politically and theoretically, of the institutional forms that urban planning has adopted over the course of its development, and of how (and how well) those institutional forms have responded to the contradiction between the social character of land and its private ownership and control.

In addition, recognizing this contradiction helps us to understand the patterns of alliance formation around planning issues, as well as the role of planners in mediating between different groups and group interests. For if the effort to socialize the control of urban land is potentially a threat to the whole concept of property rights, it is directly and immediately a threat to only one particular group of capitalists, those whom Lamarche terms "property capital." Included are persons who, in his words, "plan and equip space"—real estate developers, construction contractors, and directors of mortgage lending institutions.[41] It is this fraction of capital, in particular, that can be expected to oppose efforts to displace or diminish private control of urban development. Other capitalists, in contrast, may seek an expanded government role in the planning and equipping of space. For example, manufacturing capital may want government to provide worker housing and to coordinate the development of public and private infrastructure (such as utilities and railroads), and commercial capitalists may desire government restrictions on the location of manufacturing establishments. Likewise, non-owner groups have an interest in state intervention that will provide for or regulate the quality of worker housing, build parks, and improve worker transportation, for example. It is possible, therefore, for certain fractions of capital to align with non-owner groups in support of planning interventions that restrict the "rights" of urban land holders. The property contradiction thus manifests itself in the pattern of alliances around planning issues by creating, in intra-capitalist class conflict, the possibility of alliances between property owning and

[41] "Property Development," pp. 90-93.

non–property owning groups and allowing planners to function as mediators in organizing these compromises. Inasmuch as the property contradiction is inherent in the capitalist structure of society, existing independent of consciousness and will, recognition of this contradiction enables us to link the politics of planning to the structural ordering of capitalist society.

THE "CAPITALIST-DEMOCRACY CONTRADICTION" The other contradiction affecting the development of urban planning is the "capitalist-democracy contradiction." If the property contradiction is internal to capitalism in that it arises out of the logic of capitalist development, the capitalist-democracy contradiction is an external one, originating between the political and economic structures of a democratic-capitalist society. More specifically, it is a contradiction between the need to socialize the control of urban space to create the conditions for the maintenance of capitalism, on the one hand, and the danger to capital of truly socializing, that is, democratizing, the control of urban land, on the other. For if the market system cannot produce a built environment that is capable of maintaining capitalism, reliance on the institutions of the state, especially a formally democratic state, creates a whole new set of problems, not the least of which is that the more populous body of non-owners will gain too much control over landed property. This latter contradiction is conditioned on the existence of the property contradiction, in that it arises from efforts to use government action to balance or hold in check the property contradiction. Once government intervention is accepted, questions about how to organize that intervention arise: What goals should be pursued? How should they be formulated and by whom? This pattern of the capitalist-democracy contradiction following on the heels of the property contradiction is apparent in the actual history of planning, for while both contradictions have been in evidence throughout the history of planning in America, the property contradiction was a more salient generator of conflict in the earlier, pre-1940 period, while the capitalist-democracy contradiction—manifested in the controversy over how to organize the planning process—has been a more potent source of conflict in the history of planning after World War II. It should also be emphasized that the capitalist-democracy contradiction is conditioned on the formally democratic character of the state, out of which the danger of government control of urban development arises. Were it not for the majority-rule criterion and formal equality promised by the state, turning to government to control urban development would not pose such a problem for capital.

Consideration of the capitalist-democracy contradiction leads us back to Offe's analysis of the internal structure of the state. Following Offe's analysis, it can be postulated that capitalism is caught in a search for a decision process, a method of policy making that can produce decisions corresponding with capital's political and economic interests. Politically, this decision process must be capable of insulating state decision making from the claims and considerations of the numerically larger class of noncapitalists, a task made difficult by the formally democratic character of the state. Economically, this decision process must be capable of producing decisions that facilitate the accumulation and circulation of capital (for example, promoting the reproduction of labor power and coordinating the building up of local infrastructure), a function that the market fails to perform and that capitalists do not (necessarily) know how to perform. Both of these problems are captured in the concept of the capitalist-democracy contradiction. The question we are led to ask, then, is: In what ways has the development of urban planning—viewed here as a method of policy formulation—served to suppress or hold in balance the capitalist-democracy contradiction in a manner conducive to the reproduction of capitalism?

BEFORE TURNING to the historical analysis of planning, a brief summary is in order. A consideration of Nicos Poulantzas's globalist concept of the state raised two questions: first, in what ways have planners served to mediate the relationship between capital and the state, overcoming capital's failure to comprehend and act upon its class needs? and second, how does the development of urban planning as a method of policy formulation correspond with the interests of capital? In addition, we looked to the marxist literature on urban politics and planning to discover how that literature might help us to understand, or at least theorize about, how capitalism engenders and constrains demands for urban planning. That analysis led us to posit the existence of two structural contradictions, which, it was hypothesized, have influenced the course of development of urban planning and in terms of which that development must be understood. The first of these was termed "the property contradiction," described as a contradiction between the social character of land and its private ownership and control. The second (arising from efforts to cope with the first) is the "capitalist-democracy contradiction": the contradiction between the need to socialize the control of urban space in order to create the conditions necessary to maintain capitalism, and the danger to capital of truly socializing, that is, democratizing, the control of urban land. The analytical interest in both these contradictions is in understanding the structural origins of conflict observed around planning issues and discovering what institutional means have been devised to keep these contradictions in check. Employing the questions and concepts derived from this analysis, we are now prepared to examine, in the following chapters, the early history of American urban planning.

Chapter 2 deals with colonial town planning, since the history of efforts to consciously guide the development of American cities begins with the "town planting" of this era. Yet the history of city planning is discontinuous; many if not all of the community-serving features of colonial town planning were vitiated by the speculative mania that gripped American cities during the rapid urbanization and industrialization of the last two thirds of the nineteenth century. By going back to the colonial era, we have an opportunity to compare the problems of urban development as they confronted town builders in a largely pre-capitalist era, before the emergence of extensive urban land speculation, with the situation in the mid- to late 1800s, once speculation in urban real estate became rampant. In more theoretical terms, studying this period enables us to trace the historical development of the property contradiction.

One of the earliest efforts to respond to the contradiction between the social character of land and its private ownership and control was the nineteenth-century housing reform movement. Chapter 3 shows how housing reformers like Lawrence Veiller, Robert de Forest, and Jacob Riis sought to educate the "better classes" of cities about the need for tenement house regulation as a means of controlling the morality of the immigrant poor, their political and social behavior, and the spread of disease from the poor district.

A companion reform effort was the park movement that emerged after the construction of New York City's Central Park in the 1850s. Focusing particularly on the planning and advocacy efforts of Frederick Olmsted, Sr., Chapter 4 describes how this reform movement sought to alter the environment of the urban working class outside the realms of home and work, to compensate partially for the degradation and exploitation experienced

25

within these realms. This movement was more successful than housing reform, however, because the wealthy benefited directly from parks, too. It was also in the park commissions of the nineteenth century—with their own powers and duties separate from institutions of popular control—that we find a response to the capitalist-democracy contradiction.

Another attempt to impose social needs on the private control of urban development was the City Beautiful movement of the turn of the century. As detailed in Chapter 5, Charles Mulford Robinson, Daniel Burnham, and the other leaders of this movement were responding to a failure of the market system to produce a city that was scenic and attractive. If this planning orientation gained politically effective backing, it was because it corresponded with economically dominant groups' interest in creating a physical civic ideal that promoted respect for country, American culture, and capitalism. Although most such planning efforts were organized under private auspices, this chapter demonstrates that the inability of the sponsoring groups to implement their plans led to demands to governmentalize the planning function.

Coinciding with these reform efforts were a number of attempts to address the property contradiction as it manifested itself in the problem of urban population congestion. The vigorous campaign against population congestion undertaken by Benjamin Marsh and the New York Committee on Congestion of Population, the American Garden City movement, and the building of company towns were all attempts to alleviate the congestion problem either by placing curbs on land speculation or by displacing the property capitalist from his role in urban development and imposing unitary planning. However, as illustrated in Chapter 6, these efforts failed to provide a basis for the development of city planning, because they did not adequately correspond with the dominant interests in the city.

Neither did the City Beautiful, in the end, provide an adequate basis for the development of the profession and institutionalized practice of city planning. As recounted in Chapter 7, the City Practical emphasis that came to dominate planning in the period from 1910 to 1920 stemmed from a recognition of the need for some kind of collective control, organized through the state, to overcome the irrationality and inefficiency of the built environment wrought by the market system. It was in connection with this more "practical" approach to planning that an institutional response to the capitalist-democracy contradiction was solidified.

Planning in this era became a legitimate function of local government; it was organized in the form of elite-dominated local planning commissions insulated from institutions of popular control. Coming full circle, then, the concluding chapter examines how the theoretical postulates regarding state intervention and capitalism, set forth in this chapter, correspond with our observations on the history of planning.

In most of the periods or movements examined, the ideas and efforts of particular individuals are singled out for attention. This approach does not indicate a reversion to a great-man theory of history. Rather, these people are focused on because they were more articulate and effective than others in recognizing and formulating responses to the indicated contradictions, however much their thoughts and actions were shaped by the structures within which they worked. It will be shown that although these planners and planning advocates possessed a degree of independence from business groups, they helped educate those groups regarding their collective interest in the organization of the urban built environment. They did so not because they were from the business class, although most clearly were, but because they wanted to make the best of a bad bargain, to solve the problems of the city's built environment as best they could while maintaining politically effective support for planning and without transcending the limits of the property system. And in so doing, they served to maintain and stabilize that system, reproducing the contradictions of capitalist urban development anew.

TWO

Colonial Town Planting

IN MARKED CONTRAST with later periods of urban development, town planning was an essential feature of colonial America. Free from the political and economic barriers confronting planners in later eras, colonial town builders were in a position to consciously guide the development of many of America's earliest cities. Their ability to do so was conditioned on the combination of civil and political authority they possessed, the civil authority arising from land ownership and the political authority delegated by royal decree. Nearly all of these town planners had proprietary motives of one sort or another. Yet their town-building schemes were marked by a concern to provide common facilities of general benefit to the community. In addition to establishing a regular arrangement of house lots and farm parcels, their plans typically provided for an orderly street system; for generous open spaces, including a town common; and for central placement of public and quasi-public institutions, such as the administrative offices of government, the church, and the marketplace. This was true of the early Spanish settlements that spread across the southern tier of North America and up the Pacific coastline, of the French trading cities established along the St. Lawrence and down the Mississippi, and of the English and Dutch settlements that dotted the Atlantic coastline—despite the different origins of these communities.

In their effort to harness the interests of the individual to a generous conception of the interests of the community, these early planners bequeathed an auspicious legacy to modern America. Yet, in spite of the many community-serving features of colonial town planning, this era also provided the well-spring for our modern individualistic land law. America's earliest settlers came to this continent hungry for land, hoping to escape the encumbrances of feudal forms of landholding; the result, unfortunately for our cities, was that land came to be regarded as a civil liberty rather than a social resource, as a commodity rather than a collective good. This, the treatment of land as a commodity and the emergence of capitalist forms of land ownership, served to undermine many of the positive, community-serving advances of colonial town planning.

It would be a mistake, however, to see colonial town building solely in terms of its contribution to capitalist property relations. In New England, where our modern land law developed, private landholding was based upon a more equitable distribution of land than has existed at any time since. Moreover, throughout most of New England, private landholding existed in conjunction with communal or quasi-communal forms of landholding and collective management of land use. Yet the distribution of land was far from being completely equitable; differences in social rank, wealth, political influence, and occupation all corresponded with the amount of land owned. In addition, proprietary interests influenced which community interests were incorporated into the development of the town. But the preeminent proprietary interests were those of colonial authorities, land companies operating under royal charter, and individual proprietors; and these proprietary interests gave wider scope to the interests of the community than was to be the case later, once an individualistic land law took hold and land was transformed into a commodity.

This bounded concern for the well-being of the community can be seen in the New England village system and in the planning of towns and cities along the Atlantic coastline. In this chapter, the "town planting" practiced in Massachusetts Bay Colony and the planning and initial development of Philadelphia and Savannah will be used as examples of the positive accomplishments and typically encountered problems of colonial town planning. Yet the larger purpose of this examination is to show how the property contradiction unfolded over the course of the seventeenth and eighteenth centuries—how it emerged as a problem coincident with changes in the political and economic treatment of land and how these changes obstructed the development of town planning and worked to undermine many of its positive features. In addition, this chapter will show how colonial town planning was shaped by the political, economic, and cultural characteristics of the old European society, as well as by those of the new colonial one.

The old society provided the positive model of the English country village and the negative model of overgrown cities such as London, which was swollen with rural migrants "freed" from the land by the Enclosure Acts. It should be noted at this point that planning in the colonial era was an exercise in social as well as physical planning: town builders either took for granted a particular social order, incorporating that order into the plan of settlement, as in the Puritan villages of Massachusetts Bay, or they sought to create a qualitatively different order, acting in response to disturbances in the old world, as in the case of Savannah. But the political, economic, and cultural order also had a circumscribing effect, limiting what planners could accomplish and the goals they chose to pursue. At the same time, the pre-liberal society of seventeenth-century Europe facilitated town planning through the large grants of authority given to the organizers of colonial settlements. Thus, we need to take account of the antecedent conditions in the old world, as well as circumstances in colonial America, to understand fully the development of colonial towns and villages.

THE NEW ENGLAND VILLAGE SYSTEM

The seventeenth-century villages established by Puritan settlers along the Atlantic coast from Maine to Long Island were probably the most comprehensively planned of all American settlements.[1] The essential feature of the plan was the organized settlement or "plantation." Very few isolated homesteads were permitted to exist. As Sam Bass Warner, Jr., has perceptively noted, the planning problem was in harnessing the land hunger of seventeenth-century Englishmen to the task of establishing a stable community where frontiersmen might live and worship.[2] The solution was to identify the family as the basic unit of labor and production and the town or plantation as the basic unit of settlement. In this conceptual scheme, the family was envisaged as a little commonwealth and the town, a collection of families, as a larger commonwealth for which the common good was regarded as the highest goal. Added to this was another layer of loyalty in which all the towns of Massachusetts Bay Colony made up the Commonwealth of Massachusetts. Within this lattice of loyalties, as Gary Nash has observed, the "corporate whole," rather than the individual, was the "basic conceptual unit."[3]

The Puritan settlements of Massachusetts Bay Colony were compact settlements modeled after the traditional villages of the English countryside. At the center of each village, usually set

[1] This point is made by Warner, *The Urban Wilderness: A History of the American City*, p. 7.

[2] Ibid., p. 8.

[3] *The Urban Crucible: Social Change, Political Consciousness and the Origins of the American Revolution*, p. 5.

around a village green, were small house lots large enough only for a dwelling and a small garden. The house lots were laid out to provide the security of a compact settlement, as well as the advantages of village life. Usually, the house lots were set along one or two streets that adjoined a strip of fenced common land where cattle could be grazed until a church was erected. This rough village space was later transformed into the village green associated with early New England towns. Yet only the initial members of the town, those who had "convenanted" to establish the town, had rights to common land, which included not only the area at the center of the village, but also the outlying cultivated land. New inhabitants might build a dwelling and own land, but they did not automatically have rights of commonage. There thus developed a distinction between the commoners or "proprietors" who had rights to common land and the non-commoners or "inhabitants" who did not.

In the surrounding countryside, encircling the house lots, were the individual allotments of these village proprietors and the common lands of the town. Prior to the eighteenth century, when the emergence of land speculation altered the pattern of settlement, families were not allowed to establish isolated family farms. As a further assurance of compact settlement, then, farm parcels were intentionally scattered. Acting within the guidelines drawn up by the General Court of the Bay Colony—the central authority within the colony—the village proprietors set up individually owned and worked family parcels, but they manipulated the placement of these so as to "bind independent families into the social unity of an English village."[4] Here, as elsewhere, the interest of the individual was made subordinate to that of the plantation. A house built without permission from the village, if prejudicial to the "corporate whole," might be demolished and the persons removed. In addition, private lands could be taken for the purposes of settlement, but the rights of grantees were protected and provision was made for compensation in case of damage.[5] A certain dignity attached to the original lots, and "it was considered impor-

[4] Warner, *Urban Wilderness*, p. 10.

[5] Egleston, "The Land System of the New England Colonies," p. 35. On the similarity in design of early New England towns and the "pueblo" pattern of land division used in Spanish settlements in North America, see Reps, *Making of Urban America*, chap. 2. Reps writes that, although Spanish settlements existed on this continent for nearly two and one-half centuries, they were typically undermanned and underfinanced, and they had little effect upon subsequent town building (p. 54).

tant that they should not be abandoned or neglected, or even thrown together." To protect against this kind of abuse, Connecticut passed a law requiring that all dwelling or mansion houses " 'shall be upheld, repaired and maintained sufficient.' " The law also gave property owners twelve months to build on their house lots or face forfeiture.[6] In this way, early village settlers attempted to achieve community sociability, security, and an attractive spatial order while protecting against the scourge of land speculation.

Each proprietor was given an allotment of each of the kinds of land available, the size of the allotment depending upon that individual's share in the stock of the Massachusetts Bay Company. These individually owned parcels were used for cultivation, grazing, and firewood. Typically, the major subsistence crops, wheat and rye, were grown in a common field in which each family with common rights was given a strip proportionate in size to that family's house lot. These parcels were considered private property, and it does not appear that the wheat and rye fields were farmed as a community project, except perhaps in the early years when many new arrivals lacked tools or cattle. Nevertheless, the dispersion of individual parcels and the division of wheat and rye fields into individually held strips was all done with a view toward creating a community bond between family units.

Centrally important to this exercise in social and physical planning was the manner in which land was used and apportioned. Of the three classifications of property within these early settlements—house lots, individually owned and worked farm parcels, and common lands—the house lots were the most important element of the village system. They typically varied in size from as little as one-half acre for a poor bachelor to as much as twenty acres for a wealthy family. Only exceptionally were lands divided equally in terms of both quantity and quality; yet an attempt was made to give land to those who could use it, not only to prevent excessive inequality in the allotment of shares, but also to ensure that the smallest shares were of sufficient size.[7] In the initial division of land, weight was given to the size, wealth, and social status of each household. Those who had contributed to the cost of town promotion were given special consideration, as were those who could make distinct contributions to the town, such as ministers, men of wealth or political influence, and desirable artisans

[6] Egleston, "Land System," pp. 52-53.
[7] Ibid., pp. 43-45.

and tradesmen.[8] Despite such differentials, these first townships were "the most equitable allocations of resources the country ever knew."[9]

Nevertheless, friction occurred fairly often between commoners and non-commoners, especially as the percentage of commoners among freemen declined with the arrival of new inhabitants. The commoners could appeal to a higher authority, such as the court or colonial legislature, to protect their common rights from the claims of non-commoners, and it appears that higher authorities generally supported the rights of the commoners. Yet, according to Egleston, most plantations were fairly successful in dealing with the problem of rights to commonage. In most cases, there was a "moral trust" in favor of the latecomers, and, as long as the amount of common land exceeded the requirements of the commoners, this obligation generally was recognized, although sometimes only under pressure. Sometimes, the claims of non-commoners were satisfied by increasing the number of commoners, usually by allowing newcomers the right to purchase common rights. The more usual practice, though, was to grant rights to purchase individual parcels of land without extending rights of commonage.[10]

Cultural, geographical, and political-economic factors were all influential in shaping this pattern of settlement, and it is difficult to assign a preeminent role to any one element. To some degree, this organized mode of settlement came about spontaneously. Families that had lived together in England and sailed across the Atlantic together naturally sought to live together in the new country. Relying upon memory and experience and drawing upon indigenous folk traditions, they created a village world like that of rural England. The importance attached to the local church, along with the need for mutual protection against Indian attack and mutual aid in securing adequate food and shelter, also encouraged compact settlement. But the mode of settlement was not totally spontaneous; it reflected a large measure of centralized control exercised by the Massachusetts Bay Company and derived ultimately from the English Crown. This control was both civil and political in nature, arising from the Crown's grant of land and its concurrent extension of government authority to the Bay Com-

[8] Haller, *The Puritan Frontier: Town Planting in New England Colonial Development, 1630-1660*, p. 24.

[9] Warner, *Urban Wilderness*, p. 11.

[10] Egleston, "Land System," pp. 36-42.

pany. The colony's General Court controlled the pattern of settlement through provisions attached to the land grants made to individual settlers. In addition, committees were established by colonial authorities to supervise the allotment of land and the admission of new inhabitants, and groups of families were to make application to these committees for a township grant.

Yet the existence of this centralized control does not explain why such control was used to create a village system like that of rural England. The New England village system grew out of the strategic interests of both the land companies and the Crown, the cultural traditions of the Puritan community, and the land hunger of individual settlers. To the Massachusetts Bay Company, which had received land rights and a monopoly over trade between the colony and the mother country, the colony represented a business proposition. This strategic interest was fused with the Crown's interest in exercising sovereignty over portions of North America and in profiting from colonial trade relations. These two interests coincided with the interest of the Puritan community in securing a place where it might practice its religion and culture free from the disturbances it had known in Europe. For a time, this fusion of the interests of land company, Crown, and Puritan community was able to discipline and appease the land hunger of individual settlers, shaping the pattern of development and imparting to early New England settlements their quasi-communal character.

The desire of the Bay Company and the Crown to establish control of trade and development, promote commerce, and develop raw materials (namely, furs and agricultural products) for exploitation by the mother country was of crucial importance in determining the pattern of settlement. These interests were reflected in the effort to establish self-sufficient villages, in the refusal to grant land except in organized settlements, and in the limitation on lot sizes. To ensure a settlement's self-sufficiency, colonial authorities were careful to see that there were a sufficient number of families; they wanted men in whom they had confidence; and they made sure that the settlers were in effective possession of a tract of land. In the Bay Colony, townsmen were to occupy a site, erect houses, and establish a going community in two or three years. In contrast with later American practice, there was little or no holding of land for speculation. Grants of land were contingent on a plan to settle, and, as a rule, all of the land soon was occupied. In the few instances where the land of nonresident holders was allowed to lie unimproved, taxes were assessed against the land to spur its improvement. Moreover, many land grants were forfeitable if the land was not improved within a given period of time. As a further condition, the plantation was required to support a minister and a church, and lands were typically set aside for the erection of a church and school.[11]

The limitation on lot sizes, besides preventing the growth of great estates, worked in conjunction with restrictions on the location of land grants to ensure the establishment of compact settlements that were economically viable and easily defended. Farming lots originally were limited to two hundred acres (the village house lots, as already noted, were usually one-half acre), and the location of the land grants initially was limited to the immediate Massachusetts Bay vicinity. Such limitations corresponded with the interest of the Bay Company and Crown in securing effective possession of the Bay area and making the colony reasonably self-sufficient. In the words of Egleston, "No inducement, no excuse, was to be given for a loose, an isolated mode of settlement, which would enfeeble the political development of the colony," leaving it "at the mercy of its enemies, or, at best, dependent upon the protection of England for its very existence."[12]

Individual settlers had their own reasons for wanting additional land or the establishment of new settlements: immigration and natural population increase strained the resources of the initial settlements, and the colonists needed additional pasture land to accommodate their expanding cattle herds. These needs were not allowed to determine the pattern of settlement, however. The dominance of the strategic interests of the Bay Company and the Crown in controlling the development of the colony is suggested by the fact that settlers petitioning for permission to establish new settlements typically claimed that the acquisition of desirable land would prevent its occupation by others. This argument was bound to appeal to the Bay Company, especially after the French initiated attempts to colonize the area on the east side of the Bay.[13]

Despite the strategic interests of the Bay Company and Crown, however, the village system of early New England was also a product of the "shared memory and imagination" that underlay the Puritans' perceptions and yearnings.[14] Puritan leader John Win-

[11] Ibid., pp. 34, 54.

[12] Ibid., p. 23.

[13] Ibid., p. 31.

[14] Here I draw from Fries, *The Urban Idea in Colonial America*, chap. 2; the quotation is from p. 32. For a somewhat different view, emphasizing the diversity of

throp's "City upon a Hill" ideal was both a response to the transfiguration of seventeenth-century London, which had become for the Puritans a contemporary city of mammon, and an attempt to freeze in time the social and physical order of the sixteenth-century English village. The Puritan faith in order, hierarchy, and mutual dependence also was to be reflected in the Puritan town. Winthrop likened the Commonwealth of Massachusetts to the Puritan view of the family, in which a woman chose her husband who then became her lord; once accepted into the fold, one assumed an obligation to work for the welfare of the whole.[15] The uniformity of thought and opinion and the intolerance of diversity that conditioned the Puritans' sense of mutual responsibility is illustrated by the covenant of the town of Dedham. In the covenant's first passage, the townspeople agreed "to profess and practice one truth according to that most perfect rule, the foundation of which is everlasting love," while in the second passage they pledged to "labor to keep off from us all such as are contrary minded, and receive only such as may be probably of one heart with us."[16]

The value placed upon order was evident in the compact pattern of the Puritan settlements, the regular arrangement of streets, and the orderly way in which the layout of house lots, gardens, and farm parcels provided access to both nature and domestic life. An appreciation of order, hierarchy, and mutual dependence also was reflected in the prohibition against isolated settlements. William Bradford, perhaps the most zealous of Puritan church leaders, feared that isolated settlements would lead to the disintegration of the churches, the organizational and spiritual basis of Puritan society.[17] The Puritans' nucleated villages were not intended to provide for a non-farm population, nor were they designed to accommodate a population too large to gather in a single place to discuss town affairs. In this way, the Puritans sought to prevent their villages from experiencing the fate that had befallen London. Boston was allowed to become an exception, because it lacked the agricultural resources necessary for sustaining itself, and because the Puritans apparently acknowledged the need for a trading center to

---

early New England towns and the creativity of their founders, see Powell, *Puritan Village: The Formation of a New England Town.*

[15] Fries, *Urban Idea*, p. 35.

[16] Quoted in Lockridge, *A New England Town: The First Hundred Years, Dedham, Massachusetts, 1636-1736*, pp. 4-5.

[17] Fries, *Urban Idea*, p. 53.

make the colony economically viable. With the exception of Boston, however, the towns and villages of Massachusetts Bay Colony represented an attempt to "fix in time an intimate and rural world" that insulated its inhabitants from the change and disruption associated with city life.[18]

While inculcating a concern for the community as a whole, Puritan religious culture placed limits on individual profit making, delaying the growth of capitalist forms of landholding. Although asceticism was disavowed within the Puritan community, economic gain found its only justification in social and moral betterment. Hence, profits were to be just, and resources such as land were not to be used in ways that were harmful to the community. Towns were therefore justified in imposing restrictions that would enforce the individual's obligation to the community and ensure respect for order and hierarchy.

For a time, this Puritan religious culture, together with the restrictions on town development that grew out of the strategic interests of the Bay Company and the Crown, was effective in disciplining and appeasing the land hunger of individual settlers. The effectiveness and limits of this system of control can be seen in the way the Puritan villages dealt with the problem of growth. Growth took place in two ways: through the admission of new inhabitants and, when a village seemed full, through the planting of new villages, both of which were carefully controlled. New inhabitants were admitted only with the permission of existing inhabitants, who were careful not to admit persons who might become a poor relief liability.[19] As previously noted, the admission of new settlers created a problem in the division of rights of commonage, although, according to at least one historian, in most cases there was a "moral trust" in favor of latecomers.[20] Yet there were limits to a village's willingness to take in and care for the poor. When Indian tribes in Massachusetts destroyed dozens of inland communities in 1676, causing inland settlers to flee to Boston in search of safety and aid, that city's leaders petitioned the General Court to allow the eviction of these "strangers."[21] It is significant that this episode occurred in Boston, which of all the communities of Mas-

[18] Ibid., p. 49.
[19] Haller, *Puritan Frontier*, p. 19.
[20] Egleston, "Land System," pp. 41-42.
[21] Nash, *Urban Crucible*, p. 22.

sachusetts Bay least reflected the Puritan virtues of compactness, mutual dependency, and agricultural toil.

The other means of coping with population growth was through the planting of new settlements. There was apparently no arbitrary limit on the size of a village, but when the villagers sensed that their village was complete, no more house lots were granted. In this sphere, too, freedom and opportunity were organized in group rather than individual terms. Instead of turning away settlers and forcing them to set out on their own, the typical practice was for a group of settlers to break away from the mother settlement and establish a new village, usually nearby. This process also occurred when a settlement became divided by controversy. For about two generations, the ease of founding new townships when old ones were filled or divided by controversy made New England, in the words of Sam Bass Warner, a "stable system of multiplying cells."[22] By controlling growth in this manner, the Puritans demonstrated their awareness that growth was sound only so long as the community could remain a unit and maintain its common institutions. This method of community development also kept land values at a low level and prevented the engrossing of land for speculative purposes.[23]

The ability of these early villages to define freedom and opportunity in group rather than individual terms depended upon the relative absence of proprietary motives on the part of early settlers. While an element of speculation was present in almost every venture in colonial town planning, land speculation did not become the dominant motif of town building until after the Revolution.[24] Apart from the fact that many settlers came to the new land in search of religious and political freedom rather than profits, there were powerful constraints on their capacity to develop land with a view toward speculative gain, at least for a time. The early settlements were small and based primarily on agriculture. Hostile Indians and the natural barriers imposed by topography

[22] *Urban Wilderness*, p. 12. This process of expansion was not without friction, however. Robert Gross recounts how eighteenth-century Concord was split by controversy when outlying sections of the town sought to secede and form their own township. These efforts were resisted by the Concord majority since, after the separation, the remaining taxpayers would have to pay a larger share of the minister's fixed salary, and since they feared that a diminution in the size of the town would lessen its importance. See Gross, *The Minutemen and Their World*, pp. 15-18.

[23] Mumford, *Sticks and Stones: A Study of American Architecture and Civilization*, pp. 16-17.

[24] Reps, *Making of Urban America*, p. 349.

limited settlements to a narrow band along the Atlantic coast. In addition, the shortage of capital and the fact that the population was relatively sparse and immobile limited opportunities for land promotion schemes. Even in Boston, where urban real estate was appreciating in value, land speculation did not deliver large rewards until after the end of the seventeenth century, when land began to double and redouble in value.[25]

In the eighteenth century, the system of controlling land speculation and appeasing the land hunger of individual settlers began to break down, resulting in a new pattern of settlement. Pivotal at this point were the emergence of economic conditions facilitating land speculation, the relaxation of colonial controls over town development, and the rise of new forms of landholding. In 1702, paper money was introduced into the colony, which resulted in inflation and attracted to the colony a class of speculators eager to obtain town grants. Land speculation was further fueled by the victory of Britain over the French and their Indian allies in the so-called King Philip's War, bringing to a close an almost forty-year period of war and removing an important barrier against westward expansion. Furthermore, after 1713 the General Court of the Bay Colony loosened its control over town development. Having apparently become caught up in the speculative spirit itself, it made large grants to proprietors who had no interest in settling the land themselves.[26] The practice of these speculators was to lay out one township within a land grant and offer plots in it free to settlers. These house lots were larger than those in earlier village communities and were actually small farms, ranging in size from 30 to 120 acres. Typically, these allotments were laid out in long, narrow strips, giving the settlement a form like that of the *reihendorf*, or highway village, of Europe. The other townships in the land grant were divided into large farms, and the proprietors were allowed to dispose of these as they pleased, a practice that led to the establishment of isolated homes and farms. In this way, land speculation served to alter the pattern of settlement, the *reihendorf*, or strip settlement, serving as a transitional form between the compact settlements of the pre-1713 period and the isolated homesteads of a later era.[27]

This new mode of settlement also corresponded with the passage from pre-capitalist to capitalist forms of land ownership.

[25] Nash, *Urban Crucible*, p. 23.

[26] Here I draw from Scofield, "The Origin of Settlement Patterns in Rural New England," p. 655.

[27] Ibid., p. 661.

39

Here, the common pastures and common fields played a pivotal role, for once settlers were admitted to a village without rights of commonage, these common lands entered a transitional stage between being individually and collectively owned. From giving each individual with common rights a share of the town's grazing area or a strip of arable land in the common field, together with responsibility for maintaining a proportionate share of fence, it became an easy transition for the inhabitants to think of these parcels of land as their undivided property. As new settlers arrived without rights of commonage, common lands eventually were transferred from common to individual ownership. This shift meant an end to the practice of collective management of land use, since the town's control of the common fields depended upon the freemen of the town and the town proprietors being one and the same. Throughout most of the seventeenth century, the "town" was the "propriety" and, in its original conception, the town meeting was nothing but a proprietors' meeting. With the arrival of new settlers and the division of the common lands, however, the proprietors as an organized body passed out of existence and the town no longer exercised control over individual property.[28] The transition from individual to collective land ownership was further facilitated by the fee-simple land ownership practiced throughout New England, which made it easy to transfer title and helped to make possible the eventual engrossing under single ownership of substantial areas of land.[29]

Because of the failure to contain the thirst for land and the emergence of land speculation, the quasi-communal New England village system did not last beyond the seventeenth century. For a time, the system of nucleated settlements under the control of central authorities and restrained by a Puritan religious culture emphasizing rural toil and mutual responsibility was able to control these forces. But the restraint of Puritan culture could not contain the individual desire for land once (1) conditions became ripe for holding land for speculative gain, (2) a colonial land market developed, (3) colonial authorities loosened their control over town development, and (4) new forms of landholding took hold. The strength of these early settlements derived from the fact that the first inhabitants served simultaneously as settlers, town builders, and capitalists: those who built and inhabited the town were also

[28] Akagi, *The Town Proprietors of the New England Colonies; A Study of their Development, Organization, Activities and Controversies, 1620-1770*, pp. 289-90.
[29] Haller, *Puritan Frontier*, pp. 25-26.

the proprietors. As absentee land ownership "increased in leaps and bounds" after the beginning of the eighteenth century, however, the role of the capitalist or proprietor became separate from the roles of town builder and settler.[30] With this separation, a conflict emerged between the needs of the inhabitants of the town and the interests of the proprietors who, by virtue of their land ownership, controlled the town's development. It is this contradiction between the social character of land and its private use and control that provided the impulse for modern town planning. In failing to check the development of this contradiction, the New England village system suffered a fate similar to that of other colonial era exercises in town planning.

The Planning of Coastal Cities

In the present era of suburban sprawl and urban decline, some may find it surprising that many of our major cities were established and for a time developed in accordance with an overall plan. Like New England "town planters," the builders of these early cities were advantaged by the combination of political and civil authority they possessed. They were in possession of the land, either in their own name—as with William Penn's direct ownership of Pennsylvania—or as agents of the Crown, and they had all the rights and privileges pertaining to such possession. In addition, they typically possessed grants of royal authority that accorded them powers of governance. And while proprietary motives were evident in the founding of virtually all of these communities, these proprietary motives gave wider scope to the incorporation of community interests into the development of the towns than was true in the post-colonial era. The effort to secure general benefits for the community was evident in the establishment of orderly street systems; the creation of generous open spaces; the central placement of churches, meetinghouses, and public markets; and the general concern to build cities that were convenient and attractive.

Yet there were exceptions to the pattern of planned development and, interestingly, New York City (nee New Amsterdam) was one of them. This was not for want of the necessary authority to supervise the settlement established in 1626 by Protestant Walloon and Dutch settlers at the tip of Manhattan Island. Unlike the present government of New York City, the Dutch West India

---

[30] Akagi, *Town Proprietors*, p. 138.

Company had a monopoly on commercial trading privileges, as well as full government powers to dispose of land as it saw fit.[31] The Dutch director of the company had given detailed instructions to the first settlers about how to lay out the town; however, for reasons that are unclear, these instructions were not carried out. Settlers' huts and cabins were strewn about with little attention paid to uniformity, and new streets were laid out as needed, usually following the lanes naturally established by men and animals as they took the most convenient paths between houses, farms, and fort.[32] One such street was Broadway, whose irregular trajectory connected the fort at the tip of the island with the farms and estates beyond. Wall Street, by contrast, was planned intentionally—to service the wall built across the island in 1633 to protect the settlers from English attack.

The absence of planned development began to cause problems as New Amsterdam grew and land around the fort increased in value. In 1642, sixteen years after the first white settlement on Manhattan Island, the West India Company devised a plan for the division and organization of town land. Yet settlers were not always respectful of the newly established survey lines, and they often erected their houses and outbuildings on land reserved for streets. It is apparent, too, that they appreciated the speculative value of property even at this early date. Of the ten lots laid out at the lower end of Broadway in 1643, only two were ever occupied by the original grantees, although the remaining properties were later sold and built upon.[33] In response to this situation, the director general of the West India Company adopted an ordinance in 1647 authorizing the condemnation of disorderly and improper buildings. In addition, persons who had not yet built upon their allotted property were given one month to make improvements or face expropriation. Thus occurred the first of many official responses to the disorganized development of America's largest trading center.

UNLIKE New York, Philadelphia was established on the basis of an overall plan, with provisions for public open space, a regular arrangement of lots and streets, and central placement of community facilities. Whereas other colonial cities were organized by

[31] See Valentine, *History of the City of New York*, chap. 2.
[32] Reps, *Making of Urban America*, pp. 147-48.
[33] Valentine, *History of New York*, p. 43.

trading companies, Philadelphia was formally under the control of one man, proprietor William Penn. King Charles II of England, who gave Penn the Pennsylvania colony to cancel a debt owed Penn's father, made Penn the governor and royal proprietor of the colony and, purportedly, the largest private landowner in the world.[34] His vast domain of forty-seven million acres included all of what later became the states of Pennsylvania and Delaware and part of New Jersey. And, significantly, the terms of Penn's land grant gave him full freedom and authority to determine the pattern of settlement and division of land.

Originally, Penn had hoped to establish a number of small agricultural villages like those of rural England, with house lots centered on a village green and an outlying belt of agricultural land. This was his urban ideal, the model for his "greene country towne," although this phase often has been misused to describe the more cosmopolitan Philadelphia that Penn eventually founded. Yet Penn's undertaking was also a speculative one, and because of this his plan for creating semi-rural villages came to naught. Initial investors in the colony were drawn largely from the rising class of commercial capitalists; what they sought was an opportunity to practice their trade unobstructed rather than freedom to till the soil, and they were unwilling to invest in the colony unless they were given adequate space and facilities to carry on their commercial activities. Negotiations between Penn and the organized group of First Purchasers produced a formal recording of "Certain Conditions or Concessions," in which the indefinite proposal for establishing "towns or cities" was reduced to a single settlement, "a large town or city."[35] In making these concessions to commercial interests, Penn cited the speculative nature of his undertaking. "I cannot make money," he wrote, "without special concessions. Though I desire to extend religious freedom, yet I want some recompense for my trouble."[36]

As a land speculator, Penn wanted to make the town attractive to investors; and because of his centralized ownership, he could incorporate community amenities into the development of the town. The most important feature of Philadelphia's design, in terms of its influence on later towns, was its gridiron street sys-

[34] Harris, *Origin of the Land Tenure System in the United States*, p. 237.
[35] See Roach, "The Planting of Philadelphia: A Seventeenth-Century Real Estate Development," Part I, p. 9; the words in quotation marks are Penn's.
[36] Quoted, ibid.

tem.[37] Although it was Penn's surveyor general, Thomas Holme, who mapped the streets of the town, Penn had been explicit in his instructions to the first group of settlers about the need for a regular arrangement of streets. The commissioners accompanying the first settlers were, in Penn's words, to "settle the figure of the town so that the streets hereafter may be uniform down to the water from the country bounds." He also specified that the houses were to be "built in a line, or upon a line, as many as may be."[38] To achieve these objectives, Holme devised a gridiron street plan, later approved by Penn, that consisted of streets running parallel and perpendicular to one another, with equal-sized, rectangular blocks unbroken by diagonal thoroughfares. This scheme, probably conceived in 1682, closely corresponded with the gridiron plan Richard Newcourt had proposed for London following the great fire of 1666, a plan with which Penn probably was familiar.[39]

It was not the influence of this historical model but rather the advantage of the gridiron in facilitating the sale of real estate that chiefly explains its adoption by Philadelphia, as well as by later cities and towns. The advantage of the gridiron in this respect was that land lots were all the same size and shape, differing only in location; this uniformity meant ease of description in legal deeds, ease of description from the auctioneer's block, and ease of purchase. It also was especially important given that land was frequently sold, sight unseen, to distant purchasers.

Penn also wanted a spacious city, with wide streets and enough room between houses to plant a garden and to prevent the spread of fire (although these elements of his design are not apparent in the older sections of Philadelphia today). To provide adequate spacing, Penn and Holme created large blocks about four hundred feet square. Yet, because these oversized blocks contained so much inaccessible interior land, they were eventually crisscrossed with alleyways, which were later built upon, to the detriment of

[37] Philadelphia was not the first colonial city to have a gridiron design. Early New England townships followed either a squared, rectilinear plan (e.g., Plymouth, Cambridge, New Haven, and Hartford) or a linear plan with house lots placed in a line along a central street (e.g., Salem, Springfield, Providence, and Greenfield); see Fries, *Urban Idea*, p. 48. The influence of Philadelphia's design on later cities derived from the scale on which the grid concept was applied, and the fact that so many immigrants passed through Philadelphia. On the influence of the gridiron pattern on western cities in the United States, see Wade, *Urban Frontier: The Rise of Western Cities, 1780-1830*, p. 314.

[38] Excerpted in Glaab, *The American City: A Documentary History*, p. 36.

[39] Reps, *Making of Urban America*, p. 163.

the city's housing situation for decades to come.[40] Although the streets of inner Philadelphia appear narrow by today's standards, their fifty-foot width was generous in comparison with European cities of the day. And Philadelphia's two major intersecting streets, Broad and Main, were built one hundred feet wide.

Penn also was concerned about providing adequate public open space and ensuring the central placement of public and quasi-public buildings and institutions, a scheme that reflected the ideological model of the English country village. As described in Holme's *Portraiture of a City*, used by Penn to attract new investors to the colony, the initial layout of Philadelphia centered on a "Square of Ten Acres"; around it was space for various "Houses for publick Affairs," including "a Meeting House, Assembly or State-House, Market-House, School-House, and several other Buildings for Public Concerns."[41] The demand for a central business district was also accommodated, although it came about through the actions of the Free Society of Traders, a group of merchant investors in the colony. Organized as a joint-stock company, the members staked out for themselves, before Penn's arrival in the colony, what they thought would be the central area of the town.[42] Having no desire to alienate the town's incipient merchant class, Penn ceded this strategically located area to them. In consideration of the need for public open space, Holme's *Portraiture* projected a public square of eight acres in each quarter of the city. These he likened to London's Moorefields, an apt comparison since the Moorefields were the only true public square, open to all segments of the public, in the English capital.

Yet the history of Philadelphia's public squares is indicative of the power of land speculation to undermine the best-laid plans. In the first half of the eighteenth century, land speculation in Philadelphia became more lucrative than commercial trade; it was stated in 1768 that all the great fortunes made in the city in the preceding fifty years came from trading in land.[43] Thus, an early traveler to the city wrote in 1811 of the "prostitution" of Penn's

[40] See Churchill, *The City is the People*, p. 30.

[41] Reprinted as "A Short Advertisement upon the Scituation and Extent of the City of Philadelphia and the Ensuing Plat-form thereof, by the Surveyor General" (1683), in Myers, *Narratives of Early Pennsylvania, West New Jersey and Delaware, 1630-1707*, p. 243.

[42] Nash, "City Planning and Political Tension in the Seventeenth Century: The Case of Philadelphia," p. 62.

[43] Nash, *Urban Crucible*, pp. 122-23.

squares: of the five squares set aside for "public walks and the salutary recreation of future generations, not one has been exclusively appropriated to its destined object."[44] (It was not until the nineteenth century, when concern over population congestion generated renewed interest in public open space, that Philadelphia's central public squares reappeared.) In addition, this speculative fervor led to the carving up of Penn and Holme's large house lots into successively smaller units, which, once built upon, destroyed whatever remaining claim Philadelphia had to being a "greene country towne."

As the colony's biggest speculator, Penn was acutely aware of the need to attract investors to the colony; yet he disapproved of absentee landowners and opposed speculative practices that were harmful to the town. Writing to English investors in 1685, just four years after the founding of the colony, he appraised the success of his efforts at development in capitalist terms. "The improvement of the place," he declared, "is best measured by the advance in value upon every man's lot."[45] He ventured that the worst lots, without improvements, were already worth four times their original value, and that the best lots had increased their value forty times over. All the same, Penn questioned the fairness of allowing absentee landowners to profit from the efforts of others. "It seems unequal," he wrote in the same report, "that the Absent should be thus benefited by the Improvements of those who are upon the place, especially when they have serv'd no Office, run no hazard, nor as yet defray'd any Publick charge." While acknowledging that these unearned increments "certainly redound to them," he described absentee landowners disapprovingly as "great Debtors to the country," sounding what was to become a recurring theme among future town planners.[46] He also took steps to limit the detrimental effects of absentee ownership—where he could do so without jeopardizing his own land promotion efforts. When Penn arrived in Philadelphia in 1682 to settle the distribution of land, he placed the lots of absentee investors on the opposite side of the Schuylkill River from those who had come, and he told Holme that in assigning future lots he should "pleasure" those who had come, while absentee owners were "the least to be minded and

[44] Excerpted in Glaab, *American City*, p. 37.

[45] "A Further Account of the Province of Pennsylvania," letter to the Free Society of Traders (1685), as reprinted in Myers, *Narratives*, p. 262.

[46] Ibid.

taken care for."[47] Also the "Certain Conditions or Concessions" negotiated between the First Purchasers and Penn specified that land that remained unimproved to the prejudice of the rest could, upon the lodging of a complaint to Penn or his deputy, be taken by another.

Yet, with the progress of his town-building efforts, Penn's interest as a land speculator came more and more into conflict with the interest of settlers, leading to a controversy that caused Penn to remark on the "absence of brotherly love" in Philadelphia, and eventually causing him to withdraw from the colony altogether. He then became an absentee landowner himself. As an example of his financial opportunism, he reserved for himself nearly one-third of the land of the town, including a valuable section known as the "Bank" that separated front lots along the Delaware from the water's edge, thus assuring "himself and his heirs a handsome legacy."[48] This action, together with the feudal privileges he claimed (instead of selling the land free and clear he attempted to impose on land purchasers a "quitrent" that would run for one hundred years) led the First Purchasers to present him with a list of grievances in 1684. They objected among other things to the quitrent Penn sought to impose, to his reservation of the Bank for himself, and especially to his refusal to assign all of the town's land to the first group of settlers. The latter issue arose because, as an incentive, Penn originally had offered First Purchasers a bonus that would equal 2 percent of their country land. Penn held that the bonuses were in the "liberties" surrounding the town, and that the house lots in the town had been granted as a token of his largess, whereas the First Purchasers maintained that their house lots were part of the bonus and that the terms of Penn's offer obligated him to dispose of all of the town's land in bonuses, without holding house lots for sale to later purchasers of country land. According to Gary Nash, Penn "inexplicably denied" admitting late purchasers, and he refused to yield on the issue of the Bank lots.[49] With positions hardening on both sides, Penn set sail for London in 1684, and by the following year, he was openly advertising city lots in Philadelphia. This action led many colonists to conclude that Penn was seeking to extract the maximum profit from the colony, at their expense. If, initially, Penn's interest as a land spec-

[47] Nash, "City Planning," p. 63.
[48] Ibid., p. 65.
[49] Ibid., p. 71.

ulator, under the condition of his centralized land ownership, was
compatible with the community interests of the town, this ceased
to be the case in the view of the colonists once Philadelphia became a going community and Penn's interest as a capitalist became separate from his interest as a town builder.

IN CONTRAST to Philadelphia, Savannah was established in an explicit attempt to avoid the ravage of land speculation. The administrative capital of the Georgia colony, Savannah was laid out by
James Oglethorpe, a British military man and former member of
Parliament. Until 1752, Savannah and the Georgia colony were
under the control of a body of trustees, appointed by King George
II, many of whose members were British M.P.s. As revealed in the
promotional tracts of the Georgia Trustees and in sermons given
before this body, the Georgia colony was established for a variety
of purposes: to relieve unemployment in England, to Christianize
native Indians, to strengthen colonial defenses against the Spanish, to increase Britain's mercantile wealth, and to provide a place
of refuge for persecuted Protestants. Of greatest concern to the
Trustees, however, was the moral effect of the increasingly visible
poverty and new forms of wealth associated with more urbanized
commercial societies.[50] In this, the Georgia Trustees, like the
founders of earlier colonies, were responding to developments in
Europe. Yet the Georgia colony, established in 1733, a full century
after Massachusetts Bay colony and one-half century after Philadelphia, was the product of a different European society, one in
which the neoclassical idea that public virtue was a political
rather than a religious matter was gaining ascendancy, leading the
Georgia Trustees to pursue ideals unlike those of the founders of
earlier colonies.

To the Georgia colony's founders, civic virtue depended upon
citizens' ability to maintain their independence from the mon-
archy. This independence could be secured by means of two conditions: freehold tenure and the right to bear arms. The aim of the
Georgia Trustees, however, was not merely to create an agrarian
society of independent arms-bearing proprietors. The Trustees
had a "uniquely American conception of the city," as Sylvia Fries
has written; they accepted the city but endeavored to "cleanse [it]
of its economic dislocations and political corruption." They
sought to accomplish this, as evidenced by the design of Savannah,

[50] Fries, *Urban Idea*, pp. 141-42.

by fusing the city and country into a social whole, one which could "restore a viable polity sustained by the public virtue of an independent citizenry."[51] The recruitment of settlers from English debtor prisons, for which the Georgia colony is chiefly known, was emblematic of the Trustees' attitude toward the emerging commercial society. These debtors were viewed as the innocent victims of a corrupt society that rewarded connivance more than honest toil and regarded bad luck as a punishable sin.

At the center of the Trustees' effort to establish an independent yet virtuous citizenry was the colony's land policy. There was to be an equitable division of land among freehold proprietors, with protection, initially, against the conversion of land into a commodity. As originally intended, each settler was to be given a fifty-acre lot, and these lots were to lie all together. In Savannah, by Oglethorpe's order, each fifty-acre allotment was divided between a sixty-by-ninety-foot lot in the town, a five-acre garden, and a forty-four-acre farm lot in the outlying countryside. To prevent absentee land ownership, all grantees were to clear their land and establish habitations within twelve months of receiving their allotments or risk forfeiture; in addition, they were to inhabit and cultivate their land for two years thereafter. Although land could not at first be sold, it could be inherited by male heirs, and if there were no male heirs, it reverted to the Trustees. Applying strictures to themselves as well, the Trustees adopted a charter provision prohibiting themselves from profiting financially from their colonizing effort.

These were the intentions of the Georgia Trustees; yet the need for financing led them to modify their course. When appeals to private philanthropy produced more in Bibles than in pounds sterling, the Trustees turned to the English merchant community and government for financial support. Ultimately, the English government bore 90 percent of the cost of establishing the colony.[52] Their search for funding also compelled the Trustees to open the colony to financially independent settlers: in the first ten years, roughly 10 percent of the settlers fit into this category.[53] These private adventurers, like the charity grantees, were forbidden to alienate their land and were required to build upon and cultivate their lots within three years. Yet large landowners eventually succeeded in

[51] Ibid., p. 139.
[52] Ibid., p. 146.
[53] Ibid., p. 199 n. 38.

removing the restriction against the sale of land. The Trustees' intentions were also modified in regard to the slavery issue. While slaveholding was forbidden because it was deemed inconsistent with the ideal of modest freehold farms, the Trustees agreed to allow freeholders to take along one male servant or apprentice, provided they were not kept in service for more than four years. Upon completion of their service, these former servants and apprentices were guaranteed by the Trustees a grant of twenty acres. These terms implied a commitment to the independent proprietor ideal; yet on this issue, too, the Trustees eventually acceded to the demands of large landowners, ending the ban on slavery in 1750.

Despite the Trustees' failure to carry through their initial ideals, these ideals gave rise to one of the great accomplishments of colonial town planning—Oglethorpe's plan for Savannah. Although not entirely original, Oglethorpe's plan demonstrated how the virtues of sociability, bounded self-reliance, and controlled development could be incorporated into urban, or rather town, design. Savannah was essentially a city of squares: the basic unit of design was the "ward," a superblock composed of a series of smaller squares. In its original design, Savannah consisted of six wards, each with a central open space of approximately two acres. Within the four corners of each ward was a group of ten lots, called a *tithing*; thus, each ward consisted of four tithings or forty lots. The beauty of the ward concept was that it was not merely a physical design, but a social and political entity as well. The house lots centered around the ward's open space, and each ward had its own constable and minor elected officials, as well as its own common land in the surrounding countryside, all of which contributed to the building of community ties.[54] Yet self-reliance—however bounded—was also encouraged. Oglethorpe made sure that every freeholder had a five-acre plot for a garden so that each man would be able to provide for himself. This provision was in addition to the initial practice of "entailing" grants of land; that is, land could not be sold but only passed on to heirs. This practice was intended to guarantee that no man could forfeit his inheritance, through either his own misfortune or the avarice of others. Yet the ward concept was not only an attempt to integrate the realms of workplace, polity, and community; the provision that ward residents

[54] See Stevenson and Feiss, "Charleston and Savannah," pp. 8-9; for an alternative interpretation, attributing Savannah's design to military defense considerations, see Bannister, "Oglethorpe's Sources for the Savannah Plan," pp. 47-62.

were to share common land and to farm adjacent parcels in the outlying countryside was also an attempt to link the domains of town and country, making Savannah an example of true regional planning. Finally, the ward concept was a practical device for organizing urban expansion: instead of allowing formless growth, as manifested in the suburban sprawl of so many American cities today, Oglethorpe's plan was to expand Savannah through the addition of wards. And, surprisingly, given what was occurring in other cities, Savannah was able to organize its growth in this way for over one hundred years. From the original six wards, the number of wards grew to twenty-four, the last one added in 1851 when the city's population stood at fourteen thousand.[55]

PHILADELPHIA and Savannah represent two extremes of colonial town planning: in one case a city that developed as a speculative venture from the outset, in the other a city that surrendered to the forces of speculation only after its founders' ideals were exhausted. What they share, in spite of their different origins, is that in each one an effort was made to incorporate the collective interests of the inhabitants into the organization of the town. This concern was reflected, in both these and other colonial towns, in the generous open spaces created, the attention to street arrangement, the central placement of public and semi-public institutions such as the church and marketplace, and the determined effort to establish compact settlements with easy access to work and nature in the outlying farm lots and common lands. In the pre-liberal world that produced these settlements, it was taken for granted that government or such other collective institutions as existed should seek to provide for the common good; there was yet no accepted distinction between public and private that prevented local authorities from organizing the development of the town on the basis of their conception of the public interest. What Philadelphia and Savannah also share is that, in both, land speculation became the dominant motif of town development, reflecting the experience of other cities and towns in colonial America. There were many other positive accomplishments of colonial era town planning, to be sure. Boston established an attractive park-like central common and, in 1824, extended its common by creating a public garden along the waterfront. Charlestown, the one-time administrative center of Massachusetts Bay Colony, was distinguished by

---

[55] Bannister, "Oglethorpe's Sources," p. 48.

its attractive square and harbor promenades. New Haven was innovative in the large size of its central open space—one-ninth of the city exclusive of streets was reserved for public use. And Annapolis pioneered in calling for the separation of nuisance activities (such as tanning and dyeing) from the central area of the town. Yet the story is essentially the same in each case: efforts to incorporate community interests into the development of the town came under pressure from and typically were overwhelmed by the forces of land speculation, coinciding with changes in the political and economic treatment of land.

TOWARD A CAPITALIST LAND SYSTEM

If progress in town planning is the product of experience in urban living, it is profoundly shaped by the manner in which land is owned and acquired, including the legal definition of property ownership and the economic status of land. Colonial town planting was the product of an era in which the forces that foster wide-scale land speculation were largely contained. Land had yet to be completely transformed into a commodity; by custom as well as law, land was still regarded as a quasi-public resource. This attitude, in addition to the cultural norms enforcing a sense of individual responsibility for the welfare of the whole, gave the planning of this era its distinctive cast. Accordingly, the emergence of new attitudes, new political institutions, and, most important, new methods of owning and treating land brought to a close this era of town planning and, by creating a new set of problems, laid the basis for a new, capitalist epoch of town planning.

The land system that evolved in the eighteenth century was a capitalist system that emphasized the rights of individual landowners over the rights of society. Land came to be regarded as a private right rather than a social resource in the legal sphere, and as a commodity rather than a collective good in the economic sphere. The conversion of land into a commodity had to await the emergence of an urban real estate market; as previously noted, this phenomenon came about with the filling up of seaboard settlements, the accumulation of wealth by merchants, and the subjugation of the Indians along the frontier. In addition, the evolution of a capitalist land system required changes in the legal manner of owning and regarding land.

In New England, the colonists had adopted the least feudal of the available English forms of landholding, the Kentish tenure.[56] Yet throughout the colonial period, there were attempts to make English land law, the "most important area of private law in an agricultural society," serve as the basis for a social and economic order like that existing in England.[57] In all of the colonies except those in New England, land was typically, although not exclusively, granted in large holdings. Some of these tracts were granted to royal favorites who sought to establish semi-feudal relations between themselves and the colonists. Other great tracts were conveyed to speculators who hoped to sell at a profit or encourage colonization as a way of reaping monopoly trade advantages. Yet these efforts to link privilege to property were encumbered by the colonists' resistance to the imposing of a feudal system of land tenure on them, and by the defeat of the Indians along the frontier, which left so much idle land available. In short, the American colonists were not satisfied to work as employees or tenants or to "abide by land laws made for a small, densely populated England characterized by highly capitalized farming."[58]

The two feudal encumbrances on land tenure that had survived in the new world were primogeniture and entailment. There could not have been two more effective devices for maintaining aristocratic privileges. As J. Franklin Jameson has written, "The feudal ages had discovered that, if men desired to give stability to society by keeping property in the hands of the same families generation after generation, the best way to do this was to entail the lands strictly, so that the holder could not sell them or even give them away, and to have a law of primogeniture, which, in case the father made no will, would turn over his estate to the eldest son, to the exclusion of all other children."[59] By the time the Revolution broke out, Pennsylvania and Maryland had abolished primogeniture, and South Carolina had abolished entails. In New York, New Jersey, Virginia, North Carolina, and Georgia, however, primogeniture and entails flourished almost as they did in old England. In fact, the entails in Virginia were stricter than those in England. Interestingly, the New England colonies had a peculiar, somewhat more democratic, rule for distributing property in case a man left

---

[56] See Harris, *Origin of the Land Tenure System*, pp. 152-54.

[57] Horack and Nolan, *Land Use Controls: Supplementary Materials on Real Property*, p. 18.

[58] Ibid.

[59] Jameson, *The American Revolution Considered as a Social Movement*, pp. 55-56.

no will: all children inherited equally except for the eldest son who received a double share.

Although there was no violent outbreak against the land system that prevailed at the time of the Revolution, that system was rapidly altered in the years between 1775 and 1795. The new land system was quite different from the one preceding the Revolution and "in sharp contrast with the feudal tenure forced upon rural England by William the Conqueror."[60] Following the Revolution, royal restrictions on land acquisition were overturned and all the vast domains of the Crown fell into the hands of the states. The much despised system of quitrents was abolished and forbidden thereafter.[61] Moreover, in the ten years following the Declaration of Independence, all but two states had outlawed the practice of entailment, and the two exceptions were states in which entails were rare. In the fifteen years following the Declaration of Independence, every state had abolished primogeniture. In addition, the legislatures of the various states confiscated a large number of Tory estates. Finally, the Northwest Ordinances of 1784–1787 and the new federal Constitution specified that all land west of the Alleghenies would be held and would descend according to "fee-simple" tenure. The fee-simple method allowed land to be bought and sold with great simplicity: three witnesses and a written document were all that was needed for a binding transaction; land could be passed on to heirs in the same manner—with three witnesses and a written document; resident and nonresident landowners were to be taxed equally, while federal land was tax-exempt; and no private property was to be seized without due process of law. An individual's property was not to be disturbed except for important public purposes, and then only after a full hearing and just compensation.[62]

These legal changes at once signified and completed the transition to an individualistic, capitalist land system. It is ironic that this transition occurred when it did, just as the social character of land was becoming more evident with the evolution of towns into cities and the emergence of an urban form of life. As new problems appeared with the growth of cities—problems of housing and population congestion, sanitation and waste removal, water supply, public open space, streets and transportation, and the control of

---

[60] Harris, *Origin of the Land Tenure System*, p. 394.
[61] Horack and Nolan, *Land Use Controls*, pp. 19-20.
[62] Warner, *Urban Wilderness*, p. 17.

nuisance activities—the difficulties of relying upon an individualistic land system became more evident. It was through efforts to
respond to these problems that the discontinuous history of urban
planning reasserted itself and the modern—capitalist—era of urban planning was inaugurated. Yet the various problems arising
from the contradiction between the social character of land and its
private use and control did not affect every group; nor were these
groups equally capable of drawing attention to the problems that
did affect them, although grounds existed for intergroup alliances.
Which face of the property contradiction government responded
to, how it responded, whether it responded at all—these depended
on the relative power of the various groups within the city. It is to
such efforts to fashion or refashion the government role in urban
development that we now turn.

THREE

Early Housing Reform

ON MARCH 28, 1856, New York City's *Daily Times* editorialized that New York's experience, "like that of the cities of the old world, is that the avarice of capitalists renders governmental interference for the protection of the poor and unfortunate an absolute necessity."[1] The *Times'* commentary was inspired by the report of a state legislative committee appointed to study New York City's tenement house problem. The committee had concluded its report by stating that "[t]he tenant house is the legitimate point at which to commence the positive work of social reform."[2] Indeed, it could be said that the American "welfare state" began with efforts to improve housing conditions in nineteenth-century American cities. The report of the legislative committee described filth, dilapidation, overcrowding, degradation, dark rooms, offensive privies, lack of water, high rents, and exorbitant profits that were nearly unbelievable by present standards. These deplorable conditions were a direct result of the treatment of land as a commodity and the absence of government restrictions on the use of land—although early reformers were slow, or else refused, to grasp the connection between the "land question" and the housing problem. The housing problem was also related to exploitation in the workplace and below-subsistence wages, although this connection too was obscured, reflecting what Ira Katznelson has termed the "parcelization" of class relations in America that separates the issues and conflicts of the workplace from those of the living place.[3]

In the history of early housing reform, we can see how a response was fashioned to one of the earliest manifestations of the contradiction between the social character of land and its private use and control, or what has been termed the property contradiction. In addition to showing how early housing reform measures responded to the property contradiction, this chapter provides an account of the individuals and groups who fashioned this re-

---

[1] Quoted in Wood, *The Housing of the Unskilled Wage Earner*, p. 34.
[2] Quoted, ibid.
[3] "Considerations on Social Democracy in the United States," pp. 95-97.

sponse, as well as the interests that guided their efforts. It will be shown that these reforms were the work of a new breed of educated professional, best epitomized by Lawrence Veiller, and were supported by business groups and merchant-dominated organizations. Veiller (pronounced VAY-ay) was a model of the "planner" before the term came into the vocabulary of reform. In spite of, and partly because of, his difference of attitude and sense of separation from the city's business class, he helped to educate members of that class about their enlightened corporate interest regarding the city's ill-housed tenement poor. The result of this appeal to and education of the rich was a larger government role in urban development in the form of restrictions on the owners and builders of tenement (that is, working-class) housing.

Behind this government intervention was a desire on the part of middle- and upper-income groups for control—of the morality of the largely immigrant urban working class, of their political and social behavior and orientation toward work, and of the spread of disease from working-class quarters. This relates to Manuel Castells's argument, cited in Chapter 1, that the growth of state intervention (urban planning) is a response to capital's need to ensure the "reproduction of labor power"—the renewal of workers' capacity to produce value for capitalists. It will be argued, however, that the housing reforms adopted in the nineteenth century were less a product of capital's need to reproduce labor power, which implies the centrality of capital's economic or workplace-related needs, than of capital's need to maintain its position of hegemonic class leadership and stimulate worker acceptance of capitalism. It was not its economic needs directly but the political and ideological needs of capital that made limited housing reform possible. Yet these reforms were, for two reasons, marginal. First, housing reform ran afoul of the "property rights" of that fraction of capital (Lamarche's "property capital") responsible for the design, construction, finance, and management of worker housing. Second, and more important for understanding the limited progress of housing reform in the United States in comparison with the industrialized nations of Europe, the housing problem did not significantly mobilize American workers politically in the nineteenth century. Housing issues stimulated an elite-based reform movement which, coupled with a fragmented, ad hoc, episodic working-class politics, reflected not only the generally lower level of mobilization of American workers, but also the failure of labor organizations prior to the early twentieth century to address the housing problem as a class or worker issue. Thus, if capital had a political and ideological interest in ameliorating the housing problem, the fact that worker mobilization on this issue was marginal, despite deplorable conditions, rendered capital's interest marginal, too.

As a response to the property contradiction and an example of government intervention in the built environment, housing reform falls within the compass of city planning as analytically defined. Yet housing reform in America has a history distinct from that of formal city planning. Although, as discussed in Chapter 6, the cause of housing reform provided the impetus for the organization of a national city planning movement, the two movements remained formally separate: each had its own leaders, national organizations, philosophies, and reform agendas.[4] Indeed, this separation of housing reform and formal city planning is a key difference between urban planning in the United States and Europe. It is therefore important to take account of how housing reform developed as a form of city planning, and how and why the two movements remained apart. This chapter examines the main lines of development of housing reform from the mid–nineteenth century to the early 1900s. Other responses to the housing problem, such as employer-built housing and the effort to incorporate housing concerns into formal city planning after the beginning of the twentieth century, are recounted in Chapter 6.

CAPITALISM AND THE RISE OF THE CITY

Understanding the origins of housing reform necessitates understanding the changes taking place in the nineteenth-century American city. This era was, in Eric Hobsbawm's celebrated phrase, the dawn of the "Age of Capital"—an era in which a revolution in the organization of production led to the ascendancy of a new class, the men of capital, and to profound changes in the way people lived and worked.[5] The impact of this revolution can be seen in the changing determinants of urban growth.

Since colonial days, the dominant cities along the Atlantic— New York, Boston, Philadelphia, and Baltimore—had relied upon trade as the primary source of urban wealth. In the tradition of classic mercantile cities, they had taken advantage of their nodal

[4] For a discussion of this separation, see Marcuse, "Housing in Early City Planning," pp. 153-76.
[5] *The Age of Capital, 1848–1875.*

location along important trading routes and their special trading privileges to "buy cheap and sell dear." However, this reliance upon trade and the control of trade as the primary source of wealth began to be replaced, around the middle of the nineteenth century, with new forms of wealth based upon control of production. First in the textile mills of Massachusetts in the 1840s, then in eastern seaboard cities in the following decades, large numbers of workers were assembled in factories and set to work at machines. The factory owners, having purchased the workers' labor power as well as the raw materials and machines at which they worked, became the owners of the product of the workers' labor, while simultaneously gaining control of the process of production, expanding and curtailing output to meet the demands of the market. As the seaboard cities became centers for the manufacture of commodities, new cities to the west developed a manufacturing base to complement their commercial functions. Many of these cities specialized in particular commodities: Pittsburgh produced glass; Louisville, textiles; Cleveland, iron goods; and Chicago, meat and agricultural products. In the thirty-year period surrounding the Civil War the pace of production-related change quickened: between 1859 and 1889 the number of wage earners increased from 1.3 million to 4 million; the number of industrial establishments from 140,000 to 355,000; and the value of manufactured products from less than 2 billion dollars to more than 9 billion.[6]

The rise of manufacturing cities built around new forms of production was facilitated by a number of developments. The growth of the interurban railroad network commencing in the 1830s widened markets and stimulated specialization of production in both agriculture and manufacturing. Whereas the earliest industrial establishments had located away from coastal population centers to gain access to waterpower and a docile rural labor force, expanded use of the steam engine and the replacement of waterpower by coal enabled factories to locate inside larger cities. (Conversely, the development of electrical power in the latter part of the nineteenth century facilitated the movement of factories away from urban areas.) The production of interchangeable parts and the development of a machine tool industry provided the base for mechanized factory production. As will be detailed below, immigration from abroad, which increased dramatically in the 1840s following

[6] The statistics are from U.S. Department of Commerce, Bureau of the Census, *Historical Statistics of the United States, 1789–1945.*

the Irish potato famine and surged higher in the 1880s with the arrival of immigrants from southern and eastern Europe, provided a cheap labor pool, replacing the farm women of New England as the preferred industrial workforce while deepening the market for finished goods. And not least, the emergence of joint-stock companies, legally protected by limited liability laws, made possible the centralization of capital necessary for large-scale factory production.[7]

Although the United States was far from being an urban nation on the eve of the Civil War—in 1860 only one-fifth of the population lived in cities of 2,500 or more—the three previous decades experienced the most rapid urban growth in the nation's history. Between 1830 and 1840, the total number of urban residents grew by 64 percent; between 1840 and 1850, by 92 percent; and between 1850 and 1860, by 75 percent. Chicago's explosive population growth provides an extreme example of what was happening nationally. In 1832, Chicago consisted of little more than a score of log cabins, two taverns, a store, and Fort Dearborn. Yet two years later it had a population of 4,000; by 1848, it was a city of 20,000; in 1865, its population stood at 180,000; and in the next twenty years its population quadrupled. By 1880, there were seventy-seven cities in the United States with a population over 25,000 and twenty urban centers with 100,000 or more inhabitants. In that year, New York City's population reached 1 million. Through the 1880s the boom continued unabated; Chicago's increase of 600,000 in that decade topped all others, including increases of more than 300,000 in New York, 240,000 in Brooklyn, and 200,000 in Philadelphia.[8]

Most of the urban population growth was the result of immigration from abroad, although internal migration from farm to city was also taking place. Again, the figures are startling. Between 1820 and the early 1920s, when restrictive legislation sharply reduced immigration, more than 33 million people entered the United States. The period of greatest immigration was between 1880 and 1920, when an average of 6 million people arrived in each

[7] See Chudacoff, *The Evolution of American Urban Society*, pp. 28-36; Warner, *Urban Wilderness*, pp. 64-84; and Gordon, "Capitalism and the Roots of the Urban Crisis," pp. 86-90.

[8] The statistics are from Chudacoff, *American Urban Society*, p. 56; Robert A. Walker, *The Planning Function in Urban Government*, p. 6; Urbanism Committee of the Natural Resources Committee, *Our Cities: Their Role in the National Economy*, p. 1; and Scott, *American City Planning*, p. 2.

decade. These later immigrants were mostly from southern and eastern Europe, and they concentrated in the ghettos of northeastern industrial cities. In fact, throughout this period of mass immigration, there were more urban dwellers among those of foreign birth and parentage than among persons of native parentage. By 1920, 48 percent of all urban residents were either foreign-born or the children of foreign-born parents; in cities of 100,000 or more, which together housed almost one-quarter of the nation's population, 58 percent were of foreign birth or parentage.[9]

The vast majority of these immigrants moved simultaneously from Europe to America and from the country to the city. For most, it was also a transition to a new system of production. Unable to practice the subsistence farming made possible by a rural existence, they became dependent upon selling their labor power for a wage. This situation provided American capitalists with a cheap supply of unskilled urban labor to man the factories, build the railroads, canals, factories, and houses, and accomplish the variety of other jobs essential to the development of industrial capitalism. The concentration of immigrants in cities also tended to push up land values, stimulate the construction industry, and increase the value of private real estate holdings. At the same time, it provided a constantly expanding consumer market for the goods-producing industries.[10]

By the middle of the nineteenth century, the consequences of haphazardly concentrating large numbers of people in a small area were already manifesting themselves in intolerable living conditions and repeated epidemics. Whole neighborhoods became blighted as houses were cut up into tiny apartments to house the new urban working class. Poor sanitation and overcrowding in worker districts spawned an assortment of social ills, ranging from communicable diseases such as smallpox, yellow fever, and tuberculosis to alcoholism, delinquency, prostitution, and suicide. By 1850, there were 135.6 persons per acre in New York, 82.7 in Boston, 80.0 in Philadelphia, and 68.4 in Pittsburgh.[11] In 1905, New York had 122 blocks with a density of 750 persons per acre and 39 blocks with 1,000 or more to the acre. An investigation conducted in that city in 1908 by the Neighborhood Workers Association

[9] The statistics are from David Ward, *Cities and Immigrants: A Geography of Change in Nineteenth-Century America*, pp. 52-57.

[10] See O'Donnell, "Industrial Capitalism and the Rise of Modern American Cities," pp. 91-128.

[11] Chudacoff, *American Urban Society*, p. 66.

showed that nearly 50 percent of the families with which they had contact lived 4 or more to a room.[12] In New York, as in other large industrial cities, buildings with no sanitary provisions beyond the privy and the gutter were so crowded together that many dwellings virtually were without light and air. None of the large cities, moreover, made adequate public provision for disposal of sewage until late in the nineteenth century. Even in 1900, Philadelphia and St. Louis had twice as much street mileage as sewer mileage.[13]

Dramatic changes also were occurring in the realm of work: the subordination of people to machines, the intensification of labor and extension of work hours, the emergence of new and unprecedented hierarchies of skills, and the increased vulnerability to layoff and depression. But the effect of capitalist industrialization on the way people lived was likewise profound. In an earlier era, an employer might have felt an obligation to ensure proper living conditions for his workers; but the system of wage labor released the employer from that ancient responsibility, leaving the worker to fend for himself in a housing market dominated by speculators and shysters. As David Gordon has written, the life of the worker became "shot through with chance."[14] Secure employment, good health, decent living conditions, and freedom from want were all placed beyond workers' control. This change inevitably led to demands for assistance from government and other collective institutions such as the church, and it was during the latter half of the nineteenth century that most of the basic institutions of urban America were built up. Among the services and institutions developing in this period were almshouses and settlement houses, insane asylums, local public education, and full-time professional police forces. It was also in this era that new forms of government regulation emerged; among the first and most important of these were restrictions on the construction and maintenance of urban housing.

Chronology of Early Housing Reform

With the exception of earlier fire regulations, housing restrictions aimed at improving the quality of urban housing were not adopted

---

[12] Marsh, *An Introduction to City Planning: Democracy's Challenge to the American City*, p. 15.

[13] Robert Walker, *Planning Function*, p. 7.

[14] "Roots of the Urban Crisis," p. 91.

in the United States until the mid–nineteenth century.[15] These efforts began in New York, which probably had worse housing conditions at the time than any other American city, due largely to its status as the principal port of entry for European immigrants.[16] As a leading housing reformer wrote, New York is "the city in the United States in which improper tenement conditions began earliest and proceeded farthest."[17]

More accurately, one might say housing policy began in New York/New Amsterdam in 1647, when the director of the Dutch West India Company authorized the condemnation of disorderly and improper buildings, or in 1676, when the Common Council voted that "all the ruinated and decayed houses which are untenentable within this city" be "disposed off" to those willing and able to repair them.[18] Yet these colonial acts were discontinuous with the later history of housing reform. A better starting point is 1834: in that year, a city health inspector's report attributed New York's high death rate to the deplorable conditions found in its tenement houses.[19] No cause for the city's increasing death rate appeared "so prominent as that of intemperance and the crowded and filthy state in which a great portion of our population live, apparently without being sensible of their situation," the report declared. Although the last phrase implied that the victims were partly to blame, the report pointed an accusing finger at the city's tenement landlords, observing that there was "serious cause to regret that there are in our city so many mercenary landlords who only contrive in what manner they can stow the greatest number of human beings in the smallest space."[20] Eight years later, a report issued by another health inspector, Dr. John H. Griscom, was even more detailed and insistent about the link between slum housing

[15] Concern over fire hazards, usually following some conflagration, led to the enactment of building regulations in a number of early cities, e.g., Boston in 1679 and Charleston in 1740; see Bridenbaugh, *Cities in the Wilderness*, p. 472.

[16] That housing reform in the United States began in New York City is generally recognized; see, e.g., Wood, *Housing of the Wage Earner*, pp. 29-46, and James Ford, *Slums and Housing*, p. 121.

[17] De Forest, "Introduction: Tenement Reform in New York Since 1901," in de Forest and Veiller, *The Tenement House Problem*, 1:xxx.

[18] On the 1647 act, see Valentine, *History of New York*, p. 32; the passage for the 1676 law is from James Ford, *Slums and Housing*, p. 37.

[19] This is the date cited by housing reformer Lawrence Veiller; see Veiller, "Tenement House Reform in New York City, 1834–1900," in de Forest and Veiller, *The Tenement House Problem*, 1:71.

[20] Quoted, ibid.

conditions and death and disease. Griscom, who became a leader in the cause of housing reform, observed that the city's worst housing was found in cellar lodgings and rear court buildings. There were, he noted, 7,196 persons making their residence in 1,459 underground rooms and 6,618 families living in courts or rear buildings.[21] In examining these filthy holes, "it is almost impossible to maintain the proper degree of calmness," Griscom wrote.

> You must descend to them; you must feel the blast of foul air as it meets your face on opening the door; you must grope in the dark, or hesitate until your eye becomes accustomed to the gloomy place, to enable you to find your way through the entry, over a broken floor, the boards of which are protected from your tread by a half inch of hard dirt; you must inhale the suffocating vapor of the sitting and sleeping rooms; and in the dark, damp recess, endeavor to find the inmates by the sound of their voices, or chance to see their figures moving between you and the flickering blaze of a shaving burning on the hearth, or the misty light of a window coated with dirt and festooned with cobwebs—or in search of an invalid, take care that you do not fall full length upon the bed with her, by stumbling against the bundle of rags and straw, dignified by that name, lying on the floor, under the window, if window there is;—all this, and much more, beyond the reach of my pen, must be felt and seen, ere you can appreciate in its full force the mournful and disgusting condition, in which many thousands of the subjects of our government pass their lives.[22]

Yet, like so many early discussions of the housing problem, Griscom's horrifying description was accompanied by a weak, even nonsensical, analysis of the source of the problem. At its root, the problem was the "subjection of the tenantry to the merciless inflictions and extortions of the sub-landlord"—persons who rented buildings from their presumably more respectable owners and then subdivided them, converting them into tenements. Yet his remedy was inconsistent even with this diagnosis: the really important thing was that only "medically educated" men should be

[21] See Veiller, "Tenement House Reform," p. 73.
[22] Griscom, *The Sanitary Conditions of the Laboring Population of New York, with Suggestions for its Improvements*, p. 8.

appointed as city health inspector and to the city's numerous health warden positions.[23]

Prior to the Civil War, the principal source of organized opposition to New York City's rapidly deteriorating housing conditions was the New York Association for Improving the Condition of the Poor. Founded in 1843, the AICP sought to coordinate and bring a sense of direction to the city's numerous private charities. It owed its origin to the discovery, during the depression of 1837, of the organizational weakness of New York's existing private charity structure. Although membership in the AICP was open to all who could pay an annual fee, the members were predominantly middle-class Protestant merchants and professional men, along with shopkeepers and artisans.[24] According to historian Roy Lubove, who extensively examined the AICP, the members of the association were motivated by a sense of Christian benevolence, combined with a concern for the threat to order and to middle-class standards of morality posed by the ill-housed immigrant poor. Unfortunately for the poor, the members' Christian belief in the dignity and brotherhood of man "was compromised by the middle class ethos which harshly condemned the poor for their imperfections," wrote Lubove.[25] Article II of the AICP's Constitution described its general objective as "the elevation of the moral and physical condition of the indigent"—which led it to attack unwholesome and unsanitary living conditions as well as what it termed "indiscriminate charity."[26] Although, judging from its many tracts, the association believed poverty was caused by the indolence, improvidence, and intemperance of the poor, it leaned toward a philosophy of physical environmental determinism in examining the slum and its consequences, apparently without recognizing any contradiction.[27] The association was consistent in one respect, though: whatever caused poverty, the AICP believed the moral reformation of the poor was necessary for their salvation.

[23] Ibid., pp. 6, 43-44.

[24] Lubove, "The New York Association for Improving the Condition of the Poor: The Formative Years," p. 313. Lubove, having examined the backgrounds of the chief officeholders and advisory committee members of the AICP, observed that merchants predominated, followed by artisans and retailers and a scattering of lawyers, doctors, and manufacturers (p. 313).

[25] Ibid., p. 315.

[26] Ibid., pp. 316-17.

[27] On this point, see Lubove, *The Progressives and the Slums*, p. 6.

In a succession of annual reports, the AICP reviled the slums for their deleterious effect upon health and morals. Their reports argued that the fetid atmosphere of the slum was a breeding ground for disease and disorder, and that these ills posed a threat to the larger society. "Physical evils produce moral evils," the AICP declared. "Degrade men to the condition of brutes, and they will have brutal propensities and passions."[28] The overcrowding of population that caused whole families to sleep and dress in the same room, often in the company of lodgers brought in to supplement the family income, was singled out for particular condemnation. Here was a threat to middle class standards of morality of the first order, defying as it did all attempts at decency and modesty. This kind of overcrowding "breaks down the barriers of self-respect, and prepares the way for direct profligacy," the AICP declared.[29] Although the health dangers of bad housing were frequently noted, it was the slum's effect on the morality and social behavior of the poor and the consequent threat to political and social stability that most disturbed the AICP. The association's social control perspective was evident from its statement in 1856 that, unless the conditions of the poor were improved, they would "overrun the city as thieves and beggars—endanger public peace and security of property and life—tax the community for their support, and entail upon it an inheritance of vice and pauperism."[30]

In 1856, twenty-two years after a city health inspector first called attention to New York City's deplorable housing conditions, the state of New York finally acted. Following an outbreak of cholera, the state legislature appointed a select committee to examine conditions in "tenant houses" in New York and Brooklyn. The appointment of this legislative committee contributed to the "discovery" of the poor by New York policy makers.[31] Wanting to make a "thorough personal inspection," the committee members toured the city's slum districts with a group of reporters and

[28] Quoted, ibid.
[29] Quoted, ibid., p. 7.
[30] Quoted, ibid.
[31] One is reminded here of Engels's description of how the working-class district in Manchester was hidden in the 1840s. The city was "peculiarly built," he wrote, "so that a person may live in it for years, and go in and out daily without coming into contact with a working-people's quarter or even with workers, that is, so long as he confines himself to his business or to pleasure walks." See Engels, *The Condition of the Working Class in England*, p. 84.

a police detail for protection. They "penetrated to localities and witnessed scenes which, in frightful novelty, far exceeded the limit of their previously conceived ideas of human degradation and suffering."[32] Completed four months later, the committee's report expressed shock at the deplorable conditions discovered and condemned the capitalist "avarice" and "public lethargy" they deemed responsible for these circumstances.[33] The report described how thousands of poor persons, mostly German and Irish immigrants, were being herded together "like cattle in pens" in dilapidated houses left behind by "the wealthy who have moved up town." In explaining how these conditions arose, the committee cited the role of real estate speculators: as immigration increased and property values and rents rose in the lower wards of the city, "it was soon perceived, by astute owners or agents of property that a greater percentage of profit would be realized by the conversion of houses and blocks into barracks, and dividing their space into the smallest proportions capable of containing human life within four walls." This was done, the commission wrote, and these buildings "soon became filled, from cellar to garret, with a class of tenantry living from hand to mouth, loose in morals, improvident in habits, degraded or squalid as beggary itself."[34]

Like the AICP, the legislative committee viewed the tenement slum as a problem of social control. "Of a surety, we must, as a people, *act* upon this foreign element, or it will act upon us," the committee warned.

> Like the vast Atlantic, we must decompose and cleanse the impurities which rush into our midst, or . . . we shall receive their poison into our whole national system. American *social virtue* has deteriorated . . . through the operation of influences connected with the influx of foreigners, without corresponding precautions to counteract them.[35]

These words attest to the concern over the consequences of failing to address the needs of the poor. Contributing to this apprehension were a number of events. A cholera epidemic in 1854, vaguely traceable in contemporary accounts to housing conditions, caused 2,509 deaths. Commercial distress in 1857 led the city's Common Council to distribute food to the poor—at a time when bakers'

[32] Excerpted in James Ford, *Slums and Housing*, p. 131.
[33] Quoted in Lubove, *Progressives and the Slums*, p. 10.
[34] Excerpted in James Ford, *Slums and Housing*, p. 132.
[35] Quoted in Lubove, *Progressives and the Slums*, p. 10.

wagons were being attacked in the streets—to prevent rioting.[36] The AICP, noting in 1858 that there were 25,000 unemployed who, with their families, represented approximately 100,000 persons in distress, warned: "The rich must shell out to the poor, or the musket will be the resort."[37]

Further evidence of the consequences of the slum was provided by New York City's "draft riots" of 1863, a cataclysm of violence that was precipitated by opposition to Civil War conscription practices and in which over 1,000 persons were killed. The impact of this violence upon the consciousness of New York's upper classes was described by housing reformer Lawrence Veiller.

> When in these troublous times, during our Civil War, the tenement poured forth the mobs that held fearful sway in the city, during the outbreak of violence in the month of July, then, for the first time, did the general public realize what it meant to permit human beings to be reared under the conditions which had so long prevailed in the tenement houses in New York City.[38]

A New York journalist who toured the streets during the disturbances expressed amazement "that so much misery, disease, and wretchedness could be huddled together and hidden by high walls, unvisited and unthought of so near our own abodes."[39] The upper classes were quick to respond to this breach of order. In the spring of 1864, a Citizen's Association was created by a group of New York's foremost citizens. This body in turn appointed a Council of Hygiene, whose membership included a number of leading physicians, and charged it with preparing a complete report on sanitary conditions in the city. The thoroughness of the council's investigation, which divided the city into twenty-nine districts and assigned a prominent physician to study the sanitary conditions in each district, was an indication that science was coming to be viewed as a tool of social reform. The findings and recommendations included in the council's report led directly to the creation, in 1866, of the Metropolitan Sanitary District and Board of Health of New York and, in 1867, to the enactment of New York and the nation's first tenement house law.

The 1867 tenement house law was a landmark in the history of

[36] See James Ford, *Slums and Housing*, p. 129.
[37] Quoted, ibid.
[38] "Tenement House Reform," p. 92.
[39] Quoted, ibid.

housing reform. Applying to all buildings housing more than three families, it required among other things a window in every sleeping room, an approved fire escape, and at least one water closet or privy for every twenty occupants. Basement or cellar rooms were not to be occupied without a permit from the Board of Health, the building owner's name and address was to be posted inside the building, and at least ten feet of rear open space was required unless an exception was granted by the Board of Health. Unfortunately, this first law did not do away with all the conditions it proscribed. While it had enormous symbolic value as a demonstration of the public's right to place restrictions on the builder and tenement landlord, it proved largely unenforceable and ineffective. Part of the problem was the enormity of the task of bringing so many old buildings up to code. It is estimated that, before the adoption of the law, fifteen thousand tenement houses had been built, with little regard for the health and safety of occupants.[40] Furthermore, too many matters were left to the discretion of the newly organized Board of Health. It was given too little manpower and funding and proved corruptible in the face of enormous pressures brought to bear upon it by disgruntled code violators. Also, in limiting the law's reach to buildings with more than three families (which is how the "tenement" was legally defined), some of the worst housing in the city was exempted.[41] In 1871, the AICP reported that, although conditions had "greatly improved" as a result of the legislation, "it is still the disgrace and curse of the city, that half of its inhabitants live in [tenement] houses, from which proceeds three-fifths of the crime and three-fourths of the mortality."[42]

Another attempt to ameliorate housing conditions was through the building of model tenements. Here, innovations were sought in both the financing and design of low-cost housing. The AICP pioneered in this effort, albeit without much success. Believing adequate worker housing could be built at an affordable price while still returning a profit, the association constructed a model tenement in 1855. Christened the Workingmen's Home, it was a substantial brick structure, six stories tall and "somewhat prison-like in appearance," covering six city lots.[43] Later renamed the Big Flat, this giant tenement was the largest multiple dwelling built in

---

[40] Ibid., p. 96.
[41] Lubove, *Progressives and the Slums*, p. 26.
[42] Quoted in Veiller, "Tenement House Reform," p. 97.
[43] Bremner, "The Big Flat: History of a New York Tenement House," p. 54.

New York City before the 1880s. Robert M. Hartley, executive secretary of the AICP and the man principally responsible for the Workingmen's Home, described its apartments as "commodious and well-ventilated."[44] This description was accurate only in comparison with the typical lodgings of the poor: except for apartments facing the street, the building's three-and-one-half-room apartments had only two windows, one opening on the courtyard and the other on the hall. It was not long before this model tenement deteriorated into one of the worst slums in the city. In 1867, the AICP sold the building, and in the 1880s the association described it as unfit for human habitation.[45] Another effort to build model tenement housing was that of philanthropist Alfred White. In the late 1870s, White tried to show that decent low-income housing could be built at a profit by combining innovations in building design and limited dividend financing. Drawing from the experience of the Industrial Dwellings Company in London, White constructed two square blocks of model tenements, grouping his buildings around a central courtyard, a design innovation at the time. The project earned a 7.5-percent dividend and did not immediately deteriorate into a slum as the AICP tenement had done. Yet, despite the efforts of White and others, innovations in the design and financing of housing had little appreciable effect upon the housing conditions of New York City's lower classes.

Design innovations were sometimes counterproductive, as in the infamous "dumbbell plan," specifically created for New York City's I-shaped building lots. The dumbbell plan earned its name because the building was tapered on the sides to allow for air, light, and ventilation, giving the structure a dumbbell shape from above. This plan, which became synonymous with the worst of New York's housing conditions, was the winner of a design competition sponsored by a plumbing trade journal, the *Sanitary Engineer*, in 1879. Contestants were asked to prepare a design for an ordinary New York City lot twenty-five by one hundred feet in size; the design was to be "for a house for workingmen, in which may be secured a proper distribution of light and pure air, with an arrangement of rooms that will yield a rental sufficient to pay a fair interest on the investment."[46] The prize committee, consisting of the president of the Board of Health, two ministers, an architect,

---

[44] Ibid., p. 55.

[45] Lubove, *Progressives and the Slums*, p. 9.

[46] Quoted in Jackson, *A Place Called Home: A History of Low-Cost Housing in Manhattan*, p. 45.

and a manufacturer, concluded that the "requirements of physical and moral health" could not be satisfied on a one hundred-foot lot. Abandoning principle, however, it went ahead and awarded the five hundred-dollar prize to the designer of the dumbbell plan, James Ware.[47] The *New York Times* editorialized that if these were the best plans available "they merely demonstrate that the problem is insoluble." Similarly, Lawrence Veiller wrote at the turn of the century that New York City was still "reaping the evils" of the prize plan of 1879. "It is this plan which has produced a system of tenement houses unknown to any other city, which has produced the evil of the air shaft—a product solely of New York, and one which makes our housing conditions the worst in the world."[48]

Toward the end of the nineteenth century, the quest for reform began to show results. A tenement law adopted in New York City in 1879 limited the percentage of a lot that could be occupied by a tenement building (the law obviously pertained only to new construction). The publication in 1890 of Jacob Riis's *How the Other Half Lives* stimulated further awareness of the conditions of the tenement poor and led to the appointment, in 1894, of a legislative committee whose six hundred-page report on slum housing turned the tenement into front page news. Following the social and political turmoil of the 1890s, a decade that also saw the consolidation of greater New York and a resulting increase in the size of the city's tenement problem, the state appointed another investigative commission, the Tenement House Commission of 1900. The far-reaching recommendations of this commission led directly to the adoption of New York State's epochal Tenement House Law of 1901, the most important advance in restrictive housing legislation of this era. This legislation provided the basis for model tenement laws drafted by Lawrence Veiller for adoption in other states and led to a wave of housing enactments in cities and states across the country. Among other things, the new ordinance established a separate Tenement House Department for New York City, outlawed the notorious dumbbell apartment, and set requirements for air, light, and ventilation that led to the widespread inner-court layout of apartment buildings in New York and other cities. It was also the basis for New York's distinction be-

[47] Quoted, ibid., p. 51.
[48] *New York Times*, March 16, 1879; quoted in Veiller, "Tenement House Reform," p. 102.

tween "old law" and "new law" apartments, since two sets of standards were prescribed, one for older buildings erected before 1901 and another, higher set of standards for newer buildings. The higher minimum standards for new law apartments—regulating air, light, fire protection, and sanitation—were an important advance in housing policy, although these newer apartments typically were beyond the financial reach of all but the best-paid workers. If the 1901 ordinance was of little immediate benefit to the city's lower classes, however, it was plainly harmful to the owners and builders of tenement houses. These groups had fought strenuously against the law and had worked for years, with mixed success, to dilute its provisions.[49]

The two men most closely associated with the 1901 New York State ordinance were Lawrence Veiller and Robert de Forest. Veiller was the first of the full-time reformers. Roy Lubove describes him as the forerunner of a new breed—the "professional technician of reform." He was, in Lubove's words, a "tough-minded realist and an expert manipulator of public opinion, legislative draftsman, organizer and strategist of pressure groups."[50] Between 1879 and 1917, Veiller probably did more than anyone else to shape the housing movement in New York State and the nation.[51] As secretary of the New York State Tenement House Commission of 1900, he drafted New York's 1901 ordinance and laid the plans for New York City's Tenement House Department. During the short-lived reform administration of New York City Mayor Seth Low, a former Columbia University president, Veiller and de Forest were the Tenement House Department's first two commissioners. De Forest was the nominal chief of the department and Veiller served as his deputy, although it was Veiller who effectively ran the department. In addition, Veiller, and to a lesser extent de Forest, exercised continuing influence over the Tenement House Department through their long association with New York's Charity Organization Society, de Forest serving as president of the organization and Veiller as chairman of its Tenement House Committee.[52]

[49] See Lubove, *Progressives and the Slums*, pp. 166-74; Jackson, pp. 129-33; and Wood, pp. 43-45.

[50] "Lawrence Veiller and the New York State Tenement House Commission of 1900," pp. 677, 664.

[51] Here, and in the following discussion of de Forest, I draw from Lubove, *Progressives and the Slums*, and also from his "Lawrence Veiller and the Tenement House Commission."

[52] For the contribution of the Charity Organization Society to housing reform,

Although they worked closely in the cause of housing reform, Veiller and de Forest had different backgrounds and played different roles in their many reform efforts. Veiller was the educated professional—the planner. A product of New York's City College, he became interested in social problems after reading the works of English social critics such as Ruskin and Carlyle. Upon graduation in 1890, he became involved in relief work, served as a plan examiner in the New York City Building Department, and, at the age of only twenty-eight, was appointed secretary of New York State's Housing Commission of 1900. De Forest, by contrast, is best described as a reform-minded business leader. A lawyer with an admiration for Theodore Roosevelt's sense of social responsibility, he remained active in the business world despite his many organizational activities, serving as counsel and director for a score of banks, railroads, and insurance companies. In contrast to Veiller's role as the housing activist, de Forest contributed to housing reform as the director of a number of charitable and philanthropic organizations. In addition to serving as head of the Charity Organization Society, he directed at one time or another the Russell Sage Foundation, the Welfare Council of New York, and the New York Conference on Charities and Corrections. The division of labor between Veiller and de Forest is evident in the different roles they played in the founding of the National Housing Association (NHA) in 1910. Veiller proposed the idea of organizing the association to de Forest while the latter was president of the Russell Sage Foundation. With de Forest's backing, Veiller organized the association under the auspices of the Russell Sage Foundation, and de Forest agreed to be its first president. As with the Tenement House Department, however, it was Veiller who effectively ran the organization.

Another man who played a decisive role in the struggle for housing reform was author Jacob Riis, who directed public attention to the plight of the ill-housed immigrant poor. Yet Riis was a breed apart from men like Veiller and de Forest. A former carpenter turned police reporter, he lacked their college education and class background, which was perhaps responsible for his different approach to the problem of the slum. Riis's approach was to sensationalize slum housing conditions, thereby promoting remedial action through an appeal to public conscience. Veiller and de Forest were more cynical, however; they believed improved condi-

see Watson, *The Charity Organization Movement in the United States*, pp. 287-93.

tions would be achieved only through government regulation and appeals to the enlightened self-interest of the city's upper classes.

The example of housing reform in New York City prompted similar efforts in other cities and states and led to the emergence of a national housing reform "movement" in the first decade of this century. (The term "movement" is used in a restricted sense, because the push for restrictive housing legislation never acquired the status of a mass movement with a broad base of active participation. It was, and remained, an elite-based reform movement, although a mass constituency of potential beneficiaries was claimed by the elite activists who led the movement.) Following New York State's precedent-setting 1901 ordinance, Pennsylvania, New Jersey, and Connecticut wrote similar codes, and between 1905 and 1908, Chicago, Boston, Cleveland, and San Francisco adopted municipal housing ordinances. In fact, most of the housing legislation adopted between 1901 and 1920 was based on the New York State law or on model laws drafted by Veiller, who often personally assisted communities in preparing housing codes. In addition, the formation of the NHA in 1910, with de Forest as its president and Veiller as the director and real force behind the organization, helped popularize the cause of housing reform. By 1914, de Forest could report that twelve states and eleven cities had adopted housing ordinances, and that housing reform efforts were underway in eighty-two cities in the United States and five cities in Canada.[53]

NORMS FOR INTERVENTION

A good place to begin the analysis of housing reform is with the norms used to promote and defend government intervention. From this viewpoint we gain a sense of the interests that guided the movement. Contemporary legal historian Lawrence Friedman has distinguished between two approaches to housing reform: a "social-cost" approach, emphasizing the cost to society of the slum, and a "social welfare" approach, stressing the slum's effect on its inhabitants.[54] The social-cost approach clearly predominated in the period examined here, in large part because slum residents were not organized to use their own power to force housing

---

[53] See de Forest, "A Brief History of the Housing Movement in America," pp. 10-11.

[54] *Government and Slum Housing: A Century of Frustration*, p. 4.

improvements.[55] What effort there was to promote housing improvements out of an articulated concern for the welfare of slum residents was mostly the work of religious groups. Yet these groups appear to have been motivated as much or more by a concern that the immoral ways of the slum dweller would spread beyond the slum, as by a Christian concern for the brotherhood of man. In all, the housing ordinances of the late 1800s and early 1900s were less a response to the needs of the poor than to the perceived threats—political, sanitary, and social—to the larger community of allowing those needs to go unmet. These threats seemed all the more menacing because of the social and political turmoil of the 1890s, a decade marked by economic failure, labor strife, and political insurgency and unrest.

Guided by a philosophy of physical environmental determinism, the reformers of this period asserted the right of the community to guard against the multiple threats of the slum over the rights of the private builder and tenement house owner. These reformers—these planners-in-embryo—were searching for and articulating norms to guide and justify a larger government role in urban development in order to alter the balance between the private ownership of land and its appurtenances (that is, buildings) and their private use and control. One of the most powerful norms asserted was the right of the community to be free from disease; or, more accurately, the right of the better off to be free from the diseases bred by the circumstances of the poor. The problem of disease was one of the earliest recognized "externalities" of the slum. Yet, like the connection between overcrowding and the treatment of land as a commodity, the association between disease and poor housing was not immediately grasped; it took the discovery of the germ theory of disease in the 1870s to establish a scientific link between housing conditions and the epidemics of cholera and typhus that recurrently swept the city.[56] The germ theory of disease

[55] The most outspoken advocate for New York City's tenement poor in his era was Benjamin Marsh, Secretary of the New York Committee on Congestion of Population. Yet even Marsh was separated from the poor, relying on the power of his moral arguments with elite audiences rather than on the organized power of the working class and tenement poor to secure housing improvements. He did not become active in housing reform until after the turn of the century, when he played an important role in establishing a national city planning organization. His activities are recounted in Chapter 6.

[56] Following Pasteur's pioneering examination of microorganisms in the 1850s, his student Lister discovered in 1869 how antiseptic surgery could save lives. Yet it was not until the 1870s that Pasteur demonstrated in the case of anthrax the

thereafter became a "powerful engine of social reform."[57] Most of the important housing legislation emerging after 1900 resulted from an alliance between health and housing reformers. As Peter Marcuse has pointed out, however, the very success of public health measures in controlling the spread of disease served to deprive the housing reform movement of one of its main props, causing more emphasis to be placed upon the social consequences of the slum.[58]

Concern about the slum's social consequences translated into a social control interest in ameliorating housing conditions. This was the most powerful interest behind the attacks on slum housing. At the individual level the social control interest was in controlling crime. Yet, unlike today, the crime issue was of less concern than the threat of mass upheaval, the promotion of immigrant assimilation, and the renewal (physical, normative, and political) of the industrial workforce. The fact that arguments for housing reform were so often couched in these terms attests to the upper-class interests guiding these reforms, as well as to the weakness of other institutions of social control, which made the housing system all the more important politically. We can discern efforts to appeal to these interests in the arguments used by housing reformers.

Dr. John Griscom's 1845 report on tenement house conditions in New York City—a report which laid the foundation for much future discussion of the housing problem—clearly adopted a "social control" approach. On the opening page, Griscom observed that the poor health of the city's pauper class was the precursor of habits and deeds that "give employment to the officers of police, and the ministers of justice."[59] He discussed the social consequences of slum housing under three headings: the immoral ways of the poor, the need to produce good citizens, and the maintenance of a healthy and contented workforce. Particularly worthy of note are his comments on the latter. "Labor is wealth," he as-

---

etiological relationship of a germ to a disease, and it was not until the 1880s that vaccinations began to be developed. For a brief discussion of this subject, see Ravenel, "The American Public Health Association: Past, Present, Future," pp. 15-17.

[57] Friedman, *Slum Housing*, p. 5.

[58] See Marcuse, "Housing in Early City Planning," pp. 166-68. Cf. Peterson, "The Impact of Sanitary Reform upon American Urban Planning, 1840-1890," pp. 13-39. Peterson notes how the preventive sanitation movement of the mid–nineteenth century, which was known then as sanitary reform, was undercut from the 1890s onward by bacteriologically based concepts of public health (p. 14).

[59] *Sanitary Conditions*, p. 1.

serted. "The manufacturer, the artisan, the builder, *all*, depend upon the skill and strength of those employed to do their work." From this argument it followed that labor of the most "insignificant kind" should be "protected, improved and facilitated."[60] In support of this view he cited Massachusetts educator Horace Mann's statement that

> [a]ll investments to preserve or increase the public health, would be reimbursed many fold, in an increased capacity for production. One of the most important items in a nation's wealth, consists in the healthfulness and vigor enjoyed by its people. All agriculturists and manufacturers must feel the force of this remark in regard to their own workmen; and they would feel it still more, if they were obliged at their own expense to support these workmen during all periods of sickness or incapacity to labor; and this is the relation in which the state stands to its citizens.[61]

Apparently, Griscom, drawing from Mann, was invoking capital's interest in reproducing its workforce as justification for government intervention in housing. Relying on the market—and thus on property capitalists—to organize housing was costly for workers as well as for their employers, he warned. Yet there were other, more political arguments for housing reform.

Jacob Riis is perhaps best known for his concern over the immorality of slum life. Particularly troubled about the slum's effect on children, he argued that government should offer alternatives to the gang life of the slum by building playgrounds and providing recreational facilities. Yet he also directed attention to the slum's threat to political and social order and to the protection of property. In fact, he began *How the Other Half Lives* by noting a Police Association report that 80 percent of the crimes against property during the draft riots of 1863 were committed by persons whose homes failed to provide the "ordinary wholesome influences of home and family."[62] The message to the city's propertied class was clear: ignore the housing needs of the property-less at the peril of your own property. Riis also presented the tenement as a threat to the political order; he noted, for example, that New York's former mayor and political boss William Marcy ("Boss") Tweed was

---

[60] Ibid., p. 39.

[61] From Horace Mann, Sixth Annual Report of the Board of Education of Massachusetts; excerpted in Griscom, *Sanitary Conditions*, pp. 39-40.

[62] Pp. 1-2; Riis was quoting the Secretary of the Prison Association of New York.

"born and bred" in a Fourth Ward tenement. But it was the threat of poverty and distress translating into an attack on wealth and property that prompted some of his most sensationalistic prose. He observed that the tenements "had bred their Nemesis, a proletariat ready and able to avenge the wrongs of their crowds." These "restless, pent-up multitudes," as he described them, "hold within their clutch the wealth and business of New York, hold them at their mercy in the day of mob-rule and wrath." As proof of this power of the poor, he cited the city's many provisions against mob violence. Noting that the tenements already harbored three-quarters of New York City's population, he asked "what will the harvest be" when the next generation doubles the city's population, spawning a "vast army of workers, held captive by poverty, [for whom] the very name of home shall be as a bitter mockery?"[63]

But it was Lawrence Veiller more than anyone else who provided the elite rationale for restrictive housing laws. In appealing for support, he consistently used the conservative "stake in society" argument: he believed housing improvements were justified by the need to incorporate the immigrant poor into the existing order of society. "The modern city is the most important factor in destroying a conservative point of view on the part of the working people," he declared.[64] As part of his effort to gain upper-class support, he insisted that housing improvements not be seen as charity. Like the AICP, Veiller believed charity would only subsidize the slothful ways of the poor, and that it was an ineffective motivation for reform. He was similarly conservative in defending the limits of housing reform, rejecting the idea of government-built housing as "socialistic." "[I]t is not a part of the function of government to engage in the construction and operation of tenement houses," he asserted.[65] He also did not believe housing conditions could be improved by increasing wages, comparing such thinking to a belief in "flying carpets, wishing caps, and magic philters."[66]

METHODS OF INTERVENTION

As Lawrence Veiller's remarks make apparent, the interests guiding housing reform were reflected not only in the norms used to justify intervention, but also in the methods of intervention that

[63] Ibid., pp. 3, 16, 19-20.
[64] "The Housing Problem in American Cities," p. 255.
[65] Ibid., p. 257.
[66] A Model Housing Law, p. 3.

78

were adopted and not adopted. It is, particularly, in the methods that were not adopted that we see how the guiding interests were also limiting interests. In practice, there were two basic approaches to housing reform, restrictive legislation and the building of "model" tenements, although only the first of these was supported by Lawrence Veiller and the NHA. A third possible strategy, government-constructed housing, was eschewed by almost all housing reformers until after World War I.

This situation contrasted with the practices in the industrialized nations of Europe. In England, national legislation acknowledging public responsibility for building and renting low-cost housing was adopted as early as 1851, although a constructive housing policy was not initiated until the passage in 1890 of the Housing of the Working Classes Act. Further, national legislation adopted in 1909 made it obligatory for local authorities to engage in housing construction whenever there was a shortage of worker housing; the legislation also made available loans with favorable terms to support housing construction. This 1909 legislation reflected a shift in initiative on housing matters, from the Tory philanthropists who directed the course of reform policy in the nineteenth century to the Fabians, labor and consumer organizations, and the Labour Party, which dominated housing policy after the turn of the century. In Germany, early housing policies were more varied due to the greater powers of municipal government. In contrast with the situation in the United States, by the 1870s, socialist worker organizations in Germany were demanding municipal land measures, municipal housing, and aid for cooperative societies. And, unlike American cities, when German municipalities began purchasing land, exercising control over land use, and constructing low-cost housing, they did so by retrieving medieval powers and responsibilities. The greatest stimulus to the construction of worker housing in Germany was the adoption of Bismarck's social insurance legislation in the late 1880s, which provided public funds for housing construction. In Belgium an 1889 act made loans available to building societies to facilitate worker homeownership, and in 1894 a similar act was adopted in France.[67]

In the United States, however, housing policy remained limited, essentially until the New Deal, to restrictive legislation. This was the most conservative approach to housing reform—conservative

[67] See Bauer, *Modern Housing*, app. to Part Three, and Wood, *Housing of the Wage Earner*, chap. 5.

because it entailed the least government intervention in the system of privately produced housing. Municipalities relied on the market for the location, production, distribution, and management of housing. The "reform" was that government was to set minimum standards—rules within which the market would continue to operate. Above these minimum standards, the pursuit of profit and the forces of supply and demand were to determine the quantity and quality of housing. Only this conservative approach to housing reform was recognized as legitimate and effective by Veiller and the NHA, which he led. By its constitution (written by Veiller), the NHA was officially committed to this approach and this approach alone.[68]

Although restrictive housing ordinances were symbolically important as assertions of the community's right to regulate the builders and owners of tenement housing, they failed to produce any housing. When tenement laws were enforced, housing conditions improved, but "new law" apartments typically were beyond the financial reach of workingmen.[69] Moreover, the enforcement of restrictive laws worked to decrease the supply of housing by forcing the condemnation of buildings that were not up to code. Needless to say, no provision was made for rehousing persons forced out of condemned buildings. These problems not only added to overcrowding, but also made restrictive legislation politically difficult to enforce. As Edith Wood, an early twentieth-century commentator on housing policy, wrote: "The best restrictive housing legislation is only negative. It will prevent the bad. It will not produce the good. Especially, it will not produce it at a given rental. And rental is a despot. A high standard of restrictive legislation will not be enacted, or if enacted, will not be enforced, when its enforcement will leave a considerable number of people homeless."[70] Housing reform leader Robert de Forest was aware of these limitations of the restrictive approach, yet he found it preferable to government-built housing. He was fearful of reforms that might limit the construction of new tenements, or that would require such extensive changes in old tenements that their owners might put them to other uses. "Reform of such a kind would harm most the very persons it sought to aid," he wrote with Lawrence Veiller.[71] Here was the problem: how to constrain the profit mo-

[68] National Housing Association, *Constitution and By-Laws*, p. 4.
[69] See Jackson, *Place Called Home*, chaps. 11-12.
[70] *Housing of the Wage Earner*, p. 20.
[71] "The Tenement House Problem," in de Forest and Veiller, *The Tenement House Problem*, 1:7.

tive while relying on it to produce worker housing. The restrictive approach involved the application of a bourgeois solution to a problem arising from the capitalist treatment of land and its appurtenances, bringing to mind Engels's statement that "the bourgeois has only one method of settling the housing question after *its* fashion—that is to say, of settling it in such a way that the solution continually poses the question anew."[72]

The other response to the housing problem, as noted previously, was the construction of model tenements. The attempts at such a solution varied considerably. One was the Octavia Hill plan, named after the pioneering work of Miss Octavia Hill in London. Instead of building a new tenement house, a philanthropic association purchased an existing one and made improvements in the building to afford tenants better air, light, and ventilation. The association then continued to manage the building to ensure that the occupants did not fall into sinful ways or the building into disrepair. Its most successful application in the United States was in Philadelphia, where an Octavia Hill Association was created in the 1870s to purchase and manage housing according to the principles of the original Octavia Hill experiment in London. A second scheme was the attempt to build decent housing for the poor and to charge below-market rents, requiring that the operation be subsidized from some source. Yet a third plan, represented by Alfred White's previously mentioned model tenement project, was to demonstrate that decent low-income housing could be built and operated at a profit by taking advantage of good management and innovations in building design and housing finance.

Although generally opposed to the model tenement approach, Veiller commended the Octavia Hill experiment, citing it as a worthwhile attempt at using private initiative to address the housing problem. Yet he was highly critical of the other two methods, believing they were inadequate to the task of housing reform given the enormity of the problem, and that they only diverted attention from the one effective solution, restrictive legislation. Ever adept in the use of statistics to support his claims, Veiller noted that between 1842 and 1905 the net result of the model tenement movement in New York City was the construction of approximately two hundred tenement houses of ordinary size, while in the same period speculative builders, unrestricted by proper legislation, had built over fifty thousand "indescribably bad . . . ten-

---

[72] *The Housing Question*, p. 68.

ement houses."[73] He also objected to the semi-philanthropic approach that involved subsidizing rents because of its connotations of charity, and because he believed the supervision associated with such projects violated tenants' privacy. Depriving tenants of their privacy, he argued, would drive away the most upstanding and leave only the least desirable, a mark of failure in his view.[74] Interestingly, both these criticisms also applied to the Octavia Hill approach that Veiller commended, although he seemed unaware of this.

What these model tenement efforts shared was an attempt to remove low-income housing from the speculative market. This was true even of Alfred White's scheme, since he was seeking to demonstrate that worker housing could be built for a profit—if enormous profits of the sort speculative builders typically received were not expected. Using the most effective management techniques (methods unlikely to be available to the typical urban jerry-builder), White's capitalist experiment produced a 7.5-percent return, a respectable profit but well below that common for speculative builders.[75] Although the model tenement concept was an effort to remove low-income housing from the speculative market, it was forced to compete for capital in conventional market terms by demonstrating its attractiveness as an investment, despite the innovation in limited dividend financing. It was this constraint imposed by the need to attract capital in normal market terms that rendered the model tenement approach so ineffective in producing better housing. Interesting from an historical standpoint as an attempt to produce better and cheaper worker housing through the alchemy of capitalism, philanthropy, and technology, the model tenement effort, as Veiller correctly noted, never threatened the system of speculatively built housing.[76]

HOUSING REFORM ASSESSED

The most important substantive interest underlying restrictive housing laws was the interest in social control. This, broadly, was

[73] "The Housing Problem," p. 261.

[74] Ibid., p. 263.

[75] See ibid., pp. 264-65; Veiller, "The Speculative Building of Tenement Houses," in de Forest and Veiller, The Tenement House Problem, 1:370-74; and Lubove, Progressives and the Slums, pp. 38-39.

[76] On how this model tenement experience contributed to the design and management philosophy behind twentieth-century public housing, see Birch and Gardner, "The Seven-Percent Solution: A Review of Philanthropic Housing, 1870-1910," pp. 403-38.

the interest to which Griscom, Riis, and Veiller sought to appeal in building support for housing reform. But "social control" for what purposes and on whose terms? Manuel Castells argues that capital's interest in "reproducing labor power" provides the motive for state intervention in the field of urban planning. The course of capitalist development leads to the accumulation of capital, to the concentration of the means of production and workers in space, and to the proletarianization of workers. This process, in turn, generates demands for "collective forms of consumption" organized or guaranteed by the state. To the extent that the state complies with these demands, it is because such intervention corresponds with capital's interest in maintaining a healthy and contented workforce—this is Castells's argument.[77] We have seen that state intervention in housing in the United States indeed corresponds with the rise of factory cities and the transformation of workers into a proletariat. Yet, judging from the arguments used by housing reform proponents, the desire to renew labor power does not appear to have been the chief energizing force behind the adoption of restrictive housing legislation, although it was a significant force behind employer-built housing (discussed in Chapter 6). That Castells's European-derived explanation works no better in regard to early housing reform is no doubt due, in part, to the extensive immigration in this period. It must be remembered that approximately six million immigrants arrived in each decade between 1880 and 1920. With this large supply of replacement workers, employers could be relatively indifferent to the living and working conditions of their extant workforce. Capitalists undoubtedly have an interest in renewing workers' capacity for labor, but what this interest requires them to do, what forms of state intervention become necessary, surely varies with historical circumstances. In the period examined here, immigration, by continually replenishing the industrial reserve army, lessened capital's need for a housing policy linked to the renewal of labor power.

It makes more sense to say that it was capital's interest in maintaining its position of political and ideological leadership—its class hegemony—that made possible restrictive housing legislation ("made possible" because it is a question of which interests permitted this breach of property rights, rather than what motivated individuals like Lawrence Veiller, who supplied the leadership for the adoption of these reforms). Castells's explanation could be stretched to include capital's interest in maintaining its

[77] *Urban Question*, p. 431.

political and ideological leadership if we consider that reproduction of labor power depends on capital's ability to maintain its political ascendancy and the dominance of capitalist beliefs (for example, belief in the rights of property, fairness of the market, and limited freedoms of capitalism). But this makes Castells's explanation too all-purpose, besides obfuscating an important distinction. For it was not so much capital's economic or workplace-related needs (which Castells's explanation emphasizes) as its political and ideological needs that made limited housing reform possible. In mediating the relationship between capital and the state, between capitalists as individuals and their collective political needs as a class, these housing reformers—these planners-in-embryo—sought to appeal to capital's political and ideological interest in reform, and at the same time to educate members of that class as to why their interests dictated an ameliorative response to the housing problem. Thus we find Jacob Riis invoking the threat of a militant proletariat in arguing for an attack on the slum, all the while protecting the system of privately produced housing by failing, or refusing, to envisage an alternative to it. On the opening page of *How the Other Half Lives*, he referred to the tenement problem as the product of a housing "system" that had "come to stay." "Nothing is left," he advised, "but to make the best of a bad bargain." Lawrence Veiller, the college-educated professional, was more explicit about the limits of the system of privately produced housing and more willing to defend it against its political-economic alternative. In a list of "Do's and Don't's" in his book *Housing Reform*, he included "Don't urge the municipal ownership of tenement houses" and "Don't confuse the fields of public and private effort" with "Don't let your city become a city of tenements" and "Don't tolerate alley dwellings."[78] He believed government had a duty to see that its citizens were not denied the "ordinary conveniences of life," but he thought this should be accomplished through "proper regulation" rather than through direct government provision. Government construction of housing, he feared, would drive capitalists from the field, leaving government with a larger responsibility than it could handle and paving the way for other forms of "socialism." "If municipal tenement houses are desirable and proper," he derisively asked, "why not municipal butcher shops, municipal grocery stores, municipal clothing establishments, municipal barber shops?"[79]

[78] Pp. 193-95.
[79] "The Housing Problem," pp. 257-59.

In attempting to solve the tenement problem within the limits of the system of privately produced housing while simultaneously defending those limits, Veiller, Riis, and others contributed to the maintenance of that system, albeit not without some compromising of capital's interest. Restrictive housing legislation placed a legal upper limit on housing exploitation by providing a critique of laissez-faire capitalism, a defense of human decency, and at best a marginal improvement in the housing conditions of the urban working class—none of which should be disregarded. Yet it also served a systems-maintenance function. It did this by displacing more radical interpretations of the housing problem, by providing an ideological defense of the system of privately produced housing, and by offering better paid workers who could afford "new law" housing a material stake in society, while creating the illusion of greater progress in housing reform.

It might be objected that Griscom, Riis, and Veiller were only trying to make housing reform palatable to the dominant powers of the city, and that their own motivations and the "real reasons" for housing reform were different. But whatever the motivations of these early reformers, housing reforms were limited by the interests of the upper-class groups that these reformers sought to educate. It was in this sense that these interests were guiding—guiding because they determined what was necessary and possible. These reformers did not simply shape their arguments to fit the conscious or unconscious interests of the city's dominant class; they also shaped their proposals to fit dominant interests, eschewing the constructive approach that prevailed in Europe because they deemed it too radical. And in failing to question the limits of the system of privately produced housing, they helped to reproduce that system and its problems.

That restrictive legislation did no more to improve housing conditions was a commentary on both the inability of capitalism to solve the housing problem (as Engels recognized so clearly) and the inability of the working class to enforce its definition of adequate housing. The stricture imposed by capitalism was both "structural" and "political": structural because it emanated from the principle of property rights that restrictive legislation threatened, political because the efficacy of this stricture depended on the size, cohesiveness, and organization—in short, the political power—of that fraction of capital directly threatened by tenement codes. If restrictive housing law helped to shore up the capitalist system, it was nonetheless contradictory in its implications for capital; indeed, it was not embraced by all members of the business community. Certain sectors of capital were clearly and quite intensely opposed to government restrictions on housing. The coalition formed in opposition to New York State's epochal Tenement House Law of 1901 included, in Veiller's words,

> the building interests of the city, the speculative builders, the material men, the institutions which made loans on such property, the architects who had to learn their trade all over again and did not like it, combined with the owners of the existing tenement houses who found that they were required to spend in some cases over $1,000 to make their houses comply with the law.[80]

That this broad group of property capitalists was opposed to tenement codes was not (necessarily) because they were less enlightened than other capitalists, but because they had different immediate interests at stake. The sacrifice of property rights required to maintain the system of property rights fell on a particular fraction of capital, namely those who built, owned, and operated tenement housing; and they were predictably resistant to the terms of that sacrifice.

The character of housing policy depends not only on the capacity of property capitalists to thwart or reshape the purposes of that policy, but also on the capacity of the ill-housed to press their case for housing improvements. The latter was an important reason why nineteenth-century housing reform was so limited: the political pressure exerted by the working-class poor on the housing issue was itself limited. It was the pressure of the mob more than of a cohesive political force, of an episodic attack on property more than of a revolutionary upheaval, of a failure to incorporate the tenement poor into the political order more than a concerted attack on that order. By contrast, in England and Germany "constructive" housing legislation was adopted in this period by dint of organized pressure from the working class. As Ira Katznelson has observed, the failure, on the whole, of early trade union and socialist movements in the United States to address housing and urban land issues reflects a distinctive feature of American class relations: the language and experience of "class" have been limited to the workplace, whereas local politics more often is based on ethnic and territorial affinities. The result of this "bifurcation of consciousness" has been that labor and worker organizations

[80] Quoted in Lubove, *Progressives and the Slums*, p. 167.

have not treated consumption issues—issues arising in the living place rather than in the workplace—as class or worker issues.[81] There was a current in the early American socialist movement that advocated municipal ownership, although the issue then was public utilities. This program was rejected by the mainstream of the movement as "middle-class reform"; it was believed that socialists would have to win state power before government ownership would benefit the working class.[82] Except for the efforts of Benjamin Marsh (recounted in Chapter 6), the only other leftist program focusing on housing was that of Henry George, who advocated "single-taxation" of land during his campaigns for mayor of New York City in 1886 and 1897.[83] Not until the 1930s did labor organizations begin to push the housing issue, culminating in the adoption in 1937 of the Wagner-Steagall Act, the first constructive housing legislation in the United States. And, as Eugenie Ladner Birch has noted, these legislative efforts owe much to the leadership of two women, Catherine Bauer and Edith Wood, as well as to the involvement of non-labor organizations such as the American Association of University Women, the Regional Plan Association,

[81] *City Trenches: Urban Politics and the Patterning of Class in the United States,* pp. 18-19.

[82] The Social Democratic Party, which was organized in 1898 by Eugene Debs and Victor Berger and eventually became the American Socialist Party, split off from the older Socialist Labor Party in part because of the belief of Debs, Berger, and others that municipal ownership of local utilities—municipally owned housing was apparently not part of the debate—could advance the cause of socialism. In the first decade of this century, the center-left faction of the Socialist Party argued that only the Socialist Party could bring about the kind of municipal ownership that would benefit the working class. Opposed to this outlook was the Milwaukee Social-Democratic Party, one of the most successful local party organizations in electoral terms; it saw middle-class interest in municipal ownership as part of a rising tide of socialist consciousness. See Kipnis, *The American Socialist Movement, 1897-1912,* pp. 62-66, 167-70.

[83] Amy Bridges shows how the leaders of reform movements concerned with the "land issue" sought alliances with worker organizations in ante-bellum New York, but the issue there was the disposition of western land rather than the ownership and control of urban land; see Bridges, *A City in the Republic: Ante-Bellum New York and the Origins of Machine Politics,* chap. 6. Cf. Foner, *History of the Labor Movement in the United States,* vol. 1, chap. 10, on the role of (western) Land Reformers, Owenites, and Associationists in representing worker interests. Bridges describes spokesmen for these groups as "radicals" on the grounds that they sought to ameliorate current conditions as well as to reorganize society, whereas Foner judges them "utopians" because, in his view, they diverted workers' energies away from the political struggle over their more immediate (workplace-related) economic needs.

the National Association of Housing Officials, and the National Public Housing Conference (an offshoot of socialist Norman Thomas's Committee on Civic Affairs), with which these women were associated.[84]

Finally, early housing reform efforts also provided an incipient if nonetheless formative response to the capitalist-democracy contradiction. For in addition to whether there should be controls on tenement housing, the issue of who was to control those controls arose. Veiller's response was to rely upon expertise combined with the appearance of public representation, albeit without any form of direct accountability. This formula is implicit in Veiller's instructions to local communities on how to carry out a program of housing reform. The most important thing was that "the facts be known in a strictly accurate and scientific way," he counseled. To supervise the collection of facts and oversee the program of reform, he recommended the appointment of a citizens committee whose members were well known in the community and familiar with various sides of the housing problem. He further suggested that the committee have an architect, a builder, a real estate man, a physician, a lawyer, a settlement worker, and representatives of the municipal building and health departments. "Such persons," he maintained, "will bring to the service of the committee expert knowledge and advice along the lines of the special experience of each. Moreover, a committee thus constituted will have peculiar weight with the public." The next step was to hire a trained investigator. This was critical—"a committee had better postpone its work for a year or even two years in order to obtain the services of such persons, than to undertake an investigation without a proper executive."[85]

Veiller's faith in expertise, tempered by a concern for acquiring public legitimation but without resorting to democratic forms of control, was to become characteristic of city planning. In this formula, the reliance on expertise cloaked with a mantle of legitimation was regarded as an alternative to the unseen hand of the market system and the populist danger of democracy, setting the pattern for subsequent responses to the capitalist-democracy contradiction. It was in the appointment of park commissions charged with supervising the planning and construction of urban parks that this formula was first institutionalized, and it is to parks and park planning that we now turn.

[84] "From Civic Worker to City Planner: Women and Planning, 1890-1980," pp. 149-72.

[85] "The Housing Problem," pp. 267-68.

FOUR

Parks and Park Planning

IN THE VIEW of an English observer, America experienced a "veritable rage of park making" in the 1890s.[1] Following the construction of New York City's Central Park in the 1850s, large urban parks were built before the turn of the century in Boston, Cleveland, Baltimore, St. Louis, San Francisco, and Chicago. As one early commentator wrote, this "liberality" in the construction of parks is hard to understand in view of the "niggardly and short-sighted policies" of most municipal governments and their frequently corrupt administrations.[2] The preceding chapter should, however, help us to understand the success of park building efforts. In many ways the park movement was a continuation of the efforts that gave rise to housing reform, albeit in different form. Instead of intervening in the housing system, planners, with similar social control objectives in mind, attempted to alter the environment outside the home, thereby avoiding the difficult business of regulating private capital—at the expense of enlarging the public sector. Park building was unlike housing reform, however, in that parks provided direct benefits for the wealthy class, too. The wealthy were able to benefit both from the use of public parks and, in the case of surrounding landowners, from the enhanced land values resulting from park construction; and these benefits contributed to the political success of the park movement.

Park planners and landscape architects were not simply responding to the failure of the market system to produce a socially adequate urban form. They also helped to formulate a response to the capitalist-democracy contradiction, contributing to the view and practice of planning as a method of technical decision making removed from institutions of popular control. This is the issue touched upon at the close of the last chapter: the attempt to insulate government intervention in the built environment from popular participation, and the contribution of planners to that effort. The institutional vehicle for this elite form of planning was the governmentally independent park board or park commission, a

---

[1] Earl of Meath, *Public Parks in America*, p. 3; quoted in Blodgett, "Frederick Law Olmsted: Landscape Architecture as Conservative Reform," p. 888 n.66.

[2] "Chicago Parks and their Landscape Architecture," p. 19.

forerunner of the city planning commissions that sprang up after 1900 and the prototype for the independent boards and commissions that populate municipal government today. Landscape architects and park planners, notably Frederick Law Olmsted, Sr., played a seminal role in promoting the adoption of these institutions for planning. These park commissions typically were charged not only with supervising the design of parks, but also with employing work forces to construct and maintain parks, making contracts for park work, levying taxes and borrowing funds through the sale of bonds, altering or revising park plans, and enacting regulations governing park use. As Olmsted approvingly noted, park commissions usually were authorized to carry out these functions "all on their own unrestricted responsibility, rendering only annual account of their doings and outlays."[3] These bodies were, in effect, mini-governments for park purposes, combining the centralized methods of control of the private business corporation with responsibilities and powers that were public in character.

The promoters and practitioners of park building—Frederick Law Olmsted, Sr., Andrew Jackson Downing, Horace W. S. Cleveland, Charles Eliot, and George Kessler—were, like Lawrence Veiller, professional technicians of reform. They considered themselves landscape architects, although as the first professionals to whom the title was applied, they came from a variety of educational and occupational backgrounds. Writing in 1890, Horace Cleveland defined landscape architecture as "the art of arranging land so as to adapt it most conveniently, economically and gracefully, to any of the varied wants of civilization."[4] The existence of this field implied a recognition that the treatment of land as a commodity and the reliance upon the market system to organize urban development failed to produce a socially adequate urban form, and that conscious intervention was necessary to "adapt" land to the "wants of civilization." This is not to imply that these landscape architects desired to reorganize society. They merely recognized that the built environment wrought by the market system was incompatible with the maintenance of the existing structure of society, a lesson they helped teach the city's business class.

Although their language was that of aesthetics—with exceptions to be noted—the ends sought by these landscape architects

[3] Olmsted, Sr., *The Park for Detroit*, p. 16.
[4] *Landscape Architecture as Applied to the Wants of the West*, p. 5.

were clearly social. Despite some variation in purpose, their overriding objective was the socialization and control of the new urban working class. This aim corresponds with that of housing reformers, except that landscape architects placed more emphasis on mitigating the effects of work. Public parks were seen by reformers as a way of diverting workers' attention from the world of work, while partially compensating them for the alienating and debilitating effects of that work. At a more political and ideological level, the park was intended to elevate the sentiments of the urban immigrant working class by stimulating appreciation of American culture, capitalism, and country. In promoting parks in these terms, these early park planners helped educate the city's business class about the need for state-organized forms of collective consumption as antidotes to the anarchic effects of the market system.

CAPITALISM AND PARKS

It is important to understand the economic and social conditions that gave rise to and shaped the nature of the park idea. It originated in the eighteenth-century landscape movement, as represented in the work of William Kent and Humphry Repton, whose landscape designs sought to romanticize nature in keeping with similar tendencies in art and literature. Underlying this interest in nature were the changes that occurred in the system of production and consumption of the eighteenth century. As Raymond Williams has pointed out, the "discovery" of rural landscape by royalty and the nobility and the creation of deer parks and landscaped pleasure gardens for their use corresponded with the emergence of capitalist forms of agriculture which, together with the enclosure acts, discharged much of the peasantry from the countryside.[5] The arranged landscape of this era succeeded in creating, as Williams writes, "a rural landscape emptied of rural labour and of labourers . . . from which the facts of production had been banished." He describes this arranged landscape as "an effective and still imposing mystification."[6] And as David Harvey states, it combined "elements of necessity and pure hoax": necessity because of man's need to establish a relationship with nature, hoax because this

[5] See Williams, *The Country and the City*, chap. 12.
[6] Ibid., p. 125.

91

landscape concealed the source—in the organization of production—of man's lost relationship to nature.[7]

The building of urban parks open to all was an attempt to make
rural landscape accessible to the working class. It is in this sense
that the public park was linked to the desideratum of social control. The park movement began in western Europe, where the separation of the peasantry from the land and the concentration of
this class into large cities were more pronounced than elsewhere.
In England, the landscaped gardens that existed before this time
were the property of royalty and the nobility, and the public was
admitted only by their grace. With the growth of London, however, a number of royal parks, including St. James Park, Green
Park, Hyde Park, and Kensington Gardens, were transferred to
public use. Similarly, the French Revolution led to the opening up
of the royal gardens of Paris. However, there had not yet been established the principle of municipal responsibility for the provision of public open space.[8]

Before going further, we should draw a distinction between the
term *park* and the older concept of the *public square. Park* will refer to a large tract of land set off so that citizens might enjoy rural
landscape—it was tracts of this sort that historically were the possession of royalty and the nobility. The *public square*, by contrast,
had always been considered the ground of the people, theirs by ancient right, whether it was a central square, a market, a forum, a
shaded walk, or common land used for pleasure or pasturage. This
feudal custom of establishing public squares had even been transferred to North America. The Spanish royal ordinances of 1573,
which guided the development of Spanish settlements in the New
World, called for the establishment of a central market and public
square; these were also essential features of the Spanish settlements that spread across the southern tier of North America and
up the Pacific coastline.[9] Moreover, as related in Chapter 2, the
central common was a fixture of early New England towns.

The building of public parks in England grew from a recognition

[7] "Class Struggle Around the Built Environment," p. 287.

[8] For a brief discussion of the European origins of the park movement, see
Olmsted, Jr., and Kimball, eds., *Frederick Law Olmsted, Landscape Architect,
1822-1903,* 2:3. This lengthy volume is the best source on Olmsted's work in landscape architecture and park planning; it consists of extensive excerpts of his writing, supplemented by commentary on his professional work and the history of park
planning.

[9] See Reps, *Making of Urban America,* pp. 29-32, 54.

of the importance of parks to urban land speculation and to the health, comfort, and social order of the growing working-class population of manufacturing towns. Indicative of the emphasis on social and health concerns was an English magazine's description, in 1839, of St. James Park as the "lungs of London."[10] In 1841, landscape architect J. C. Loudon took up the plea for a public park on London's crowded east side; his appeal, together with public pressure, led to the founding of Victoria Park in 1844, East London's first "people's park."[11] In Germany, as in England, the demand for public parks was formulated in terms of the need for places of recreation and the desire to improve the physical appearance of the city, and it coincided with the rise of manufacturing towns with large working-class populations. The first park built as a public park in Germany was constructed in Magdeburg in 1824. Berlin built a public park in 1840, as did Frankfurt, Dresden, and Leipzig in the 1850s and 1860s, the same period in which New York City's Central Park was constructed.[12]

European progress in park building did not go unnoticed in the United States. Andrew Jackson Downing and Frederick Law Olmsted, Sr., the leading figures in the early park movement in this country, were keen observers of park developments in Europe; moreover, through their travels and commentary, they provided an important link between European and American park building. Downing came to the park movement through an interest in landscape gardening, having published an influential text on that subject in 1841.[13] His practical experience, which was in the planning of country estates, reflected both his ties to the wealthy class and the limited opportunities for practicing landscape gardening on a large scale in his day. In the 1840s, he became interested in the landscaping of cemeteries, seeing the cemetery as a place where landscape design could be made a public art. A number of attractive park-like cemeteries had been established on the edge of major cities by this time. Mount Auburn, near Boston, was built in 1831, followed by Laurel Hill on the outskirts of Philadelphia and Greenwood outside New York. These rural cemeteries served not

[10] *Blackwood's Edinburgh Magazine*, August 1839, pp. 212-27, quoted in Olmsted and Kimball, *Olmsted*, 2:8.

[11] See French, "The First 'People's Park' Movement," pp. 25-29.

[12] Olmsted and Kimball, *Olmsted*, 2:10-11.

[13] Downing, *A Treatise on the Theory and Practice of Landscape Gardening*. On the objectives guiding Downing's work, see John William Ward, "The Politics of Design," pp. 51-85.

only as burial grounds, but also, in the years before they became covered with grave markers, as public pleasure grounds for those able to travel to them. Downing sought to promote the building of rural cemeteries and to draw the lesson of their use as public pleasure grounds through his position as publisher of the *Horticulturist*, a journal devoted mostly to the practical aspects of landscaping. Noting that nearly thirty thousand persons had visited Laurel Hill in a single season, he asked, "Does not this general interest . . . prove that public gardens, established in a liberal and suitable manner, . . . near our large cities, would be equally successful?"[14]

For Downing, as for others, the ends served by romantic cemeteries and public gardens were as much social as asthetic. Mount Auburn, for example, was intended expressly as a counterpoint to the enervating forces of the commercial world. As Joseph Story said at the cemetery's consecration, "The rivalries of the world will here drop from the heart; the spirit of forgiveness will gather new impulses; the selfishness of avarice will be checked; the restlessness of ambition will be rebuked."[15] For his part, Downing argued that attractive pleasure grounds would stimulate a mutual "love of natural beauty," helping to break down "barriers of class, wealth and fashion" and to "civilize and refine the national character."[16]

Downing's contribution to the park movement might have been greater had he not died—in a steamboat fire—at the young age of thirty-seven. (He died in 1853, the same year New York State authorized the taking of land for Central Park.) Part of his contribution to park building was his influence on Frederick Olmsted, Sr., a friend and close follower of Downing's work. Olmsted, the co-designer of Central Park, was undoubtedly the single most important figure in the development of American park planning. A professional technician of reform and a member of the genteel class, he was a planner of parks, a promoter of elite-dominated institutions for park planning, and an educator of the bourgeoisie as to its interests concerning the urban working class.

Olmsted was part of a "gentlemanly cosmopolitan elite" active in various areas of reform in the period surrounding the Civil

[14] "Public Cemeteries and Public Gardens," p. 11.

[15] Quoted in Bender, "The 'Rural' Cemetery Movement: Urban Travail and the Appeal of Nature," p. 198.

[16] See Downing, "A Talk About Public Parks and Gardens," p. 155, and Downing, "Public Cemeteries," pp. 10, 12.

War.[17] In addition to his activities in the field of park planning, he joined with other members of the elite in a publishing venture with *Putnam's Magazine* and helped to launch the *Nation* and the American Social Science Association (ASSA). He also helped found the United States Sanitary Commission, predecessor to the American Red Cross, and took a leave from his position as New York City's park superintendent during the Civil War to serve as secretary of the sanitary commission from 1861 to 1863. The social outlook that prompted these many involvements is perhaps best exemplified by the charter of the ASSA, which stressed the "responsibilities of the gifted and educated classes toward the weak, the witless, and the ignorant."[18] Behind Olmsted's many activities, in the view of historian Geoffrey Blodgett, was a "profoundly conservative concept of reform," the goal of which was to promote "social order and cohesion."[19] This concept of reform was also conservative in that it advocated the establishment of centralized forms of administration, reflecting Olmsted's belief that democracy should respond to the cues of a trained and civilized elite—an attitude that also found expression in his view of planning.

Olmsted was a man of many talents and experiences.[20] He was an expert horticulturist, a skilled and artistic landscape designer, a well-traveled observer of nature, and a knowledgeable and perceptive analyst of society. These talents were the product of a rich and varied life. He was thirty-seven before entering the field of landscape architecture, having previously worked as a store clerk, sailor, farmer, and journalist. The son of a prosperous Hartford merchant, he was sent to Yale but dropped out because of failing eyesight. He then drifted from occupation to occupation, spending a great deal of his parents' money along the way. With parental funds, he established in the 1840s a widely acclaimed model farm on Staten Island, then moved from there to journalism, which he combined with extensive traveling while allowing his farm to go to ruin. It was during a trip to Europe in 1850 that he visited his first public park, People's Park in Birkenhead, England; the result

[17] Blodgett, "Olmsted and Conservative Reform," p. 871.
[18] Quoted, ibid., p. 875.
[19] Ibid., pp. 870, 872.
[20] The best and most detailed biography of Olmsted, although less satisfactory than the Olmsted-Kimball volume as a source on his work, is Roper, *FLO: A Biography of Frederick Law Olmsted*.

of this trip was a short monograph, published in 1852.[21] His growing reputation as a writer subsequently garnered him a commission from the *New York Times* to travel through the American South and report on economic and social conditions there. The result was a much-read series of articles on the institution of slavery, in which he argued that a slave-centered economy was weakened by the absence of incentives for labor or industrial development. This utilitarian analysis corresponded with his later argument that parks were needed to counter the psychological drain of urban life and the commercial world. His articles on slavery, later collected in a two-volume work, were deemed influential in promoting abolitionist sentiment in the North and were favorably cited by Marx in *Capital* and, more recently, by Malcolm X.[22]

At a time when an anti-urban bias dominated American intellectual life, Olmsted was anything but anti-urban. His position is apparent from a paper he presented to the ASSA in 1870, which nicely shows that he understood the relationship of his work to the larger process of social development. In his essay, he argued that human progress and the growth of cities were inextricably linked. Rural life was made dreary, he believed, because it failed to take advantage of advances in culture and technology. "[I]f you have ever had part in the working up of some of the rare occasions in which what stands for [rural] festivity is attempted, you will hardly think that the ardent desire of a young woman to escape to the town is wholly unreasonable," he stated. Moreover, the growth of cities was bound to increase in the future. Recognizing that "the further progress of civilization is to depend mainly upon the influences by which men's minds and characters will be affected while living in large towns," he asserted that the task ahead was to prepare for this growth.[23]

If cities and the progress of civilization were linked, Olmsted be-

[21] *Walks and Talks of an American Farmer in England.*

[22] Olmsted's writings on the ante-bellum South were published under the title, *The Cotton Kingdom; A Traveller's Observations on Cotton and Slavery in the American Slave States.* Marx's citation of Olmsted appears in *Capital: A Critique of Political Economy*, vol. 1, p. 196 n. 1. Malcolm X cited Olmsted's analysis of slavery as an important contribution to his own understanding of the black experience in America, in Malcolm X and Haley, *The Autobiography of Malcolm X*, p. 175.

[23] Olmsted's paper was published the following year as "Public Parks and the Enlargement of Towns," in the *Journal of* [the American Association of] *Social Science*, quotations, pp. 6, 10.

lieved that further progress required the application of technology to the problems of urban life as a whole. The growth of cities, which was itself the product of advances in technology, posed problems—problems that threatened the civilizing influence of the city; yet this threat only confirmed the need to apply technology to the problems of urban life. Olmsted saw his work as a step in this direction. In this respect, his analysis was remarkably consistent, even circular: technological advance was the source of the problem and, prospectively, the answer as well. The greatest source of difficulty in his view was not the intractability of the problems of the city, for he had faith in the capacity of science to produce technically effective solutions. Rather, it was that neither the market system nor existing forms of government decision making followed the logic and procedure of the method of technical problem solving that he esteemed.

Olmsted's objectives in park building were clearly social. He saw the park as an antidote to the "enervating" forces of urban and commercial life. City life affects the "mind and moral strength," producing "a peculiarly hard sort of selfishness," he wrote. This is because city dwellers continually encounter one another but, feeling no common bond, seldom communicate. Every day urban residents see "thousands of their fellow-men, [meet] them face to face, and yet have had no experience of anything in common with them," he observed.[24] Here he anticipated by almost twenty years Louis Wirth's "discovery" that urban life contributes to the breakdown of "primary social relationships," causing individuals to view one another in instrumental terms, as objects rather than subjects.[25]

A more apt comparison, however, is with Engels's analysis of industrial Manchester. Writing one-quarter century before Olmsted, Engels noted how people moved past one another on the crowded streets of Manchester "as though they have nothing in common" save the tacit agreement that "each keep to his own side of the pavement." Continuing, he remarked that:

the brutal indifference, the unfeeling isolation of each in his private interest becomes the more repellent and offensive, the more these individuals are crowded together, within a limited space. And, however much one may be aware that this isolation of the individual, this narrow self-seeking is the funda-

[24] Ibid., p. 11.
[25] See Wirth, "Urbanism as a Way of Life," pp. 1-24.

97

mental principle of our society everywhere, it is nowhere so shamelessly barefaced, so self-conscious as just here in the crowding of the great city. The dissolution of mankind into monads, of which each one has a separate principle, the world of atoms, is here carried out to its utmost extremes.[26]

The conservatism of Olmsted's approach to reform is apparent in the comparison with Engels. While Engels's solution was to alter the system of production which made a virtue of selfishness, Olmsted's prescription was to provide recuperative relaxation outside the world of work. He did not explicitly address himself to the world of production, preferring to focus on the characteristics of *urban* society, but his concern to banish "the facts of production" (as Raymond Williams observed about eighteenth-century landscape designers) is evident in his definition of what an ideal park should be.

> We want a ground to which people may easily go after their day's work is done, and where they may stroll for an hour, seeing, hearing, and feeling nothing of the bustle and jar of the streets, where they shall, in effect, find the city put far away from them. We want the greatest possible contrast with the streets and the shops and the rooms of the town which will be consistent with convenience and the preservation of good order and neatness. We want, especially, the greatest possible contrast with the restraining and confining conditions of the town, those conditions which compel us to walk circumspectly, watchfully, jealously, which compel us to look closely upon others without sympathy. Practically, what we want most is a simple, broad, open space of clean greensward, with sufficient play of surface and a sufficient number of trees about it to supply a variety of light and shade, this we want as a central feature. We want depth of wood enough about it not only for comfort in hot weather, but to completely shut out the city from our landscapes.[27]

It was the desire to strike a contrast with the world of work that led Olmsted to oppose the use of parks for active forms of recreation, an attitude he shared with Downing.[28] While Olmsted con-

[26] *Condition of the Working Class*, p. 64.

[27] "Public Parks," p. 22.

[28] See Downing, "A Talk About Public Parks," p. 157. The desire to make parks places for peaceful relaxation rather than active recreation did not originate with

ceded that recreational activities such as baseball and trotting exercised a "mitigating influence," he maintained that what was needed was an influence that "acting through the eye, shall be more than mitigative, that shall be antithetical, reversive and antidotal." Such an influence was found, he believed, "in what . . . will be called the enjoyment of pleasing rural scenery."[29]

Although Olmsted viewed park benefits mostly in psychological and political terms, from time to time he acknowledged that there were economic benefits, too. He declared, for example, that parks countered the "drawbacks" of urban living that "deduct much from the wealth-producing and tax-bearing capacity of [the people of large towns], as well as from [their] wealth-enjoying capacity."[30] Yet this was never the crux of Olmsted's argument for parks; more likely it was added as a concession to pecuniary interests. Moreover, the economic benefits he cited were ones he regarded as aggregate or community benefits (although others might question just how aggregate they were). With progress in park building, however, it became apparent that parks also provided particularistic benefits in the form of enhanced land values for adjacent property owners. While Olmsted did not emphasize these economic benefits in his advocacy of parks, others did, and in time this rationale developed a powerful life of its own.

NEW YORK CITY'S CENTRAL PARK

Central Park in New York City was the first of the nation's large urban parks and the prototype for many later parks. Its history is important both for what it teaches about the forces that shaped park building, and for what it taught others at the time, especially the city's wealthy class, about the benefits of public parks.

It was William Cullen Bryant, editor of the *New York Evening Post*, who first proposed a large uptown park for New York City. In a propitiously timed editorial, appearing on a hot July 3 in 1844,

---

Olmsted and Downing. An ordinance adopted in Chicago in 1851 made it unlawful to play ball, cricket, or "any other game or play whatsoever" in the city's parks, on penalty of a five-dollar fine; see Knapp (planning engineer for the Chicago Park District), "Short History of the Development of Chicago Parks." The rise of the automobile altered this conception of the park: today we use urban parks for active recreation and drive to our mainly rural state and national parks for the relaxed enjoyment of scenery; see Shurcliff, "Progress in Park Design During the Last Fifty Years," pp. 621-27.

[29] *Notes on the Plan of Franklin Park*, p. 32.
[30] "The Justifying Value of a Public Park," p. 164.

just as Manhattan islanders were streaming to distant parts for the Fourth, he argued that New Yorkers needed a public pleasure ground that could be reached "without going out of town."[31] At the time, one-half million people lived in New York City. The extreme northern boundary of buildings was approximately Thirty-fourth Street, although there were yet many empty districts south of that line. While there were publicly owned open spaces in existence, these totaled only about 170 acres; the grounds actually open to the public did not exceed 100 acres; and the largest single park, the Battery, contained only 21 acres.[32]

In 1845, as Bryant continued his editorials in support of an uptown park, Downing began arguing in the *Horticulturist* for a park. Bryant and Downing had visited the parks of Europe and had written glowing reports on those they had seen. What impressed them was not only the scenic beauty of European parks, but also the fact that many were public facilities open to all. Writing in the *Horticulturist* just after a visit to Germany in 1848, Downing touted the fact that Germany's parks were "public enjoyments, open to all classes of people, provided at public cost, maintained at public expense, and enjoyed daily and hourly, by all classes of persons."[33] However, it was not just the power of journalistic persuasion that brought about the success of the Central Park campaign. As Olmsted said of Downing's writings, they could not have yielded "the seed of so large a harvest, but for their timeliness, and a condition of expectancy in the soil upon which they fell."[34]

Steps were taken in the 1850s to make Central Park a reality. Influenced no doubt by the *Post*'s editorial campaign, both mayoral candidates in 1850 supported the idea of a park. The victor, Ambrose C. Kingsland, asked the city council to approve the acquisition of park land, arguing that public funds for this purpose "would . . . be returned to us four fold, in the health, happiness and comfort of those whose interest[s] are especially entrusted to our keeping—the poorer classes."[35] The city council accepted the proposal and asked the state legislature to authorize the taking of land for the park. The location that was approved, however, was not the site of Central Park but an area known as Jones Woods on the East

---

[31] Quoted in Nevins, *The Evening Post: A Century of Journalism*, p. 194.
[32] Ibid., p. 193.
[33] "A Talk About Public Parks," p. 154.
[34] "Justifying Value of a Public Park," p. 152.
[35] Kingsland's message is reprinted in Olmsted and Kimball, *Olmsted*, 2:24-26, quotation, p. 25.

River above Sixty-eighth Street. Following the council's action, a dispute arose over whether to build a park at the Jones Woods site or at a more central location, whether to use both locations, or whether to build a park at all.

By the autumn of 1851, there were three parties to the dispute: a large and influential body of businessmen wanted no park whatsoever, a sizable group would be satisfied with Jones Woods alone, and a "growing number" desired a great central park.[36] Bryant and the *Evening Post* favored building a park at both sites, as did Downing. Completely opposed to the project was the business-oriented *Journal of Commerce*, which maintained that a park on the scale being discussed by Bryant and the *Evening Post* would be too costly, that New York City already had sufficient park land, and that the cool water and green country surrounding New York made further park space unnecessary. It also complained that the Central Park site would obstruct the street system—a complaint later voiced by Olmsted.[37] Yet, with the support of leading citizens, city hall, and the friendly part of the press, the state legislature approved the creation of both parks.

For a time, it appeared both would be developed. So much pressure was brought to bear on the legislature in opposition to building both parks, however, that the authority for the Jones Woods site was rescinded. This abrogation caused New York to lose what would have been, according to Olmsted's biographers, a "splendid waterfront recreation ground." The loss was attributed to the triumph of a "narrow commercial point of view,"[38] referring to the fact that Mayor Jacob Westervelt and a number of wealthy citizens sent a petition to the legislature arguing that the Jones Wood site "should never be taken from the purposes of commerce."[39]

Almost from the start, the park project was controlled by specialized, highly centralized, governmentally independent institutions—prefiguring the future course of park planning. Although construction of the park was initially under the control of local elected officials, the task of assembling land was delegated by the New York State Supreme Court to a specially appointed five-member Commission of Estimate and Assessment. This special commission determined both the amounts to be paid for land within the park boundaries and, since the legislature had decided

[36] Nevins, *Evening Post*, p. 198.
[37] Ibid., pp. 197, 199.
[38] Olmsted and Kimball, *Olmsted*, 2:28-29.
[39] Quoted, ibid., 2:29.

to charge adjacent owners for the benefits resulting from enhanced land values, the benefits to be assessed against the adjacent landowners. (The court awarded $5,069,693 for land taken for the park and assessed benefits totaling $1,657,590.)[40] To supervise park construction, the city council established a Board of Commissioners, consisting of the mayor and street commissioner. Fearing a lack of public confidence in this body, it also appointed a consulting board of prominent citizens and named Washington Irving the board's first president. The Board of Commissioners acquired the services of a chief engineer, Egbert L. Viele, a former army lieutenant, who at his own expense had prepared a general plan for the park. With a modest appropriation from the city council, the commission began to supervise the clearing of the park site, which at the time was deep in mire, covered with rubble, and overrun with goats abandoned by vacating landowners.

From the beginning, there was conflict over giving control of the park to Mayor Fernando Wood, a Tammany Democrat. His opponents, who included Reform Democrats as well as Republicans, opposed giving him control over the patronage and prerequisites of such a large project. When no significant progress was made in almost a year under Mayor Wood's administration, supporters of the park became wary of leaving control of design and construction to politicians whom they regarded as corrupt and inefficient.[41] They harbored this distrust despite the fact that Mayor Wood had successfully vetoed a council ordinance that would have sold park land for private development. The anti-Wood forces prevailed, however, and the Republican-dominated state legislature voted in April 1857 to remove control of the park from the mayor and city government, vesting it instead in an independent, supposedly nonpartisan, eleven-member park commission. It was this commission, a bipartisan body dominated by Republicans, that appointed Frederick Olmsted, Sr., as park superintendent, making him a deputy to Chief Engineer Viele.[42]

Of central importance in the dispute over the park was the control of jobs and patronage. For the Central Park project was a vast source of patronage—as Mayor Wood and his supporters were well

[40] Ibid., 2:30.

[41] Ibid., 2:32.

[42] On how Olmsted came to be appointed park superintendent and the stir caused by his appointment, see Olmsted, Sr., "Passages in the Life of an Unpractical Man," reprinted in *Landscape Architecture* from fragments of an autobiography left by Olmsted.

aware. (By October 1859, the park commission had authorized the employment of a daily average of 2,500 men.) While the control of so many jobs would have proved important in any year, it was especially significant in 1857 because of the financial crisis (the Panic of 1857) that had thrown thousands out of work. Had it not been for the clamor for jobs, the park project might have been stalemated by a hostile city council, since in the absence of adequate state funding, the park commission had been forced to turn to the city for support. As it was, the financial crisis put the project on tenterhooks by preventing the sale of park bonds; until the crisis eased enough for the bonds to be marketed, park laborers were paid in script that the city agreed to redeem with interest at a later date. Olmsted was aware of the importance of the park project as a source of employment but was opposed to exploiting the jobs potential of the park, even in a period of exceptional unemployment. In fact, in boasting that he had done his best to prevent excess employment at the park, he demonstrated that he was a wise choice of the anti-Tammany forces responsible for his appointment.[43]

Having become park superintendent as the candidate of Republicans and Reform Democrats on the park commission, Olmsted owed his appointment to the system of partisan politics—a system of which he was later outspokenly critical. It should also be recalled that the Wood regime had successfully defended the park against an attempt by real estate developers to take park land for private development. Yet Olmsted judged the partisan political system to be inadequate for carrying out large public works projects. For example, he believed that the Central Park site had been ill-chosen. "It would have been difficult to find another body of land of six hundred acres upon the island . . . which possessed less of what we have seen to be the most desirable characteristics of a park," he averred. Although the Central Park site was recommended by a committee of the city council and endorsed by Bryant and Downing among others, Olmsted maintained that the choice was the result of a private grudge between a city alderman and a sponsor of the Jones Woods site. The site was chosen, he contended, in an "off-hand way" by someone "not well informed or interested in the purposes of a park." Following is his version of events:

[43] See Olmsted, Sr., letter to Charles Brace, December 8, 1860, as reprinted in Olmsted and Kimball, *Olmsted*, 2:63-64.

When in the formation of the counter project, the question was reached, what land shall be named in the second bill, the originator turned to a map and asked: "Now where shall I go?" His comrade, looking over his shoulder, without a moment's reflection, put his finger down and said, "Go there"; the point indicated appearing to be about the middle of the island, and therefore, as it occurred to him, one which would least excite local prejudices.[44]

Whether apocryphal or not, this account supported Olmsted's conviction that park matters should not be entrusted to local politicians.

Olmsted was named architect-in-chief of the park, in effect, the park's chief executive officer, after he and the Englishman, Calvert Vaux, became designers of the park by winning a design competition organized by the park commission following its rejection of the plan prepared by Egbert Viele. Vaux, who had come to the United States to join Downing in a partnership just before the landscape architect's death, had asked Olmsted to collaborate in a park design. Benefiting from Olmsted's familiarity with the park grounds, they submitted under the pseudonym "Greensward" a plan that was judged the winner from among thirty-five entrants.[45]

Olmsted's belief in centralized coordination was embodied in the Greensward plan. The outstanding feature of the plan was the unity of effect in the layout of the park grounds and the arrangement of convenience and traffic facilities—a unity of effect that depended on Olmsted and Vaux's centralized control of the plan. According to its authors, the central theme of the Greensward plan was the "constant suggestion to the imagination of an unlimited range of rural conditions."[46] This theme was effected by sinking transverse roads (a design innovation), concealing park shel-

[44] "Public Parks," pp. 26-27.

[45] In making Olmsted architect-in-chief and the chief executive officer of the park, the state park commission abolished Egbert Viele's post as chief engineer. Viele responded by bringing suit against the city, claiming that the original city park commission had accepted his park plan and was therefore financially obligated to him. The court found in Viele's favor and ordered the city to compensate him for his plan. Despite some misunderstanding to the contrary, however, the court did not rule on the authorship of Olmsted and Vaux's Greensward plan. Although Viele argued in court that the ideas for the Greensward plan were stolen from his earlier plan, the court ruled only on whether the city had accepted Viele's plan and therefore owed him compensation. See ibid., 2: Appendix 3.

[46] Excerpted in Olmsted and Kimball, *Olmsted*, 2:45-47; the quotation is from p. 46.

ters as much as possible, and landscaping the various sections of the park in a manner suggestive of rural conditions. The park design was also noteworthy for its engineering feats: the traffic system was ingeniously divided to create separate traffic ways for carriages, pedestrians, galloping horsemen, and common street traffic. Yet engineering considerations were subordinated to the aesthetic element of the plan and to the desire to create a pastoral effect suggesting rural conditions. Creating this rural effect represented a greater accomplishment than it might at first seem. If the grounds had been left in their natural state, they would have looked "unkempt" rather than rural. Thus, the task was not to recreate or restore nature but to "paraphrase it," a task Olmsted and Vaux were acknowledged to have performed with great skill.[47] In effect, Olmsted and Vaux were not simply preserving nature: they were adapting it to a point of view—one aimed at creating an escape from the memories and pressures of the workaday world.

For the park to serve this social purpose, it had to be accessible to all classes, especially to the working class. Olmsted and Vaux were well aware of this: they wrote in their original plan report that "one great purpose" of the park was to "supply to the hundreds of thousands of tired workers, who have no opportunity to spend their summers in the country, a specimen of God's handiwork that shall be to them, inexpensively, what a month or two in the White Mountains or Adirondacks is, at great cost, to those in easier circumstances."[48] Emphasizing the park's public character, Olmsted referred to it as "a democratic development of the highest significance."[49] Yet not everyone supported extending this "suburban solution" to the city's laboring population, particularly not all of the wealthy class.[50] If in the larger analysis the park was a means of conservative reform, it provided, or appeared to provide, "free" amenities to the city's working class—at a significant initial cost to the city's taxpayers. Besides opposing the cost of the park, many of the city's wealthier inhabitants feared the poor would overrun the park, making it unusable by others and contributing to disorder by giving ruffians a place to congregate. For in-

[47] Caparn, "Central Park, New York: A Work of Art," p. 170.

[48] Excerpted in Olmsted and Kimball, *Olmsted*, 2:46.

[49] Letter to Parke Goodwin, August 1, 1858, excerpted in Olmsted and Kimball, *Olmsted*, 2:45.

[50] This felicitous term is from Richard A. Walker, "The Suburban Solution: Urban Geography and Urban Reform in the Capitalist Development of the United States."

stance, the *New York Herald* expressed fear that the park would be a "bear-garden for the lowest denizens of the city."[51] According to Olmsted, there was so much opposition from the wealthy that for a time it was feared they might flee the city and bring ruin to the local economy if a park were built. He related the story of one wealthy resident who complained that the proposed park was too nice for a *public* facility. "Why, I should not ask for anything finer in my private grounds for the use of my own family," the man sniffed. To which (by his account) Olmsted smartly replied, "Possibly grounds might not unwisely be prepared even more carefully when designed for the use of two hundred thousand families and their guests, than when designed for the use of one."[52]

While we do not know how the park affected workers' political attitudes, there was general agreement that it had a moderating influence on the behavior of park visitors. The *Atlantic Monthly* reported in 1861 that the park "exercises a beneficial influence of no inconsiderable value."[53] Olmsted attributed this effect to the park's pastoral character, which he believed "exercise[d] a distinctly harmonizing and refining influence upon the most unfortunate and most lawless classes of the city—an influence favorable to courtesy, self-control, and temperance."[54] Even the *Herald*, which had argued that the park would contribute to disorder, observed in 1870 that "one is no more likely to see ruffianism or indecencies in the Park than in the churches."[55] Perhaps suspecting that its critics' claims would prove true, the park commission had created early on a twenty-four member police force. Yet, as the *Herald* itself reported in defending the park, there were only about twenty arrests per million visitors. And interestingly, the most serious problem for park police was controlling the speed of the carriages driven by the wealthy through the park. As the *Herald* stated:

> We regret to say that the more brilliant becomes the display of vehicles and toilettes, the more shameful is the display of bad manners on the part of the—extremely fine-looking people

[51] Quoted in Olmsted, Sr., "Public Parks," p. 28.
[52] Ibid., p. 29.
[53] Bellows, "Cities and Parks: With Special Reference to New York's Central Park," p. 428.
[54] "Public Parks," p. 34.
[55] Quoted in Olmsted and Kimball, *Olmsted*, 2:170.

who ride in carriages and wear the fine dresses. We must add that the pedestrians always behave well.[56]

The pleasantness of the park contrasted sharply with the prevailing conditions of urban life, as evidenced by the phenomenal flow of visitors to its grounds. In the four years prior to 1870, there were over thirty million visitors by actual count. Often fifty to eighty thousand persons came on foot, thirty thousand in carriages, and four to five thousand on horseback in a single day. On Sundays during the summer an average of thirty to forty thousand persons entered the park on foot, and on a very fine day the number might reach one hundred thousand. Olmsted proudly noted that the number of visitors increased markedly when a law was passed closing saloons on Sunday, although no similar increase was noticed in church attendance.[57]

The park was likewise judged a financial success—an important lesson for neighboring property owners, who had feared the park would diminish property values because of the class of people it would attract. Yet, in this case too, the opposite occurred. Land adjoining the park's seven-mile frontage increased in value 200 percent per annum. According to Olmsted, there was universal agreement that the forty-five million dollars spent on the park had been more than offset by the additional private capital drawn to the city by the park. He wrote that the park had a "very marked effect in making the city attractive to visitors, and in thus increasing its trade, and causing many who had made fortunes elsewhere to take up their residence and become taxpayers in [New York]."[58] In 1861, a special committee appointed by the New York State Senate to investigate Central Park, after noting that land values around the park had more than quadrupuled, reported that from a financial standpoint the park was "one of the wisest and most fortunate measures ever undertaken by the City of New York."[59] Yet the Central Park commissioners continued to assert the social value of the park, writing in their farewell report in 1870 that the advance in property values surrounding the park was "but a small element of the value of the Park to the City"; its chief value, they maintained, was its effect upon the "health, happiness and com-

[56] Quoted in Olmsted, Sr., "Public Parks," p. 33.
[57] Ibid., pp. 31-34.
[58] Ibid., pp. 35, 32-33.
[59] Quoted in Olmsted and Kimball, *Olmsted*, 2:173.

fort of the people."[60] Nevertheless, the lesson of the park's economic value had been learned. When, for example, a proposal for building new parks in the city was being considered, several prominent citizens sent an open letter to the mayor in which they argued for new parks, citing the great financial success of Central Park.[61] In time, it also became apparent that the city's lower class, far from overrunning the park as earlier feared, made less use of it than did the middle and upper classes.[62]

Yet Central Park did more than demonstrate the value of building public parks; it also contributed to the development of the planning process. Specifically, it contributed to the view of planning as a centralized, elite-dominated process, separated from institutions of popular control and accountability. Although Olmsted thought Central Park was "of great democratic significance" because of its public character, he was opposed to leaving park matters to the control of local elected officials. He believed government intervention was necessary to provide collective facilities, like parks, that the market failed to provide; while tolerating this expansion of the state, however, he believed public participation in administering these responsibilities should be minimized.

A fairly coherent critique of the system of local political decision making emerges from the paper Olmsted presented to the ASSA in 1870. Regarding such matters as the location of parks, he believed that the system of local politics invited the representation of too many points of view, impeding rational decision making and often producing stalemate. In support of this view, he cited the "difficulties of equalizing benefits and damages" that prevented the planned redevelopment of New York and London following the disastrous fires that swept both cities. He also maintained that leaving control of park matters to elected officials permitted financial interests to have too great an influence. There is a greater danger in the development of parks than in most other areas of public policy, he contended, that "public opinion may be

[60] Ibid., 2:177.

[61] Ibid., 2:174. The signers of the letter included members of such well-known New York families as the Astors, the Belmonts, the Jays, the Livingstons, and the Putnams. Their names were listed under occupational headings, e.g., "Bankers," "Owners of Real Estate," "Taxpayers," and "Lawyers"; see ibid., 2:173 n. 4.

[62] Olmsted acknowledged this fact in 1881; see Olmsted, Sr., "The Spoils of the Park: With a Few Leaves from the Deep-Laden Notebooks of 'A Wholly Unpractical Man,' " pp. 422-23. Similarly, Jacob Riis observed in 1890 that few slum children ever saw Central Park; see Riis, *How the Other Half Lives*, p. 137.

led, by the application of industry, ingenuity, and business ability on the part of men whose real objects are perhaps unconsciously very close to their own pockets, to overrule the results of more comprehensive and impartial study."[63] Underlying both these concerns was a belief that park development belonged to a special category of public policies for which politics as a system based upon the pursuit of self-interest was incapable of defining and administering the public good. This judgment led Olmsted to argue that public involvement in park matters, and by implication in other large works projects, should be minimized.

> What I would urge is, that park questions, and even the most elementary park questions, questions of site and outlines and approaches, are not questions to which the rule applies, that every man should look after his own interests, judge for himself what will favor his own interests, and exert his influence so as to favor them; but questions rather of that class, which in his private affairs every man of common sense is anxious, as soon as possible, to put into the hands of somebody who is able to take hold of them comprehensively as a matter of direct, grave, business responsibility.[64]

Olmsted's model of planning is captured in his statement, in the same paper, that park matters could best be "taken up efficiently by a small body of select men." In part, this preference stemmed from a belief that a small body could better act as a trustee for the public, rising above petty differences and basing its decisions on disinterested conceptions of the public good. He also believed that a small body was better able to make decisions based on hard-headed factual analysis. As for the "select men" requirement, Olmsted felt park matters should be in the hands of persons well versed in business methods of decision making. Again and again he contrasted decision making by "off-hand common sense" (as in the location of Central Park) with decision making based upon "special, deliberate, business-like study." This attitude is also reflected in his statement that park questions should be delegated to those able to treat them "as a matter of direct, grave, business responsibility."[65]

Olmsted's belief in centralized responsibility, decision making

[63] "Public Parks," pp. 12, 26.
[64] Ibid., p. 26.
[65] Ibid., pp. 26, 31.

by a small group, and "business-like study" was partly the result of his experience with the state-appointed park commission that supervised the building of Central Park. He regarded this body as a model for the administration of public works planning; in his estimation, it had performed a herculean task in insulating the park project from most aspects of the spoils system, making it possible to plan and develop the park using superior professional know-how in civil engineering and landscape architecture. He was quick to point out that this accomplishment was not due to any special expertise on the part of the commissioners. The commission had been successful, he believed, because its members were experienced in business decision making, and because it was given a special, independent responsibility for park matters. He approvingly noted that the commission members were businessmen—"better known from their places in the directory of banks, railroads, mining, and manufacturing enterprises, than for their previous services in politics." At the time of their appointment, moreover, they knew or cared no more about parks than the average businessman, he wrote.

> If, then, it is asked, how did they come to adopt and resolutely pursue a course so very different from that which the public opinion seemed to expect of them, I think that the answer must be found in the fact that they had not wanted or asked the appointment; that it was made absolutely free from any condition or obligation to serve a party, a faction, or a person; that owing to the extraordinary powers given them, their sense of responsibility in the matter was of an uncommonly simple and direct character, and led them with the trained skill of business men to go straight to the question:
> "Here is a piece of property put into our hands. By what policy can we turn it to the best account for our stockholders?"[66]

Stressing the importance of the commission's independent responsibility for park matters, Olmsted applauded the commissioners for conducting themselves like a private board of directors, holding their sessions behind closed doors and purportedly making themselves inaccessible to the private vendors, contractors, and party men who dominated machine politics. These high-handed practices produced a howl of protest: the commission was denounced by the mayor, refused cooperation by city departments,

[66] Ibid., pp. 29-30.

threatened with impeachment and indictment, and lampooned by the press; its sessions were broken up by a mob; and it was investigated five times by legislative committees.[67]

In sum, Olmsted was instrumental not only in the design and promotion of public parks, but also in the promotion of institutions for park planning. Centralized control by a small group, business methods of study, specialized responsibility, and governmental independence—these were the presumed ingredients for successful park planning. And in the years following the Central Park project, these ingredients came to define the local planning process. The importance of Central Park to this view of planning is captured in Olmsted's comment that the "chief lesson" of the project was not its demonstration of the value of parks, but of how to carry out public works planning. "I could show you," he wrote, "that where parks have been laid out and managed in a temporary off-hand common-sense way, it has proved a penny-wise, pound-foolish way, injurious to the property in their neighborhood." It appears this lesson was also impressed upon New York City property owners. For years, landowners had been trying to agree on a system of streets for the upper part of Manhattan; a special committee had been appointed from their number, but even it had failed to reconcile conflicting interests. Observing the success of the Central Park project, the landowners asked the state legislature to make the park commission responsible for planning the streets and roads of upper Manhattan. The legislature granted their request, giving the park commission, in Olmsted's words, "absolute control of the matter, and under them it has been arranged in a manner, which appears to be generally satisfactory, and has caused an enormous advance of the property of all those interested."[68] In 1869, the powers of the park commission were expanded further; its jurisdiction was extended over Westchester County to the Yonkers city line, and it was given responsibility for the design of streets and public squares and parks; for sewerage, drainage, and water supply; and for the improvement of the Har-

---

[67] Ibid., p. 30.

[68] Ibid., pp. 35-36. Olmsted preceded Robert Moses by three quarters of a century in promoting the appointment of independent commissions for public works planning. Contrary to Robert Caro's assertion in his splendid biography of Moses, it was the park commission appointed to oversee Central Park, not Moses's Long Island State Park Commission or the Triborough Bridge and Tunnel Authority, that was the prototype for these semiautonomous governmental bodies. See Caro, *The Power Broker: Robert Moses and the Fall of New York.*

lem River, including the bridges and tunnels running over and under the river. The New York City Park Commission was also a prototype for the boards and commissions established for park planning, as for other forms of public works planning, in cities across the country.

In fairness to Olmsted's critique of the system of local politics, during his association with the Central Park project from 1857 to 1878 he probably experienced New York City machine politics at its most corrupt worst. The period from 1868 to 1871 saw the rise to power of the infamous Tweed Ring, during which time Olmsted and Vaux were frozen out of participation in park matters. This was a period in which the Tammany machine had yet to achieve the centralization of power necessary for disciplining and rationalizing the graft of minor officials and for maintaining some overall control of government policy.[69] Yet it should be remembered that Olmsted had benefited from the system of patronage politics, having become park superintendent as the candidate of the Republicans and anti-Tammany Democrats on the state-appointed park commission. Moreover, he served the interests of his political patrons by preventing the park project from becoming a font of patronage for the Tammany Democrats, even when thousands were thrown out of work by the Panic of 1857. It should also be remembered that if, in Olmsted's view, the local political system had botched the selection of the Central Park site, that same system had won approval of the park project despite formidable opposition from much of the city's wealthy class. The local political system also had proved effective in protecting the park from the land development schemes of land speculators and real estate developers.

PARK PLANNING AFTER CENTRAL PARK

The success of Central Park—socially, politically, and financially—stimulated the building of large urban parks in cities across the continent. Among the better known parks designed wholly or partly by Olmsted and Vaux were Prospect Park in Brooklyn, the Chicago South Parks, Mount Royal in Montreal, Belle Isle in Detroit, Golden Gate Park in San Francisco, and

[69] For an enlightening account of how the Tweed regime fit into the history of New York's Tammany machine, see Shefter, "The Emergence of the Political Machine: An Alternative View," pp. 14-44; for an account of Olmsted's trials and tribulations with the Tweed government, see Roper, *FLO*, pp. 329-31.

Franklin Park in Boston, along with other parts of that city's park system. Reflecting the desire to create what historian Roy Lubove has called an "urban-rural continuum," a continuous garden-city-park, the interest in parks led to the development of parkways linking different parts of the park system as well as the city and suburbs.[70] Another offshoot of park building was the construction of "romantic suburbs," so named because of their park-like, sylvan character. The best examples were Riverside, Illinois; Roland Park, near Baltimore; and Tarrytown Heights, Ohio—all designed by Olmsted, Vaux & Company. In the years following the Central Park project, the Olmsted-Vaux firm quickly became the leading landscape architecture firm in the nation. From 1875, when Olmsted and his partners began keeping records, they laid out thirty-seven public pleasure grounds and twelve suburban developments, as well as the grounds of eleven public buildings and hospitals, thirteen colleges, four large schools, four railroad stations, and twelve large private estates.[71]

There were of course other important figures in early park planning, though all seem to have worked with or for Olmsted at one time or another. Horace W. S. Cleveland, Charles Eliot, and George Kessler all made notable contributions to the park movement that emerged in the 1870s. Cleveland, from an old New England family, provided a link between park planning in the East and the Midwest. Following a stint working for Olmsted on part of the Brooklyn park system, he moved to the Midwest where he designed park systems for Minneapolis (a companion plan for St. Paul was rejected) and Omaha. In addition, he was appointed landscape architect for the South Chicago Parks, succeeding Olmsted and Vaux who had prepared a general plan of parks and boulevards for the Chicago South Park Commission. Charles Eliot, son of the famous Harvard University president, worked as an apprentice for Olmsted before starting his own professional practice and then later became a partner of Olmsted's. He played a leading role in organizing the suburban governments surrounding Boston to create a regional park system, and then in designing metropolitan Boston's system of parks and parkways. His contribution to the park movement would surely have been greater had he not died (from meningitis, while laying out the Hartford park system) at age 38. George Kessler, the youngest of this group, was a Texan with a Eu-

---

[70] Lubove in Cleveland, *Landscape Architecture*, p. x.
[71] Glaab and Brown, *A History of Urban America*, p. 234.

ropean education who worked briefly for Olmsted on the Central Park project. Returning to the West, he secured a commission to design the private grounds of the multimillionaire chairman of the Kansas City park board and was thereafter asked to plan Kansas City's park system. When completed at the turn of the century, the Kansas City park and boulevard system was the envy of cities across the country. Kessler also laid out a park system for his native Dallas in 1910.

Park building in the years following the Central Park project was motivated by conservative social purposes, combined with an interest in enhancing neighboring land values and the desire of members of the carriage set for places in which to relax and display their finery. Although comparatively few received the benefits of enhanced land values, the success of a number of park proposals turned on the lobbying efforts of this small but intense minority. In Boston, taxpayer opposition prevented implementation of Olmsted's proposed park and boulevard system for the Back Bay area—until landowners and speculators from the Back Bay pressured the city council to borrow funds to finance the project.[72] Indeed, these real estate interests knew what they were doing: Boston's park board observed in 1890 that Back Bay land values had increased 300 percent, compared with only 18 percent for the rest of the city. In New York, Boston, Philadelphia, Baltimore, and Chicago, it was reported that park and boulevard construction had boosted land values 300 to 500 percent.[73] In the years following the Central Park project, these economic benefits became part of the litany of arguments used to support park construction. Thus, we find Horace Cleveland arguing that acceptance of his Minneapolis park plan would have a beneficial effect upon property values.[74] In promoting a park and boulevard system for Kansas City, park commissioners there pointed to the increased land values resulting from Chicago's boulevard system. The Kansas City commissioners also maintained that a beautiful park system would attract to the city prosperous businessmen who would contribute to the community good by augmenting the "capitalist class . . . , that

[72] This account is from John C. Olmsted, son and partner of Frederick Olmsted, Sr.; see John C. Olmsted, "The Boston Park System," p. 44.

[73] Holden, "Parks as Investments and Educators," pp. 44, 47. For a further account of the effect of parks on land values, see Buchholz, "Acquirement of Kansas City Park and Boulevard System and Its Effect on Real Estate Values," pp. 96-105.

[74] "Suggestions for a System of Parks and Parkways for the City of Minneapolis," p. 1.

class to whose experience, ability and means the building up of a city is always largely due."[75] When promoting a park and boulevard system for St. Louis, George Kessler demonstrated his appreciation of the economic argument by collecting data from real estate men on the financial impact of the park and boulevard system of neighboring Kansas City. One realtor reported that land facing a boulevard sold for at least twice the value of land on an adjacent street, another that unmarketable land was suddenly worth sixty to eighty dollars a front foot when a boulevard was constructed nearby, and a third that "located on a boulevard" was the best advertisement for selling real estate.[76]

Yet it was the social purposes of parks that principally motivated the landscape architects who were the leaders of the park movement. Arguments supporting this point of view predominated in the journals and plan reports of park planners. A case in point is an 1898 article by Horace Cleveland on "The Influence of Parks on the Character of Children." Cleveland contended that the park's primary purpose was to provide "the occasional relief of the quiet seclusion of rural scenes"; this, he believed, was especially important for children, particularly those from the "poorer classes." For the latter, the park was viewed as an antidote to the evil influences of the slum.[77] Sometimes the focus of social control was on individual behavior. In proposing a park system for Detroit, Olmsted counseled that "one of the most important elements of value in a park" was its power to "divert men from unwholesome, vicious, and destructive methods and habits of seeking recreation."[78] More often, however, discussion centered on how parks provided protection against mass disorder, including working-class militancy. A good example of this argument is a speech by Charles Eliot on "The Need of Parks," presented before the Advance Club of Providence. Observing that the herding together of the poor produced a "degraded race of people," Eliot dwelled on the threat of anarchism.

> The tremendous competition for opportunity to work breeds
> that discontent, and anger, and despair, which lead to anarchy,
> and feeds the fires of that volcano under the city which the

[75] Report of the Board of Park and Boulevard Commissioners of Kansas City, Missouri, 1893, p. 42.
[76] Wilson, *The City Beautiful Movement in Kansas City*, p. 127.
[77] *American Park and Outdoor Art Association*, pp. 105-8.
[78] *Park for Detroit*, p. 18.

alarmists tell us is soon to break forth. Even if the volcano does not belch forth, civilization is not safe so long as any large part of the population is morally or physically degraded; and if such degradation is increasing in our great towns (and who is to say it is not?), it is plainly the duty and the interest of all who love their country to do what they can to check the drift.[79]

What was being articulated here were norms to guide and justify a larger government role in creating the built environment through the construction of collective forms of consumption: public parks. These norms and the arguments supporting them were designed to appeal to and edify the city's politically and economically dominant class. Eliot's concern here was how to avoid political and social disorder. Parks provided an outlet for the tensions that might otherwise lead to political insurrection. In addition, parks served as an active means of socialization. Chicago's parks made "abundant use of water" to attract the immigrant poor,[80] but they were also used as a locus for civic lessons and instructions in English.[81] Olmsted, too, was clearly aware that parks could be put to the service of political socialization: he advocated that labor agitators be barred from the grounds of Boston's Franklin Park, that school children be trained in dutiful respect for the peaceful innocence of the park, and that flat land outside the park be reserved for military exercises, fireworks, and balloon ascensions.[82]

It was not just the threat to political order that motivated park advocates, however. There was also a desire to provide a respite from the world of work, to partially compensate the worker for his degradation within that realm and renew his capacity for labor. This commitment corresponds with capital's interest in the "reproduction of labor power," discussed earlier, and it was a principal motivation for Frederick Olmsted. It is also evident in the remarks of Stephen Child, a Boston landscape architect and designer of industrial towns. Child's case for park building was analogous to Eliot's, except that while Eliot saw the threat to order in the slum, Child located it in the world of work. He held that laboring

---

[79] The speech was given May 9, 1890, and is reprinted in Eliot, *Charles Eliot, Landscape Architect*, p. 338. This book is a collection of the writings of Charles E. Eliot, supplemented by biographical information about the younger Eliot written by his father, Charles W. Eliot.

[80] "Chicago Parks and their Landscape Architecture," p. 19.

[81] See Mulford, "Recent Park Reports," p. 403.

[82] See Blodgett, "Olmsted and Conservative Reform," p. 886.

conditions produced a "mental drain" upon workers, making them the "prey" of labor leaders and disposing them to accept orders from labor unions "that they would never dream of doing if their minds were more active." Providing parks that were easily accessible to workers, Child contended, would help to "relieve the strain of the numerous labour troubles now confronting us."[83] He thus put a more explicitly political gloss on Olmsted's conception of the park as a place for "recuperative relaxation."

What worried Child was that existing parks were too distant from workers' residences to serve much of an antidotal influence. Writing in 1904, he estimated that not ten percent of the laboring population of commercial and manufacturing cities made use of park facilities.[84] Horace Cleveland expressed a similar concern about Chicago's proposed outer ring of parks, which were all but inaccessible to residents of the worker district.[85] The problem, as Cleveland himself observed, was not just one of park location; it lay with the organization of work as well. For in the era of the ten-hour day and the six-day work week, workers had precious little time for recuperative relaxation and peaceful communing with nature. In support of his point, he cited the 1872 report of the Central Park Commission.

> That large part of the people of the city to whom, from the closer quarters in which they are most of the time confined, the park would seem to promise the greatest advantage, cannot ordinarily leave their daily tasks, at the earliest, till after four o'clock; nor their homes, which in the majority of cases are yet south of Twenty-fifth street, before five. A visit to the Park, then, involves two trips by street cars, which with the walk to and from them will occupy more than an hour. The street cars on all the lines approaching the Park are at five o'clock overcrowded, and most members of a family entering one below Twenty-fifth street will be unable to find a seat. Under these circumstances, the pleasure of a short visit to the Park, especially in the latter part of a summer's day, does not often compensate for the fatigue and discomfort it involves, and accordingly it appears that as yet a majority of those who FREQUENT the Park are people in comfortable circumstances, and largely of families, the heads of which have either

[83] "Parks for Industrial Cities," pp. 1-4.
[84] Ibid., p. 1.
[85] *Landscape Architecture*, p. 24.

retired from business or are able to leave their business early in the day. Except on Sunday, and Saturday afternoons and general holidays, the number of residents of the city who come to the park in carriages is larger than those who come by street cars and on foot.

Continuing, the park commissioners observed that "a large majority of the visits of ordinary short daily recreation" were being made by "the comparatively small number, who can afford to use pleasure carriages or saddle horses, or of those from whose houses a walk to it is easy and agreeable."[86] Here was the irony of the public park as an instrument of conservative reform. As the Central Park commissioners recognized, there were limits to its effectiveness as a "public" solution to the degradation within the private world of work. It could not be fully compensating because the conditions of work prevented it from being so. Moreover, despite initial opposition from the wealthy to the building of public parks, in the end they themselves made more use of parks than did workers. Because the wealthy enjoyed parks, too, they were reluctant to support the building of parks in locations where they would be most effective as tools for socializing and controlling the working class.

It should be noted at this point that the political success of park proponents was greatly facilitated by the patronage potential of park construction and maintenance. As discussed earlier, this was an important factor in securing Mayor Wood's support of the Central Park project. It also helped win the support of the Pendergast machine for the Kansas City park and boulevard system,[87] and it was no doubt important in other cities as well. In this way, the local political process contributed to the development of parks—despite the criticism of Olmsted and others that that process was inadequate to the task of park building. In seeking, in the independent park commission, an alternative form of public administration, promoters of park planning sacrificed governmental support for park building while narrowing the range of interests that came to bear on park planning.

The framework for planning defended and promoted by these landscape architects was like that of the New York City Park Commission—based upon centralized control by a small group, governmental independence, special responsibility for park mat-

---

[86] Quoted, ibid., pp. 24-25.
[87] See Wilson, *City Beautiful Movement in Kansas City*, p. 52.

ters, and control by a governmental and social elite. This model of planning was defended on the grounds that park matters should be under the control of persons who were free from the influence of political motives or special interests and could act as trustees for the public. John C. Olmsted, the son and partner of Frederick Olmsted, Sr., stated forthrightly that the park movement had originated with an elite of "public-spirited, broad-minded citizens" and should stay under their control.

> If this same set of people continued ever after in control of parks it would be better both for the parks and for the people, but, unfortunately, it sometimes happens that the parks pass into the control of men who, however honest and well intentioned they may be, have not grasped the fundamental reason for the existence of large parks.[88]

One early park publication described the ideal park commissioner as someone who was intelligent, well traveled, and possessed of refined taste; who comprehended the needs of the community as a whole and would prevent one segment from gaining an advantage over another; who would not use his position to gain personal or political advantage; and who was a person of "sufficient leisure" to enable him to devote at least part of his time to the parks under his care. Further limiting social access, the article maintained that the position should be unpaid and honorary "to obtain the services of gentlemen who consider the honor connected with such a position sufficient reward for their services" and to deter "professional office-seekers."[89] Likewise, Charles Eliot wrote: "The direction of park works may probably best rest with a small body of cultivated men, public-spirited enough to serve without pay, who should regard themselves, and be regarded, as a board of trustees." Eliot excluded from consideration real estate developers and politicians, whom he deemed insufficiently public-minded.[90] To the list of qualities that park commissioners should possess, Horace Cleveland added the wisdom and courage to resist demagogues who asserted that parks only benefited the few.[91] Following the model of New York's Central Park, subsequent park boards and commissions in cities across the country were set up like mini-governments for park purposes; they combined such

[88] "The True Purpose of a Large Public Park," p. 11.
[89] Wahl, "The Duties of Park Commissioners," pp. 132-34.
[90] Eliot, *Charles Eliot*, p. 443.
[91] "Suggestions for a System of Parks for Minneapolis," p. 13.

governmental functions as the imposition of tax levies and the expenditure of public funds with private control by the select. Reflecting the private source of this system of administration, Charles Eliot proposed the board of trustees of the Museum of Art as a model for the administration of Boston's metropolitan park system.[92] Boston, Philadelphia, Brooklyn, Detroit, Chicago, Indianapolis, Kansas City, Milwaukee, Minneapolis, St. Paul, and New York all established park commissions on this model before the turn of the century. Typically, these commissions were responsible for employing park work forces and making contracts; for adopting, commencing work on, and altering park plans; and for enacting ordinances for the park and employing a special police force to enforce park ordinances. One such "strong" commission was the Chicago South Park Commission, founded in 1869. According to one observer, it was because of the commission's liberal powers that South Chicago was so well provided with parks.[93] Having five unpaid members, initially appointed by the governor and subsequently by the judge of the Circuit Court of Cook County, the Chicago South Park Commission had a variety of powers. Among other functions, it was authorized to take and improve land for park purposes; to regulate the use of parks in its domain; to exercise the right of eminent domain in taking additional park land; to control street traffic running through park grounds and to close streets within areas taken for park purposes; to assess benefits against private land surrounding parks; and to levy taxes (up to 5 percent of the assessed value of the taxable property in the district), borrow funds (but not over two million dollars), charge fees for services, and collect funds from the rental and sale of park property.[94]

It was especially the power to borrow money, possessed by some but not all park commissions, that made these bodies like mini-governments—and proved politically controversial. Frederick Olmsted, Sr., was explicit about the need to bypass city councils in securing funding for park construction and maintenance. In advising the Detroit Park Commission he declared:

[I]t has been the custom in undertaking a park, to provide for a less indirect, complex, and confused system of responsibil-

[92] Eliot, *Charles Eliot*, p. 319.
[93] "Chicago Parks and their Landscape Architecture," pp. 19-22.
[94] See Wheelwright, "The Appointment and Powers of Park Commissioners," pp. 25-29.

ity [a reference to city councils] than would otherwise have obtained, by delegating with respect to it most of the duties commonly exercised by common councils in other city business to a board of citizens selected for their supposed special capacity and trustworthiness, serving gratuitously, from interest in the park enterprise.[95]

Yet there was resistance to this circumvention of representative institutions, and it proved effective in a number of cases. Chicago's North Park Commission was authorized by the state at the same time as the Chicago South and West Park Commissions. However, it was never submitted for voter approval out of fear of taxpayer resistance; as a result, it lacked the legal status of its counterparts and could not levy taxes directly. In Boston, opposition to granting taxing power to a proposed park board and to empowering the governor to appoint a proportion of the members of the board stymied park development from 1870 until 1877. And when work finally began on a Back Bay park (the Fens), the Common Council retained control of financing. In Philadelphia, opposition to the tax assessing powers of the park commission led to special state legislation preventing the commission from making special tax assessments against abutting property, which had been an important means of financing park construction. By contrast, the Kansas City park board had the power not only to make special assessments, which it used to finance a large share of park costs, but also to control private development adjacent to parks and parkways.[96]

A number of transitional developments were spawned by nineteenth-century park planning. One was the shift from designing parks to the planning of parkways, and then to the laying out of romantic suburbs. For Frederick Olmsted, Sr., the interest in parkways grew out of the planning of traffic ways within the park. For Cleveland, parkways were a means of bringing parks to a wider section of the city and of avoiding the spread of fire—he had witnessed Chicago's destructive fire of 1871. Romantic suburbs such as those designed by Olmsted and Vaux at Riverside and Roland Park represented an extension of the planning project to the bed-

[95] *Park for Detroit*, p. 16.

[96] Knapp, "Short History of Chicago Parks," p. 2; John Olmsted, "Boston Park System," p. 44; *Thirty-First and Thirty-Second Annual Reports of the City Park Association of Philadelphia*, p. 15; and George B. Ford, "The Park System of Kansas City, Mo.," pp. 498-504.

room community, if not to the city as a whole. For those who could afford access to these park-like sylvan communities, an explicit attempt was made to separate home from work and provide for peaceful communing with nature.[97] Park planning broadened the reach of planning in other ways as well. Kessler's report for the Kansas City park board studied not only the need for parks, but also the topography and traffic patterns of the city, its population density, its industrial and residential sections, and its prospects for future growth. Corresponding with this wider purview, new planning objectives were given expression. The system of parks and boulevards designed by Kessler for Kansas City not only was used for recreation and to provide patronage employment, but also was pressed into the service of slum clearance: parkways were driven through slum areas to force the demolition of unsightly structures. Moreover, Kessler's tree-lined boulevards were laid out to protect the residential character of the city's better neighborhoods, presaging later developments in land use zoning.[98] Park planning also broadened the geographic scope of planning beyond the individual city. The Kansas City park board was a regional body, with a jurisdiction encompassing the suburban environs of the city. Likewise, the park system of metropolitan Boston was created in the 1890s, at the urging of Charles Eliot and others who recognized that the surrounding suburban governments, acting independently, could not create an integrated park system.

Park planning also stimulated a better appreciation of the need for purposive intervention to guide urban development. The conservative social purposes behind the building of public parks could not be realized by leaving the organization of urban amenities to the market system—thus, the need for government intervention. Yet neither could the development of collective facilities like parks be left to the vagaries of local politics: in the view of park planners, a method of public administration capable of coordinating activities toward the achievement of express objectives was needed. The connection between creating such institutions for park planning and realizing the common interests of capital is

[97] For Olmsted and Vaux's thoughts on the suburban ideal, see Olmsted, Vaux & Co., "Preliminary Report Upon the Proposed Suburban Village at Riverside, Near Chicago," pp. 257-77. Here (p. 262), Olmsted and Vaux describe the nation's emerging suburbs as "the most attractive, the most refined and the most soundly wholesome forms of domestic life, and the best application of the arts of civilization to which mankind has yet attained [sic]."

[98] Wilson, *City Beautiful Movement in Kansas City*, pp. 46-49.

nicely captured in Olmsted's comments on the failure to adopt Christopher Wren's plan for the reconstruction of London following the disastrous fire of 1666.

Olmsted attributed this failure to the "incredible shortsightedness of the merchants and real estate owners." Significantly, however, he did not believe the interests of these groups were antithetical to the broader interests of the city. Rather, the problem was that these groups were unable, without the aid of planners, to realize and act on their collective interests. As Olmsted wrote:

> There can be little question, that had the property owners, at this time, *been wise enough to act as a body in reference to their common interests*, and to have allowed Wren to devise and carry out a complete street system, intelligently adapted to the requirements which he would have been certain to anticipate; as well as those which were already pressing, it would have relieved the city of London of an incalculable expenditure which has since been required to mend its street arrangements; would have greatly lessened the weight of taxation . . . , and would have saved millions of people from the misery of poverty and disease.[99]

In Olmsted's view, the business class would be better off, and the larger city as well, if there existed a method of realizing the positive common interests of business in the area of urban development, of overcoming their internal competition and narrow focus of interest. Indeed, one of the lessons of park planning was that planners, in conjunction with politically insulated institutions for park planning, were necessary to realize Olmsted's "common interests" of business. This is not to say, of course, that planners have been perfectly capable of identifying the common interests of business, or even that they have been uniformly or self-consciously committed to that objective. In the City Beautiful movement discussed in the following chapter, we see both a continuation of the planner's role in educating the business class on the need for planning and a demonstration of the difficulty inherent in allowing planners to stray too far from the economic needs of their business supporters.

[99] Olmsted, Vaux & Co., "Observations on the Progress of Improvements in Street Plans, with Special Reference to the Parkway Proposed to Be Laid out in Brooklyn," p. 29 (italics mine).

FIVE

Planning the City Beautiful

"LET YOUR WATCHWORD be order and your beacon beauty"—
these words of Daniel Burnham neatly summarize the meaning of
the City Beautiful.[1] A complex cultural movement with diverse
origins, the City Beautiful signified academic classicism in public
architecture and the planning of monumental civic centers, public
building groups, grand boulevards, ornamental parks, equestrian
statues, elaborate fountains, and other such street embellishments. In the first decade of this century, dozens of cities initiated
beautification projects of this sort. Among the major cities receiving City Beautiful–style facelifts were Washington, Cleveland,
New York, Boston, Philadelphia, Baltimore, and Chicago. Politically, the City Beautiful was part of an attempt by urban economic
elites to regain or solidify their control over urban institutions; it
was, as one author has put it, the "architectural and aesthetic
arm" of the Progressive movement.[2] Thus, the quest for "order"—
Burnham's "watchword"—applied to more than architectural order (for example, regulating architectural styles, cornice heights,
and building materials). The City Beautiful was the physical civic
ideal for an attempt to create social and moral cohesiveness in a
heterogeneous urban society in which face-to-face methods of social control had proven to be unworkable.

As with park planning, City Beautiful planning represented a response to both the property contradiction and the capitalist-democracy contradiction. In asserting the need for civic beauty, both
for its own sake and for other, derivative ends, City Beautiful proponents were calling for a larger public role in urban development.
They believed that purposeful intervention was necessary to
achieve the ideals of the City Beautiful, and that this intervention
entailed, at least potentially, a recasting of the balance between
private purposes and social need in shaping the built environment
of the city. Yet the City Beautiful tradition was conservative on
the issue of property rights, reflecting its upper class basis of sup-

[1] From a speech by Daniel Burnham, quoted in Burnham and Bennett, *Plan of Chicago*, p. v.

[2] Hines, *Burnham of Chicago: Architect and Planner*, p. 138.

port. In most cases, City Beautiful planning consisted of private planning for the public sector; that is, planning by private associations for the design and location of public facilities. This activity still constituted regulation of the city building process, but instead of public restrictions being placed on private property, social needs were being asserted to guide the actions of government decision makers. The issue of controlling property rights was, however, a continuing source of tension within the City Beautiful, and the experience of City Beautiful planning contributed to recognition of the need for public controls over private development, even to achieve the ideals of urban beautification.

The goals of this planning tradition were conservative in that they reflected the desire to maintain the existing structure of society. In one respect, City Beautiful works—civic centers, monuments, grand boulevards, fountains, and the like—were an exercise in vanity on the part of the upper classes. In seeking to dress up cities with European-derived ornamentation (for example, in the use of Italian Renaissance-style architecture), they sought to link "their" cities with the great cities of the past. Yet this assessment ignores the political service of civic beautification. City Beautiful works were the physical embodiment of a legitimating civic ideal at a time of large-scale immigration, before the rise of mass communication, when the task of legitimating economic, cultural, and political institutions fell largely to local elites. These works were intended to divert attention from more threatening reform agendas and to instill the citizenry with respect for country, American culture, and capitalism. And in doing all this, they contributed to the hegemony, or class leadership, of the men of capital, since these men were the ones who made these works possible. Of course, civic beautification also offered economic benefits: direct benefits for the owners of adjacent land and, in theory, indirect benefits for the larger community through the stimulus provided for private investment. Yet, whatever the merit of these economic arguments, it was not chiefly the economic benefits of City Beautiful planning that explained its appeal to urban elites across the country.

Turn-of-the-century aesthetic planning contributed to the development of the planning process as well. Although most City Beautiful projects were initiated as private efforts, there being a naive belief that good planning would be implemented voluntarily, these efforts made apparent the need for government powers to make planning a reality. In spite of its private origins, then, City

Beautiful planning spurred the development of quasi-governmental planning commissions, independent bodies composed of local elites with special responsibility for planning matters. Correspondingly, the planning of this era stimulated an awareness of the need for experts—planning specialists—to prepare plans; in this case, it was architects rather than engineers who were the preferred experts. City Beautiful planning contributed to the view of planning as something that experts did in conjunction with elites through specialized boards or commissions formally separated from institutions of popular control. Purposeful intervention in accordance with a plan was presented as a corrective to both the market system and the system of local political decision making.

The City Beautiful was also important for what it signified about the limits of planners' autonomy from their business-class supporters. The City Beautiful ideal, however nicely it articulated with other aspects of Progressive reform, emerged from within the traditions and internal history of architecture and landscape architecture. That City Beautiful planning found support within the business community indicated that it harmonized with the needs and interests of at least some members of that community. But, in the end, the City Beautiful failed for lack of sufficient support from within the business class—the only social group with the power to make planning a reality. The response of the emerging body of planning specialists was to reorient its approach to planning. By 1915, the City Beautiful had been superseded by an approach to planning that emphasized economy and efficiency concerns, particularly in regard to the street and transit system and to the division of land use. Taking as its ideal the City Practical, this approach better corresponded with the economic needs of planning's business supporters. The story of this transition and its implications for understanding the relationship of planners to business are treated in this chapter and in Chapter 7. More specifically, the present chapter examines the flowering of the City Beautiful, while Chapter 7 ("Planning the City Practical") looks at the completion of that transition.

BURNHAM AND THE FAIR

Daniel Burnham was the leading practitioner of City Beautiful planning and one of its most effective promoters. To know Burnham, therefore, is to gain a better sense of this planning tradition.[3] His background was much like that shared by Veiller, Downing, and Olmsted. He was of respectable bourgeois origin and Yankee New England stock. When he was eight years old, his family moved from upstate New York to Chicago where his father entered the wholesale drug business and soon became prosperous. In 1865, the elder Burnham was elected president of the Chicago Mercantile Association, one of the city's earliest businessmen's associations. Befitting his class origins, Daniel Burnham was sent to preparatory school, but, despite diligent preparation, he failed to gain admission to either Harvard or Yale, the only universities he and his father thought appropriate for him. Returning to Chicago, he became a draftsman's apprentice in an architectural office, yet the love of architecture was not immediate. At twenty-three, he set out for Nevada in hopes of making his fortune prospecting for silver, a venture that ended in failure. Two years later, he returned to Chicago, still lacking a college education or any kind of professional training but now determined to become an architect. While working for a large architectural firm, he met John Root who, with an engineering degree from New York University, had the professional training Burnham lacked. The two soon formed an architectural partnership that lasted from 1873 until Root's death in 1891. During that time, they designed approximately forty million dollars' worth of buildings. Among their most famous structures in Chicago were the Monadnock Building, at ten stories Chicago's first "sky scraper"; the Rand McNally Building, the Rookery, and the Reliance Building. With their contemporaries, Louis L. Sullivan, Dankmar Adler, and Frank Lloyd Wright, Burnham and Root helped create the style of the Chicago School of Architecture.

The success of the Burnham-Root firm in the competitive world of Chicago architecture turned not just on the partners' architectural skill, but also on their ability to gain the respect of and maintain connections with the men of wealth who were doing the building in Chicago. There was a division of labor between the two partners, with Burnham serving as the firm's public relations man and manager while Root concentrated on the architectural side of the business. Their first big break came when they received a commission in 1874 to design a house for stockyards magnate John B.

[3] The best biography of Burnham is Hines's *Burnham of Chicago*. I have also consulted the more laudatory biography of Burnham by Charles Moore, who worked with Burnham as a publicist for the Washington Plan of 1902; see Moore, *Daniel H. Burnham: Architect, Planner of Cities*.

Sherman. The commission was a double success: Sherman liked the design and recommended the two young designers to his friends, and Burnham married Sherman's daughter, gaining social entrée into the upper crust of Chicago society. Moreover, the increasing prominence of the Burnham-Root firm came at a propitious time. Chicago in this period was growing at a dizzying pace; with the concentration of capital and the rise of the large business corporation, there were numerous headquarters to be designed, as well as large department stores, professional office buildings, and private homes and mansions.

Burnham the architectural businessman was quick to recognize the opportunities offered by the new age of business. Louis Sullivan, commenting on how the corporate age affected architecture, wrote, "The only architect to catch the significance of this movement was Daniel Burnham, for in its tendencies toward bigness, organization, delegation and intense commercialism, he sensed the reciprocal workings of his own mind." Burnham had confided to Sullivan that he was not content to design merely houses. "My idea," Burnham had said, "is to work up a big business, to handle big things, deal with big business men, and to build up a big organization, for you can't handle big things unless you have an organization." Under Burnham's guidance, the Burnham-Root firm pioneered in the transition from an "atelier" style of architectural practice to one based on division of labor and business management. At its peak in 1912, the Burnham firm had no fewer than 180 employees; after 1900, sub-offices were established in New York and San Francisco to maintain presences on both coasts.[4]

Burnham's belief in the virtue of bigness and his faith in centralized management based upon expertise extended to the political world as well. Although he worked with politicians in promoting his planning and building schemes and made regular financial contributions to the Republican party, he dabbled in electoral politics only once: while prospecting for silver in Nevada, he ran for the state senate on the Democratic ticket and was defeated, an experience that may have diminished his faith in electoral politics. As his biographer, Thomas Hines, has written, "Burnham believed strongly in the idea of free enterprise capitalism, shorn of its excesses and grosser injustices by 'progressive' governmental con-

[4] The Sullivan quotation is from Sullivan, *The Autobiography of an Idea*, p. 314; the Burnham quotation is also from Sullivan (pp. 285-86). On the growth of the Burnham-Root firm, see Hines, *Burnham of Chicago*, p. 269.

trol, and he worked on the assumption that, with proper regulation, reform, and receptiveness to change, the system could somehow manage to exist compatibly with political democracy." As a Republican who identified with the Progressive movement, Burnham was a centralizer who believed that planning and controls were necessary to limit the excesses of both democracy and the market system. "While basically a supporter of capitalist individualism," writes Hines, "[Burnham] also saw the need—perhaps in the interest of conserving that system—for greater social collectivization and cooperative sacrifice among individual citizens."[5]

If Burnham was the leading practitioner of City Beautiful planning, the Chicago World's Fair was its "activating symbol."[6] With its classical-designed White City, replete with Romanesque columns, reflecting pools, and monumental architecture, the Fair was an alluring expression of the norms and outlook of the City Beautiful. There was also significance in the way the Fair's White City was planned; its reliance on centralized administration, expertise, and collaboration between designers and civic boosters set the pattern for later planning efforts.

Officially known as the Columbian Exposition, the Fair commemorated (one year late) the four-hundredth anniversary of Columbus's landing in America. It was therefore more of a celebration of national accomplishment than it was a true world's fair. And more particularly, it was a celebration of the accomplishments of Chicago, the premier city of the Midwest. Typifying the urban rivalry of the day, there was intense competition over which American city would play host to the Fair. By the summer of 1889, New York, Washington, St. Louis, and Chicago were all vying for congressional designation. According to Chicago historian Bessie Louise Pierce, Chicago succeeded in attracting the Fair, in spite of the city's upstart image, because of the "I will" spirit of Chicago boosters.[7]

Promoters of a Chicago site appear simply to have out-hustled the competition. In July 1889, Chicago Mayor DeWitt Cregier appointed a committee of 250 leading citizens to work on bringing the Fair to Chicago. This committee even went to the extent of sending representatives to Paris to report on the Universal Expo-

[5] Hines, *Burnham of Chicago*, pp. xix, 172.

[6] Robert Walker, *Planning Function in Urban Government*, p. 12.

[7] *A History of Chicago*, vol. 3, *The Rise of a Modern City, 1871-1893*, p. 502.

sition being held there. Also, to underwrite the cost of the Fair, promoters created a joint-stock company with a board of directors consisting of 45 leading Chicago businessmen. This body pledged a total working capital of ten million dollars, half this amount to be raised by subscription and the other half through the sale of municipal bonds. When the criticism was heard from various parts of the country that the Chicago stockholders could not raise their pledged five-million dollar subscription, it was pointed out by a Chicago architectural publication that the wealth of the 45 directors combined totaled approximately seventy million dollars. George Pullman, manufacturer of Pullman railroad cars, was himself responsible for purchasing one hundred thousand dollars in stock. With such backing, it was difficult to imagine the Chicago boosters failing. In April of 1890, Congress passed a resolution designating Chicago as the site of the Fair.[8]

Designer-booster collaboration was the hallmark of the Fair, as of the City Beautiful planning that followed in its track. Reflecting the Fair's mixed, public-private character, two bodies were charged with overseeing the project: one consisted of the Chicago stockholders, incorporated as the World's Columbian Exposition, and the other was a national commission appointed by Congress and comprised of representatives from every state. It was principally the stockholder group, however, that superintended planning and construction work. This responsibility was further delegated to a Committee on Buildings and Grounds chaired by E. T. Jeffery, president of the Illinois Central Railroad. Burnham, who had been a consultant to the group seeking to bring the Fair to Chicago, was named chief of construction (later director of works). Jeffery drew the terms of Burnham's commission so that all other building officials and heads of departments reported directly to Burnham. This was a role well suited to Burnham's talents and his predilection for centralized management, but it is significant that this organizational model came from Jeffery and the stockholder group rather than from Burnham. As Burnham said of this centralized mode of organization, "It was urged by men who knew more about organization than I did at the time, that it was absolutely

---

[8] Burnham, "The Organization of the World's Columbian Exposition," p. 5; Hines, *Burnham of Chicago*, p. 76; Buder, *Pullman: An Experiment in Industrial Order and Community Planning, 1880-1930*, p. 147; and Moore, *Daniel H. Burnham*, p. 31.

necessary to have a chief." In his role as chief, Burham gained a reputation as a demanding but benevolent dictator.[9]

When a dispute developed between the national commission and the Chicago authorities over where the exposition grounds should be located, Frederick Olmsted and his partner Henry Codman were asked to survey possible sites and make a recommendation to the commission. Expert opinion was thus valued from the start. Earlier, Olmsted and Calvert Vaux had prepared a general plan for Jackson Park on Chicago's South Side, one of the Fair sites under consideration; and Olmsted and Codman recommended the Jackson Park location, along with a lakefront area adjacent to downtown Chicago, as the dual sites of the Fair. Eventually, however, the Jackson Park location, alone, was decided upon. Olmsted and Codman thereafter agreed to serve as consulting architects for the design of the exposition grounds. In the fall of 1890, a general scheme for the grounds and buildings was prepared through the combined efforts of Burnham, Root, Olmsted, Codman, and engineer Abram Gottlieb. After initially recruiting top architects from New York, Boston, and Kansas City to work on the Fair, Burnham acceded to the request of the Chicago stockholders and brought several leading Chicago architects into the project as well. Those recruited included Richard M. Hunt, George B. Post, and William R. Mead of New York; Robert S. Peabody of Boston; Henry Van Brunt of Kansas City; and Dankmar Adler, Louis L. Sullivan, F. M. Whitehouse, S. S. Beman, Henry Ives Cobb, and W. L. B. Jenney of Chicago. Root died shortly after the general plan for the Fair was prepared and was replaced as chief architect by Charles Atwood. Also a member of the design group was the French sculptor Augustus Saint-Gaudens. Burnham and his design collaborators worked under the supervision of the Fair's stockholders and the national supervisory body, but because of their prestige, they were given a relatively free hand.

The designers' most fundamental planning decision was to adopt a uniform neoclassical architectural style and sixty-foot cornice height. It was these features, together with the treatment of the Fair's park-like open areas, which were integrated into the overall design of buildings and land use, that distinguished the Fair from real-world American cities, creating what one architectural critic called its "triumph of ensemble." Yet the Fair was also sig-

[9] Burnham, "Organization of the Columbian Exposition," p. 5; the quotation is from Hines, *Burnham of Chicago*, p. 79.

nificant for the collaborative effort that went into its design. Sculptor Saint-Gaudens commented that the Fair represented "the greatest meeting of artists since the 15th century." However immodest this remark, Saint-Gaudens's comparison was apt in that the Fair represented a return to the kind of collaborative undertaking characteristic of an earlier era of artistic and architectural endeavor. As architectural historian Christopher Tunnard has written, "The Renaissance principle of collaboration was consciously if briefly revived in an age otherwise characterized by its 'rugged individualism.' "[10]

The Fair's model city became known as the "White City" because its buildings were all bathed in white paint. Harmoniously arranged in height, bulk, and location, the exhibition halls were grouped around a central Court of Honor, filled with water, that served as a reflecting pool and a means of access to the principal Fair buildings. A system of canals and lagoons spread outward from the Court of Honor, enclosing and linking together the exhibition halls. Monumental in size, these halls covered two hundred of the Fair's six hundred acres. Besides the Administration Building, there were halls labeled Agriculture, Manufacturers and Liberal Arts, Electricity, Machinery, Mines and Mining, Transportation, Fisheries, and Horticulture. There was also a Music and Fine Arts Building and a Women's Building, the latter designed by Sophia Hayden of Boston. In addition, there were thirty state headquarters buildings and twenty buildings for foreign governments.

With their glittering white facades, neoclassical architecture, and monumental size, these buildings and the reflecting pools and statues surrounding them imparted a mystical quality to the Fair. As one magazine commentator rhapsodized in an article entitled "Our Dream City":

> The Fair! The Fair! Never had the name had such significance before. Fairest of all the world's present sites, it is. A city of palaces and spaces of emerald reflected in shining links of water which stretch in undulating lines under flat arches of marble bridges, and along banks planted with consummate skill.

[10] Burnham, "Organization of the Columbian Exposition," pp. 5-8; on the distinctive features of the Fair's design, Schuyler, "Last Words About the World's Fair," pp. 292-93; Saint-Gaudens, quoted in Moore, *Daniel H. Burnham*, p. 47; and Tunnard, "A City Called Beautiful," p. 31.

But the Fair was also a place for fun and amusement. Stretching outward from the Fair alongside the new campus of the University of Chicago was the fabulous Midway. Here visitors encountered the first Ferris wheel, watched the titillating dancing of Little Egypt, and sampled dozens of other amusements. The garish exotica of the Midway was instrumental in attracting over twenty million paid admissions during the Fair's six months of operation.[11]

As an ideological model "for what a great city might be," as one commentator enthusiastically described it, the White City suffered numerous limitations. It directed attention to the visual disorder of the physical city while ignoring the economic and social city. In demonstrating how the organization of buildings and land use could be made a deliberate work of art, it contributed to a revival of neoclassical architectural styles still evident today in museums, libraries, and other public buildings dating from this period. Yet this revival has been described as having had a retrograde influence on American culture and architecture. Probably the severest critic of the Fair's architecture was Louis Sullivan, designer of the giant Transportation Building, the one major structure not built on neoclassical lines. Sullivan later described the Fair's neoclassical architecture as a "virus [that was] snobbish and alien to the land." A more "natural" architecture, more in keeping with American traditions (more like his own), would have been preferable, Sullivan maintained. Others have said that the neoclassical style was a result of the designers' common Beaux Arts architectural training. Except for Burnham, who was American-educated, they all had been exposed to classical styles in their European architectural training, and there was no other style so well suited to the Fair's colossal buildings. This explanation signifies that the architecture of the Fair and of later City Beautiful works grew out of the traditions and internal history of the architectural profession. Yet this explanation overlooks the psychological and political appeal of neoclassical architecture: no other style appealed as much to the vanity of the designers and stockholders controlling the Fair, and no other style had as much power to confer historical legitimacy on their efforts.[12]

[11] Wheeler, "A Dream City," p. 833; figures on attendance, Hines, *Burnham of Chicago*, p. 117.

[12] John Adams, "What a Great City Might Be—A Lesson from the White City," pp. 11-12; Sullivan, *Autobiography*, p. 235; on Sullivan's critique of the Fair, Crook, "Louis Sullivan and the Golden Doorway," pp. 250-58; on how the design

Nor was the ideological model of the Fair relevant to the issue of controlling private development. The Fair's success in demonstrating how the city could be made a deliberate work of art depended on the centralized ownership (public and private) of its buildings and grounds: the Fair was located on public park ground and its buildings were owned by a joint-stock company. In this respect, the Fair and the tradition of City Beautiful planning that it stimulated were analoguous to earlier nineteenth-century planning efforts, such as the planning of cemeteries, university campuses, and private real estate developments, all of which took advantage of centralized land ownership to impose overall design coordination. By using the controls made possible by centralized land ownership, the institution of private property and the desire for coordinated development were kept out of conflict.

As a planning model, the Fair demonstrated the value of relying upon expertise, collaborative effort, and centralized administration, and it thus prefigured subsequent planning efforts. For control by the market system, the Fair substituted control by design experts working in a designer-client relationship with local civic boosters. Within this relationship, the designers had considerable freedom of action. Burnham said of the deference shown to the designers that it arose from Chicago businessmen's habit of "entrusting great works to men trained in the practice of such undertakings."[13] His belief in the need for expertise to complement business decision making was evident in a note sent to the businessman chairing the Fair's ceremonies committee. He wrote: "Men of business . . . cannot expect to evolve new ideas, which alone should be tolerated. How can you expect to reach any but familiar stock conclusions?"[14]

The reliance on expertise and collaborative effort, fused with centralized coordination, engendered a collectivist spirit on the part of those who worked on and wrote about the Fair. Indicative of the power of monumental public art to stir feelings of patriotism, one commentator compared the Fair's ability to stimulate concerted effort to the pitch of national consciousness felt in time of war. "Once again now, but this time in the interest of beauty

---

group's training influenced its choice of an architectural style, Schuyler, "Last Words," pp. 293-94; Tselos, "The Chicago Fair and the Myth of the 'Lost Cause,' " p. 265; and Karlowicz, "D. H. Burnham's Role in the Selection of Architects for the World's Columbian Exposition," p. 253.

[13] Burnham and Bennett, *Plan of Chicago*, p. 6.

[14] Quoted in Hines, *Burnham of Chicago*, p. 110.

and of peace," wrote Alice Freeman Palmer, "we have studied the art of subordinating fragmentary interests to those of the whole." Palmer was commenting specifically on the role of the Lady Board of Managers in organizing the Fair's "Women's Exposition." Wherever pettiness and personal considerations entered into these efforts, they have "flawed the beautiful whole and flecked the honor of us all," she observed.[15] Likewise, Henry Adams was so impressed with the Fair that he devoted a whole chapter to it in his *Education*, writing that "Chicago [the Fair] was the first expression of American thought as a unity."[16] Along the same lines, another commentator declared that the Fair taught a lesson in the meaning of citizenship. The "source and secret" of the Fair in this regard was that "the best were called upon to produce the best." Not only were the best design artists assembled for the Fair, he noted, but the whole enterprise was administered by the "foremost businessmen in Chicago."[17]

The collectivist spirit of the Fair entailed mild tolerance of organized labor, but only on the condition that it not exercise its collective power. As director of works for the Fair, Burnham had a paternalistic attitude toward labor. He intervened in a number of cases to keep workers on the force when their part of the project was completed, and he professed not to be anti-union. Yet he refused to accede to workers' demands for a union shop and gave standing orders to the Fair's security force to keep labor agitators off the grounds. However, Burnham did accept the principle of arbitration of worker disputes, though this concession was probably intended to prevent a crippling strike—he had only two years to complete work on the Fair. The *Inland Architect*, a Chicago architectural publication and the voice of Chicago architects, agreed with organized labor on the need to standardize wages on the project. Yet, when unionized workers attempted to achieve this end by threatening a strike, the *Architect* denounced the unions as "un-American institutions" and condemned union leaders for attempting to use "the compulsory methods of the old world." The similarity between Burnham's centralized control of the Fair and "old world" forms of dictatorial control apparently escaped the *Architect*.[18]

[15] "Some Lasting Results of the World's Fair," pp. 519, 520.
[16] *The Education of Henry Adams: An Autobiography* p. 343.
[17] John Adams, "What a Great City Might Be," p. 12.
[18] Hines, *Burnham of Chicago*, pp. 103-5; "Organized Labor and the World's Fair," p. 54.

Although the term *City Beautiful* had not yet been coined in 1893, the Fair provided the conceptual ideal for the City Beautiful planning that followed. As it is commonly told, visitors to the Fair were so impressed by what they saw that they returned to make improvements in their own cities on the model of the White City. This activity led to the planning of civic centers, public building groups, radial boulevards, and monuments and other street embellishments, all emblematic of the City Beautiful.[19] A number of objections can be raised to this tracing of events, however. First, it describes only the elite response to the Fair. For the masses who flocked to the Fair, it was not the uplifting splendor of the White City but the garish exotica of the Midway that captured their attention. While the White City left a legacy of monumental architecture, the Midway stimulated an industry of traveling carnival shows and new attractions for popular resorts, a far different model of urban recreation than either Central Park or the White City.[20] Second, the translation of the Fair's heritage into concrete planning efforts was a slow process that took almost a decade, due largely to the economic depression of the mid-1890s. It was not until the replanning of Washington in 1902 that the first concrete attempt was made to apply the lessons of the Fair. Third, the emergence of a City Beautiful movement depended on the formation of a number of national and local organizations and on the diligent propaganda efforts of lay activists within these organizations, some of whose efforts predated the Fair. To understand the development of the City Beautiful movement, we need to discover how these diverse efforts came together in the period encompassing the turn of the century.

PROGRESSIVE ENVIRONMENTAL REFORM

It was in the decade between the Fair and the replanning of Washington that the ideals of the City Beautiful were defined and articulated, transforming the spirit of the Fair into a well-organized elite movement and laying the foundation for the first organized effort to promote city planning. Like the Progressive move-

---

[19] This is the way the history has been passed down within the planning profession; see, for example, the article by George B. Ford, chairman of the Town Planning Committee, American Institute of Architects, "The Architectural Side of City Planning," pp. 299-300.

[20] On the influence of the Fair's Midway, see Kasson, *Amusing the Million: Coney Island at the Turn of the Century*, pp. 23-28.

ment with which it was vaguely associated, the City Beautiful movement had diverse origins. Charles Mulford Robinson, the leading evangelist of the City Beautiful, wrote that the end of the nineteenth century witnessed "a general realization of the shortcomings of our cities, from an aesthetic point of view, and a surprisingly common awakening of a wish to improve them."[21] Because of Robinson's leadership role, this analysis might be understood as the movement's own interpretation of its origins. Yet Robinson's depiction of the movement as a response to spontaneously expressed desire fails to take account of the organized efforts to promote this awakening, including his own vigorous propagandizing. Historian Jon Peterson argues that the City Beautiful movement arose from three different spheres of reform—municipal art, civic improvement, and public landscape and outdoor art—each with roots predating the Fair and each with its own constituency.[22] It should be noted, however, that there was also an important similarity between these reform efforts: in each of them, middle-class reformers sought to impose social control and moral order through environmental reform. By reviewing the history of these reform endeavors, we gain a more profound sense of the origins of the City Beautiful.

The municipal art movement is the most commonly recognized point of origin for the City Beautiful and the one most closely associated with the inspiration for the Fair. By all accounts, this movement began in New York City in the early 1890s. While interest in the adornment of public buildings and the erection of monuments, statues, and the like had been developing for some time, it took organizational form on the eve of the Fair with the founding of the Municipal Art Society of New York. Architect Richard M. Hunt, one of the principal designers of the Fair, played the lead role in organizing the Society, and its membership was drawn mostly from art circles. For this group, municipal art meant principally two things: piecemeal adornment of public buildings, streets, and parks (for example, frescoes, sculptings, and works of stained glass), as opposed to comprehensive schemes for beautifying the city, and coordination between allied artists—architects, painters, and sculptors—in the design and execution of these adornments. Although municipal art activities slowed during the depression years of the 1890s, by the decade's end municipal art

[21] "Improvement in City Life III: Aesthetic Progress," p. 771.
[22] "The City Beautiful Movement: Forgotten Origins and Lost Meanings," p. 416.

societies had been formed in Philadelphia, San Francisco, Cincinnati, Baltimore, and Brooklyn. Art professionals also were becoming organized; this period saw the founding of the National Sculpture Society, the National Association of Mural Painters, the Fine Arts Federation, the National Art Club, and the Architectural League of America, which organized a National Committee on Civic Improvements and Embellishments.[23]

It was in connection with municipal art that the City Beautiful term was born. Borrowed from the arts and crafts movement in England, the term was given prominent display in the December 1899 issue of *Municipal Affairs*, the magazine of the Reform Club of New York. It thereafter became the conceptual ideal and something of a shibboleth for municipal art advocates and proponents of other local improvements. In recognition of the spread of enthusiasm for municipal art, a national conference was called by the Baltimore Art Society in 1899 to discuss "subjects related to the artistic development of cities." There, conferees from New York, Boston, Chicago, Philadelphia, and Washington were told in the opening address: "Beauty in high places is what we want; beauty in our municipal buildings, our parks, squares and courts; and we shall have a national school, when, and not until when, art, like a new Petrarch, goes to be crowned at the capitol." These words were prophetic, since Washington, D.C. was indeed the first example of City Beautiful planning.[24]

Another legacy of the municipal art movement was the appointment of quasi-governmental art commissions—forerunners of the independent plan commissions which began to be appointed in the first decade of this century. Formed at the urging of local art devotees, these bodies were composed of patrons of the arts and art professionals. Their task, as they themselves defined it, was to supervise the city's art acquisitions (fountains, statues, and frescoes, for example) to ensure that they constituted "art" and reflected good taste.

Yet the municipal art movement was concerned with more than aesthetics. Like the larger City Beautiful movement it helped launch, it justified planning not only in aesthetic terms but also in

[23] On the formation of municipal art groups, see Peterson, "City Beautiful Movement," pp. 416-20, and Robinson, "Improvement in City Life," pp. 780-81.

[24] The term *City Beautiful* was first used in the United States in Charles Lamb, "Civic Architecture from its Constructive Side," p. 72; on the Baltimore Art Society's conference, "Baltimore Municipal Art Conference," pp. 706-13; opening address, Blashfield, "A Word for Municipal Art," p. 593.

terms of such goals as cultural uplift for the lower classes, urban economic growth, and the stimulation of patriotism. In some cases, the issue of private control of development was addressed head-on. An 1877 article in the *American Architect* cited private enterprise as the "greatest enemy" of efforts to enhance the appearance of the city—words scarcely imaginable in the *Journal of the American Institute of Architects* today. More commonly, the complaint was directed against one or another aspect of private enterprise without addressing private development per se. Thus, municipal art advocates spoke out against garish commercial displays, the gridiron street system, uncontrolled smoke stacks, and, occasionally, land speculation. These complaints led to some recognition of the need for public controls over development. For example, a 1901 article in the *American Architect* called for "specific laws" governing the height and character of buildings along great avenues, as well as for controls over flag, electrical, and trolley poles; curbs and drinking fountains; signs beyond a specified size; and all kiosks. Yet there was considerable vacillation on the property issue, as happened in later City Beautiful efforts. J. F. Harder, an architect who sought to fuse aesthetic ideals with more utilitarian concerns, complained in *Municipal Affairs* that in New York City's gridiron street system "[e]very consideration of economy of inter-communication, future financial economy, sanitation, helpfulness and aesthetics was left out of reckoning." The larger problem, he declared, was that American cities had not been built with "deliberate intention." Overcoming this problem would entail restrictions on individuals and corporations, interfering "with that liberty which is the essence of American institutions"; yet he believed this interference was justified in terms of "the greatest good for the greatest number of people." But Harder stopped short of proposing controls on development, believing that planning would be adopted by the force of its own logic. "The mere establishment of a comprehensive general proposition for improvements," he wrote, "will result in voluntary conformity to it in many cases where such conformation will be simpler and more economical than to do otherwise."[25]

For J. F. Harder, aesthetic planning was valuable for aesthetic reasons, for its contribution to "civic pride," and for its capacity to enhance the efficiency of the city's street and transit system. Re-

[25] "The Shaping of Towns," p. 195; C. Howard Walker, "The Grouping of Public Buildings in a Great City," pp. 11-13; Harder, "The City's Plan," pp. 35, 25, 30.

garding the latter, he wrote, "Utility is economy, but artistic utility is greater economy." As noted previously, however, advocates
of the municipal art movement commonly justified planning in
other than aesthetic terms. Edwin H. Blashfield, in his opening address at the Baltimore Municipal Art Conference, emphasized that
public art could serve as a "public and municipal educator" by
commemorating the memory of the wise and strong and stimulating reverent thoughts on the part of the citizenry. On a "lower
plane," he added, "municipal art has swelled the revenues of cities." While Blashfield appeared reluctant to cite municipal art's
economic benefits, another conference speaker urged the audience
to "appeal first, last and at all times to your citizens on this [eco-
nomic] ground."[26]

These arguments corresponded with those made by Baron von
Haussmann to justify the redevelopment of central Paris in the
1840s. Haussmann developed the concept of "productive ex-
penses," holding that the expenditure of public funds for great
boulevards, ornamental parks, street adornments, and other forms
of public architecture would contribute to the common good by
enhancing land values, encouraging tourism, and stimulating private investment. (His other contribution to the planning lexicon
was the concept of "creative destruction," which he used to justify
the demolition of slum housing as part of his beautification efforts.) George Kriehn, a leading voice in the municipal art and City
Beautiful movements, echoed Haussmann's arguments. Citing
Paris as the preeminent City Beautiful, he wrote in *Municipal Affairs* that a program of planned civic beautification would pay by
attracting a more desirable class of residents to the city, encouraging tourism, and enhancing real estate values. Thus, we see the
emergence, at the turn of the century, of the argument used today
to justify downtown redevelopment projects and the building of
civic centers, coliseums and the like—that such projects will redound to the community economic good.[27]

For Kriehn, as for most other municipal art advocates, however,
the value of "civic art" was more political and cultural than economic. In particular, it was seen as a spur to civic patriotism. Citing the example of French monuments recalling the days of Napo-

[26] Harder, "City's Plan," p. 30; Blashfield, "Municipal Art," p. 582; Frederick
Lamb, "Art for the People," p. 712.

[27] On Haussmann, see Moses, "What Happened to Haussmann?" pp. 57-66 (this
article is also interesting for the parallels it reveals between the careers of Haussmann and Moses); Kriehn, "The City Beautiful," pp. 594-601.

leon, Kriehn averred that monuments could teach glory better than could books. "Nothing would be a more effective agent in making good citizens of our foreign population than such monuments. Many of them cannot read English books, but they can read monuments which appeal to the eye," he wrote.[28] It was not just national patriotism but the cultivation of a sense of local civic pride, a sense of belonging and an acceptance of the existing order of things, that was desired. Kriehn, Blashfield, Harder, and kindred activists presented municipal art and civic adornment as expressions and means of inculcating this kind of civic patriotism.

The organized effort to promote local civic improvements was a second source of inspiration for the City Beautiful movement, and one that complemented the municipal are movement. Whereas municipal art societies were composed of patrons of the arts and art professionals, civic improvement associations initially were organizations of local elites, mostly women who came from small- to medium-sized cities.[29] The inspiration for these associations could be traced to Andrew Jackson Downing's writings on rural landscaping in the 1840s. They had a small-town orientation and concerned themselves with piecemeal, small-scale projects; indeed, they promoted everything from flower beds to electric lights and sanitation improvements. These small-town associations acquired national organization in 1900 when an Ohio publisher, after running a series on local improvement associations in his magazine *House and Flower*, called a national meeting of these organizations in Springfield. The result was the formation of the National League of Improvement Associations, with its headquarters in Springfield. Most of the member associations were located in New England, although by 1900 several dozen associations existed in California and a number had been formed in the South Atlantic states. In this region, the Seaboard Airline Railroad sought to organize an improvement association at every stop along its line from Portsmouth, Virginia to Atlanta, Georgia as part of an attempt to attract northern industry.

Under the guidance of the association's second president, Charles Zueblin, a University of Chicago sociologist with a zeal for reform, an attempt was made to connect these ad hoc local improvement efforts with the larger Progressive movement. Sym-

[28] Kriehn, "City Beautiful," p. 600.
[29] This discussion is drawn from Peterson, "City Beautiful Movement," and Wilson, "J. Horace McFarland and the City Beautiful Movement," pp. 315-34.

bolic of this attempt, the association's name was changed at its second annual convention to the American League for Civic Improvement, and its headquarters was shifted to Chicago. Corresponding with the increased emphasis on "civic" rather than "village" improvement, member associations emerged in urban centers such as Chicago, St. Paul, and Milwaukee. By 1902, the League had 232 individual members, many of them important opinion leaders, and 148 association members.[30]

The third source of the City Beautiful was the interest in outdoor art and public landscape. This interest originated in the park movement, whose social engineering orientation was explored in the preceding chapter. In 1897, the American Park and Outdoor Art Association (AP&OAA) was formed to give focus and support to the interest in urban landscaping and beautification. Organized principally by landscape architect Warren Manning, the association consisted of landscape architects, park superintendents and commissioners, and informed laymen. Originally conceived as an organization to promote park development, the AP&OAA soon broadened its interest in landscaping to include the proper aesthetic development of city streets, home grounds, and public buildings. The AP&OAA also advocated beautifying school grounds, spoke out against billboards, and promoted efforts to control urban ugliness, giving it common cause with municipal art societies and local improvement associations. By 1903, the AP&OAA had 786 individual members and 33 association members.[31]

By 1900 to 1901, the interests in municipal art, civic improvement, and outdoor art were nationally organized. Although these interests were organized separately, activists from the representative organizations began interacting at national conferences and meetings, exploring their common interest in the City Beautiful and its many different meanings. Eventually, the term became associated with everything from tree planting to the building of monumental boulevards. As Jon Peterson has written, it was this "mingling of organizations and ideas [that] gave the City Beautiful its complexity as an ideal and its vitality as a cause."[32] This interweaving of concerns took organizational form in the merger of the AP&OAA and the American League for Civic Improvement in

[30] Peterson, "City Beautiful Movement," p. 423.

[31] On the AP&OAA, see Peterson, "City Beautiful Movement," pp. 425-26, and Wilson, "J. Horace McFarland," pp. 320-21.

[32] "City Beautiful Movement," p. 426.

1904; from their merger, the American Civic Association was born.

A key participant in the merger of these two organizations and the president of the American Civic Association for its first twenty years was J. Horace McFarland. Because he was a businessman who had participated in Harrisburg, Pennsylvania's city beautification program, McFarland has been presented as an example of the "lay" origins of the City Beautiful.[33] He might more appropriately be regarded as an example of business's support for civic beautification. He was a prosperous printer and real estate developer who came to appreciate the value of beautification efforts from his own experience. As a real estate developer, he had used attractive landscaping schemes to his benefit in developing Harrisburg's prestigious Bellevue addition and a Pennsylvania resort in which he was involved. He also was aware, as an employer, of the advantages of environmental management. His printing plant, which employed 150 men by 1916, was covered with ivy and surrounded by a carefully manicured lawn. To point up the value of these improvements, he once contrasted the careful "adornment" of his factory—where "no labor difficulty has ever vexed the air"—with a nearby large shoe factory that was "hideously bare" and experienced "constant friction" between management and labor.[34] Thus, for McFarland the City Beautiful meant generalizing urban improvements from the suburban tract and factory to the city as a whole. His perspective as a businessman gave him a more utilitarian view of the City Beautiful than that held by the design professionals associated with the movement.

While McFarland was a tireless campaigner in support of the City Beautiful, traveling the country to give his "Crusade Against Ugliness" speech, the ideas of Charles Mulford Robinson were more influential in charting the movement's course, in addition to being more coherent and sophisticated. Robinson had been a reporter for the *Rochester Post Express* when he wrote a seminal article, appearing in the *Atlantic Monthly* in 1899, which surveyed local improvement efforts. In this article and in a subsequent book, *The Improvement of Towns and Cities*, Robinson helped lay the foundation for a broader City Beautiful movement by making activists in one field of urban improvement aware of the work of

---

[33] My source on McFarland is Wilson, "J. Horace McFarland."
[34] Quoted, ibid., p. 318.

others in related fields. There were, by his count, over 110 urban improvement societies active in 1901 (this number included a handful of societies in England and Belgium). He insisted that these should not be understood as separate organizations but as "one brotherhood in the joyous and earnest crusade for beauty of town and city." In *The Improvement of Towns and Cities*, Robinson went beyond reportage to set forth an agenda for "aesthetic progress." This agenda is best indicated by the organization of the book: one chapter was devoted to improving gridiron street plans (by adding diagonal boulevards and circular drives); five chapters dealt with enhancing "street beauty," covering such topics as the burial of electrical wires and the control of advertising; and four chapters were concerned with outdoor art, from the building of ornamental parks to methods of historical preservation. In a 1903 book, *Modern Civic Art*, Robinson extended his focus to the business district and, in a final section, called for "comprehensive planning" to guide the city's development. On the basis of these and other publications and Robinson's vigorous promotion of the City Beautiful cause, he emerged as the movement's principal ideologist.[35]

In Robinson's writing, we find the three principal elements of the City Beautiful: the emphasis on beauty and aesthetics, the vacillation on the issue of property rights, and the underlying social control orientation. Let us consider these elements in turn. First, in regard to Robinson's emphasis on aesthetics, the point is not that he was indifferent to other concerns; indeed, he dealt briefly with the tenement house problem and the need for a more efficient street system. It is rather that he spent very little time on these subjects, justified not giving them more consideration, and, in general, subordinated sanitation and circulation concerns to the quest for civic beauty. For example, Robinson devoted a chapter of *Modern Civic Art* to the tenement house problem, arguing in those pages that population congestion could be reduced both by improving transportation, so that workers would not have to live so close to where they worked, and by relocating factories to the periphery of the city, after the model of the English Garden Cities. He did not call for tenement regulation, however; in fact, he defined the tenement problem as outside the scope of "civic art,"

---

[35] "Improvement in City Life," pp. 771-78; *The Improvement of Towns and Cities or the Practical Bases of Civic Aesthetics*, pp. viii-xii; *Modern Civic Art or the City Made Beautiful.*

thereby prefiguring the future separation of housing reform and formal city planning. "Civic art need only concern itself with the outward aspect of houses," he declared, "for such details—sociologically pressing though they are—as sunless bedrooms, dark halls and stairs, foul cellars, dangerous employments, and an absence of bathrooms, civic art has no responsibility, however earnestly it deplores them." Similarly, although he remarked upon the waste and inefficiency created by the rectangular street system, his more basic objection was that the gridiron did not provide attractive vistas for viewing monuments and other works of public architecture. His solution, to cut diagonal boulevards through the city, was also his response to the slum problem. Following Haussmann, he proposed driving boulevards through slums to force the removal of unsightly structures and (in theory) to generate improvements in the surrounding area. He gave no attention to the need for new housing or business space for those displaced by this class-biased "creative destruction"; he also failed to consider whether slum residents would benefit from such projects.[36]

Second, on the property question Robinson was cautious, restricting planning, for all intents and purposes, to the public sector. Like municipal art proponents, he spoke out against unsightly billboards, polluting smokestacks, overhead electrical lines, and the unregulated height of "sky scrapers." But although he called for government regulation in these areas, his principal emphasis was on controlling the location, design, and arrangement of *public* facilities—streets, civic centers, monuments, and the like. He called for a "comprehensive general plan" that would cover the "future development of all the public and semi-public institutions," the aim being to impart a "recognizable uniformity to those structures of the town that have a like public character and perform a like public function and are built from the public means."[37]

The third element of the City Beautiful articulated in Robinson's writings was the orientation toward social control. Robinson did not value civic art entirely for its own sake; he saw civic improvement as having economic as well as social and political effects. In his survey of local improvement efforts that appeared in the *Atlantic Monthly*, he declared that the economic argument for

[36] *Modern Civic Art*, pp. 257-58; "The Street Plan of a City's Business District," pp. 233-47.
[37] *Modern Civic Art*, p. 286.

city beautification was "not needed" but could not be passed over since it had been referred to so often. He then recited Haussmann's argument that civic improvements would help attract wealth to the city and aid in the retention of existing wealth, all to the economic benefit of the larger community. However, of greater importance, Robinson believed, was the "sociological value" of urban improvements in producing "the larger happiness of the greater masses of the people." He wrote: "The happier people of the rising City Beautiful will grow in love for it, in pride for it. They will be better citizens, better because better instructed, more artistic, and filled with civic pride."[38]

What Robinson was calling for here was the creation of a physical civic ideal that would help stimulate local patriotism, an idea that ran throughout the City Beautiful experience. As historian Paul Boyer has written, the City Beautiful sought to bring order, harmony, and moral cohesion to urban America—an effort Boyer seems to applaud, albeit without defending the nature of the society for which cohesion was sought. "Fundamentally," writes Boyer, the City Beautiful "sprang from the conviction that a more livable and attractive urban environment would call forth an answering surge of civic loyalty from the urban populace, and that this in turn would retard or even reverse the decay of social and moral cohesiveness which seemed so inevitable a concomitant of the rise of cities."[39] The centrality of this concern with promoting local patriotism is apparent in the concrete examples of City Beautiful planning to which we now turn. We also see in these examples how ties were forged between planners and business groups, how the lay movement promoting civic beautification grew dependent upon experts to realize its ideals, and how City Beautiful planning vacillated on the property issue.

CITY BEAUTIFUL PLANNING

The replanning of Washington exemplified the major themes of City Beautiful planning. Substantively, it dealt with two main problems: the grouping of public buildings and the creation of an integrated park system. Except for its proposal for a regional park system, the plan focused upon the central area of official Washington, without taking account of the vernacular city, a city noto-

---

[38] "Improvement in City Life," pp. 784-85.
[39] *Urban Masses and Moral Order in America, 1820-1920*, p. 264.

rious for its rundown alley dwellings inhabited largely by the city's growing black population. It was also a plan for public facilities; with one exception—the call for removing railroad tracks from the Mall—private development was ignored. As a plan for official Washington, the predominant aim was to promote national patriotism by glorifying the nation's capital. To achieve this end, the designers took as their model the cities of old, feudal Europe, an ironic source of inspiration for the supposed citadel of republican government.

If the Fair had a fantasy-like quality, Washington was unique among real-world American cities. It was a city of monumental buildings that had been laid out by a Frenchman, Pierre L'Enfant, who was influenced by the baroque style of eighteenth-century Europe. Like the Fair, Washington was largely devoid of industrial and commercial complexes; moreover, it contained large expanses of government-owned land. And in being under the control of Congress, it was governed by a body of autocratic colonial rulers, much as the Fair was presided over by a central council of administration. In the way it was governed, Washington was closer to the Paris of Haussmann and Napoleon III than was any other American city. The central difference was that the autocratic control of Washington was fragmented within the committee structure of Congress, which posed a problem in implementing the plan. But at least the planners would not be thwarted in their efforts by Washington residents.

In the replanning of Washington, architect-planners and politicians formed an alliance that complemented the alliance forged between planners and civic boosters in other cities. Indeed, the very concept of replanning Washington grew out of the conjunction of the one-hundredth anniversary of the relocation of the capital to Washington and a national meeting of the American Institute of Architects (AIA) in Washington in 1900.[40] Various proposals for replanning the capital city were put forward at the architects' convention, and a legislative committee was formed to

[40] The best, most detailed source on the replanning of Washington is the National Capital Planning Commission (NCPC), *Worthy of the Nation: The History of Planning for the National Capital.* See also the two biographies of Burnham: Hines, *Burnham of Chicago,* chap. 7, and Moore, *Daniel H. Burnham,* chaps. 10-12. I have also consulted the following contemporary accounts: Moore, "The Improvement of Washington," pp. 101-2; "Washington: The Development and Improvement of the Park System, I & II," pp. 35-36 and 75-77; and Henry McFarland, "The Rebuilding of the National Capital," pp. 3-13.

seek support for this effort. This committee found a friend and ally in Senator James McMillan of Michigan. McMillan was chairman of the Senate's District Committee and had been chairman of the Detroit Park Commission at the time Olmsted designed Belle Isle Park. Twice before, McMillan had been rebuffed in attempts to appoint a commission to propose improvements for the District, but with the support of the AIA, and taking advantage of congressional interest in commemorating the capital's centenary, he won approval for commissioning a number of experts to advise his committee on improving the capital city. Yet this panel of experts, which became known as the Senate Park Commission, or simply the McMillan Commission, was empowered only to make private recommendations to its sponsoring congressional subcommittee; it was not authorized to make a report to Congress. This restriction became a source of difficulty later on.

The AIA's role in proposing the replanning of Washington was important to the gestation of the planning movement because, having been present at the AIA convention in Washington, architects across the country were imbued with a paternal interest in the planning effort. And the membership of the McMillan Commission likewise added weight to the project. As Charles Robinson said of the commission, "The idea of an expert commission to make plans for improving a city could not have had other more prominent and appealing example."[41] Prefiguring future reliance on outside experts, none of the members of the panel was a resident of the District. Rather, they were selected on the basis of their prestige in the design community. Daniel Burnham and Frederick Olmsted, Jr., were appointed at the urging of the AIA legislative committee, and the two other members, architect Charles F. McKim and the sculptor Augustus Saint-Gaudens, were nominated by Burnham and Olmsted. This panel also linked the replanning of Washington to the Chicago World's Fair, since all the members had participated in its design, except for the younger Olmsted, who was replacing his father because the latter was too ill to join the project.

Upon arriving in Washington, the commission first studied L'Enfant's original plan for the city and then sailed to Europe (minus the aging Saint-Gaudens, who was too infirm for the trip). There, in Burnham's words, they hoped to "see and discuss parks in relation to public buildings" and to trace the origin of L'Enfant's

---

[41] "New Dream for Cities," p. 411.

concepts.[42] On their return, a division of labor was established: McKim handled the composition of the Mall and its appurtenances, Burnham concentrated on the design of Union Station, Olmsted was made responsible for a system of parks, and Saint-Gaudens advised on matters of scale and on the location of monuments and statues. The commission's plan, described by Senator McMillan as "the most comprehensive ever provided an American city," was completed in January 1902 and placed on display with accompanying models and photographs at the new Corcoran Gallery.[43]

In its emphasis on public buildings and the grounds surrounding them, the McMillan Plan (as it came to be known) set the pattern for City Beautiful planning. Public buildings and monuments were grouped in a highly concentrated central area around the White House, the Capitol Building, the Washington Monument, and two proposed monument sites, now the Jefferson and Lincoln Memorials. Strong axial relationships and broad vistas linked together the various elements of this central area. To maintain the axial character of the plan, the new Mall was tilted slightly southward to accommodate the incorrect alignment of the already-present Washington Monument. In the design of the Mall, as in other aspects of the plan, European influences predominated: the Mall was suggested by the Champs Elysées; the reflecting pool beneath the Washington Monument recalled the decorative canals at Versailles, Fontainebleau, and Hampton Court; and the monument site now occupied by the Lincoln Memorial was set in a "rond point" much as the Arc de Triomphe crowns the Place de L'Etoile in Paris. Principally the work of Charles McKim, this central element of the plan established academic classicism as the official architecture of the city. The choice of this style was not surprising, given not only the influence of the Fair, but also the fact that McKim was the leading exponent of academic classicism in the United States.

The exception to the commission's focus on public facilities was its proposal for removing the tracks of the Pennsylvania Railroad from where they crossed the Mall beneath the Capitol. The tracks were to be moved to a new depot area north of the Capitol where a union station was to be constructed. Allowing the Penn-

[42] Quoted in Moore, *Daniel H. Burnham*, p. 142. As McMillan's secretary, Moore served as the commission's publicist and as a de facto member of the commission. In addition to the biography of Burnham, he later wrote a biography of McKim.

[43] McMillan is quoted in NCPC, *Worthy of the Nation*, p. 125.

sylvania's tracks to cross the Mall had been the most egregious violation of L'Enfant's original plan, although it was a location convenient for congressional travelers (not unlike Washington's National Airport today) and one with obvious advantages for the railroad. In accordance with the McMillan Plan, Burnham approached Alexander Cassatt, president of the Pennsylvania Railroad, to ask whether he would be willing to relocate his tracks. Cassatt was agreeable, provided Congress paid to tunnel his tracks beneath the Mall, and provided a union station was built, at public expense, for the use of both the Pennsylvania and the Baltimore and Ohio, which the Pennsylvania had just purchased.[44] The massive white marble Union Station designed by Burnham was eight feet longer than the Capitol Building and contained facilities for eight railroad lines (seven for the combined Pennsylvania and Baltimore and Ohio railroads and one additional facility). To appreciate the importance of this structure, one needs to understand that rail terminals had the same significance for a city's image in this era that airports have today.

Stylistically, Olmsted's park design was unlike other elements of the plan; it was also unlike the ornamental parks characteristic of later City Beautiful planning.[45] Whereas European influences predominated in the core of the plan, Olmsted's park proposals reflected the influence of the Boston metropolitan park system he had helped to plan. This was apparent, for one, in his proposal for linking existing park land to an interconnecting system of scenic parkways. It was also evident in his recommendation for a regional park system (like the one proposed for Boston), extending to the outlying areas of the District and across the Potomac River as far as Mt. Vernon and Great Falls. And, indicative of the younger Olmsted's sociological approach to planning, the plan called for neighborhood parks and the development of parks for recreational purposes and other, less formal uses. This scheme was in contrast with the patriotically minded monumentalism, formality, and ornamentation of other aspects of the McMillan Plan.

Despite the humanizing influence of Olmsted's park proposals, the McMillan Plan was essentially a federal plan: a plan for federal buildings and federal land, inspired by the desire to make Washington a great national capital and to stimulate feelings of patri-

[44] On Burnham's dealings with Cassatt, see Moore, *Daniel H. Burnham*, pp. 154-55, and Hines, *Burnham of Chicago*, pp. 148-49.

[45] On the significance of Olmsted's park proposals, see NCPC, *Worthy of the Nation*, p. 125.

otism. The greatest shortcoming of the plan was its failure to address the effects of private development, although the proposals for expanding the government office park in central Washington did entail the taking of private land, with compensation. (On the recommendation of a jury of condemnation, Congress appropriated 2.5 million dollars—half the amount requested by private landowners—to purchase land for buildings which would house the Departments of State, Justice, and Commerce and Labor.) Seven years after the completion of the plan, Henry B. F. McFarland, president of the Commissioners of the District of Columbia, remarked on the plan's failure to take account of private development. He observed that "[u]nfortunately private building in Washington has not as a whole reflected the same esthetic ideas" as the plan's proposals for official Washington. As a remedy, he proposed adopting building restrictions "in the interest of beauty." McFarland also noted that Washington suffered from severe housing difficulties. The problem was not only the existence of the miserable alley dwellings inhabited by the capital's swelling black population. An important employer interest of the federal government had been overlooked in the McMillan Plan: as congressional testimony indicated in 1909, Washington did not have adequate and affordable housing for low-paid government clerks. Yet, despite these failings, Charles Robinson wrote of the plan that it touched on "almost every problem involved in the improvement of cities."[46]

Even as a plan for official Washington, however, the McMillan Plan has been criticized. The National Capital Planning Commission (NCPC), itself a legacy of the McMillan Plan, has observed that the plan was based upon "static models of the city, largely devoid of human reference, [which] gave credence to the notion that 'McMillanism' spelled vacant streets and oppressive architecture."[47] The NCPC's complaint is that, because the streets along the Mall are lined with museums and office buildings, they lack the gaiety of life one finds, for example, along the commercial and residential streets flanking Paris's Champs Elysées. The implication is that this was a planner error, the result of errant design principles or a failure to understand the French model of the Champs

---

[46] Henry McFarland, "Rebuilding the National Capital," pp. 5, 8-9; on Washington's housing conditions, see the report by the president of the United States Homes Commission, Army General George M. Sternberg, "Housing Conditions in Washington," pp. 62-63. See also Robinson, "New Dreams," p. 411.

[47] *Worthy of the Nation*, p. 129.

Elysées. Yet this technical-determinist explanation overlooks the political objective of the McMillan Plan: the purpose was not to create a gay city, but to glorify, educate, and commemorate, to do for national patriotism what later City Beautiful plans would seek to do for local patriotism.

Despite being a government plan prepared for a committee of Congress, the McMillan Plan encountered many of the same problems of implementation as did City Beautiful plans prepared under private auspices. By 1909, only the removal of the tracks from the Mall, the building of Union Station, and the grouping of public buildings around the Mall had been carried out. Further implementation was delayed by the costliness of the building, landscaping, and land acquisition called for in the plan; by the fact that the commission had been authorized by the Senate District Committee and not by the full Congress; and by the implacable opposition of House Speaker Joe Cannon. Difficulties with implementation were compounded by the death of Senator McMillan the summer following the completion of the plan, leaving it without an effective spokesman in Congress. In 1910, however, President William Howard Taft appointed a Fine Arts Commission, with Burnham as its chairman, for the purpose of reviewing public works improvements to determine whether they conformed with the McMillan Plan. Under the commission's guidance, the Lincoln Memorial and the adjacent Arlington Memorial Bridge were built at the foot of the Mall, as proposed in the plan. Then, in keeping with the McMillan Commission's recommendation that a permanent park commission be appointed, the National Capital Park Commission was established in 1926 with a mandate to implement nearly all of the original commission's remaining park proposals. In addition, legislation adopted in 1926, 1930, and up through Lyndon Johnson's presidency has carried out other parts of the plan.[48]

Because Washington was a national capital without a significant private business establishment, the McMillan Plan was marked by collaboration between planners and politicians. In the preparation of Cleveland's Group Plan, on the other hand, we see the formation of the business-designer alliance that typified City Beautiful planning; we also see a continuation of many of the substantive themes of the McMillan Plan.[49] Inspired by their visit

[48] Ibid., pp. 130-33.

[49] The text of the plan report can be found in "The Grouping of Public Buildings at Cleveland," pp. 13-15. For the history of this planning effort, see Hines, *Burnham of Chicago*, chap. 8, and Robinson, "New Dreams," pp. 412-17.

to the Chicago Fair, a number of Clevelanders active in civic affairs returned home with the idea of creating a building group like that of the model White City. It was a timely idea, since Cleveland was set to build a post office, county courthouse, city hall, and library all at the same time. Members of the newly created Cleveland Architectural Club became interested in the idea, as did the Chamber of Commerce, and the two groups joined in a propaganda effort. The architects held a competition for the design of a building group, and the Chamber held public meetings at which prominent architects spoke on the merits of a public building group. Popular sentiment on the issue was "assiduously cultivated," as Charles Robinson wrote. Tom Johnson, Cleveland's mayor and a Progressive politician of national reputation, also supported the concept of a building group. Johnson, a so-called "light and water socialist," was an advocate of municipal ownership of electric utilities and water services, a position regarded by some at the time as a dangerous step towards socialism.[50]

Working together, the local AIA chapter and the Cleveland Chamber of Commerce won state approval for the appointment of a panel of experts to design the city's building group. The experts' salaries were paid by the state, and they were given complete control over the location and style of public buildings. Recruited for the panel were Daniel Burnham and two New York City architects: Arnold W. Brunner, who had already been designated to design Cleveland's post office and federal building, and John M. Carrère. Their plan was typical of City Beautiful efforts in its emphasis on the aesthetic relationship of buildings and grounds. Covering a tract five blocks in length and two in width (save at the waterfront, where it widened to four blocks), the plan provided for a grouping of the designated public buildings together with a new headquarters for the Chamber of Commerce and a union station.[51] These buildings were to be set around a central mall patterned after the Fair's Court of Honor. Also borrowed from the Fair were the design principles governing the building group: uniformity of

[50] Robinson, "New Dreams," p. 413; on Mayor Johnson's political views, reputation, and involvement in this planning effort, see Hines, *Burnham of Chicago*, pp. 158-61.

[51] The Union Station, which was to be a centerpiece of Cleveland's mall, was not built on the site indicated in the plan. In the 1920s, after Burnham's death, businessmen and real estate speculators were successful in moving the station site to an area adjacent to Cleveland's old public square, thus robbing the new mall of some of its vitality. See Hines, *Burnham of Chicago*, pp. 167-68.

architecture was of primary importance, designs were to be "derived from the historic motives of the classic architecture of Rome," one material was to be used throughout, and a uniform scale (in terms of the height, bulk, and cornice line) was to be utilized for all the buildings.[52]

Conciding with the effort to dress up the central area, the plan required large-scale slum clearance, although this endeavor was not explicitly stated in the plan report. The plan called for the taking of a "dilapidated" skid row district along the city's lakefront, following an earlier Chamber of Commerce recommendation. This area was to be the site for part of the mall and for a rejuvenated waterfront recreation area.[53] In endorsing this Chamber recommendation, the architect-planners professed to have looked at the matter from "the practical as well as from the sentimental and artistic point of view." An AIA report explained further that the area had "no buildings of great value," and that the land itself was "less costly than that which surrounds it"—arguments similar to those used by a later generation of urban redevelopment planners. The plan resembled future planning in another way as well: it was based on experts' assessment of the public good rather than on popular participation. Burnham had rejected any such participation from the beginning. During the initial stages of planning it was suggested that a large public meetings be held to solicit opinion and comment from citizens. But Burnham had objected, saying that he believed "the best way to go about it would be . . . to place the whole matter in the hands of the mayor and ask him to consult with the proper officials and proper citizens and then advise us."[54]

Wider in scope than the Cleveland Plan was Burnham's San Francisco Plan, which, although published in 1907, was prepared on the eve of the 1906 earthquake. This plan was interesting because it originated in Progressive reform, because it considered practical aspects in the redesign of the city's street system, and because it represented a lost planning opportunity due to the San Francisco earthquake and fire. Whereas the Cleveland Plan was essentially a plan for the city's central district, the San Francisco Plan called for changes in the city's street network and the creation of a city-wide system of parks; it thus became the first at-

[52] "Grouping of Public Buildings at Cleveland."
[53] The quoted term is from Frederic Howe, "The Cleveland Group Plan," p. 1548.
[54] "Grouping of Public Buildings at Cleveland," p. 14; AIA report, quoted in "Report of the Committee on Municipal Improvements to the American Institute of Architects," p. 145; Burnham, quoted in Hines, *Burnham of Chicago*, p. 161.

tempt of this era to plan for a whole city. The San Francisco Plan originated with a group of business leaders and wealthy citizens; in this case, however, they were persons who had been displaced from control of the city, and who saw the plan project as a vehicle for their resurgence. At the head of this group was James Phelan, a "Progressive aristocrat" and mayor of the city from 1897 to 1901. Phelan had been voted from office by workers angered by his use of police to intervene in the San Francisco strike of 1901.[55] Following his ouster, Phelan, along with "many prominent and wealthy citizens" (as one participant described them), formed the Association for the Improvement and Adornment of San Francisco to spearhead their planning effort.[56] The announced goals of the organization were to beautify the city's streets and other public places, stimulate "civic pride," and (curiously) "promote quasi-public enterprises."[57] It was this organization of civic boosters, Progressive idealists, and social and economic elites displaced from political leadership by the bossist working-class government of Mayor Eugene Schmitz that commissioned Burnham's firm to devise a plan for the city.

The plan prepared by Burnham and his Ecole des Beaux Arts–trained assistant, Edward Bassett, went beyond earlier efforts not only in its geographic reach, but also in its attention to the practical aspects of the city's street system.[58] Essentially, the plan was like other City Beautiful plans: it called for radial boulevards, an outlying circular drive, a central mall, and various parks and public playgrounds. Yet the proposals for altering the city's street system were based on considerations of economy and convenience and not merely on the desire to beautify. This practicality was in response to the irrationalities of the market system: real estate developers, attempting to create as many uniform lots as possible, had clamped a rigid gridiron street system on the city in disregard for its hilly terrain. This meant that streets coursed over hills at right angles to the point of incline, as in the famous example of Telegraph Hill. Burnham and Bassett's proposed remedy was to re-

[55] On the background of the San Francisco Plan, see Hines, *Burnham of Chicago,* chap. 9.

[56] The quotation is from Herman Scheffauer, vice-president of the San Francisco Architectural Club, in Scheffauer, "The City Beautiful—San Francisco Rebuilt—I," p. 3.

[57] Quoted in Hines, *Burnahm of Chicago,* pp. 178-79.

[58] For a detailed though overly laudatory account of the San Francisco Plan, see Croly, "The Promised City of San Francisco," pp. 425-36.

claim the steepest hillsides for public use and, otherwise, to lay out streets following the contours of the hillsides. Interestingly, the site chosen for the proposed mall and public building group had the intended effect of moving the city's public center to the heart of the emerging business center. On the one hand, this move was an example of private planning being used to coordinate public facilities with private development. Yet, on the other, it exemplified the political objective of City Beautiful planners, namely their desire to create aesthetically attractive public places to stimulate local civic pride. Burnham believed that governmental and educational facilities were the "real being" of the city. By placing the mall and public building group in the "spacious *place*" at the heart of the city—there "removed from the direct flow and press of business"—they would "gain in repose and strengthen the public sense of the dignity and responsibility of citizenship," the plan report asserted.[59] It was this effort to promote both civic pride and attention to aesthetics that marked this plan, in spite of its other, more forward-looking aspects, with the stamp of the City Beautiful.[60]

Although the plan was favorably received by Mayor Schmitz, who ordered copies printed at public expense, it had not received official sanction before the earthquake and fire that leveled four square miles of the city seven months after the plan's completion. This complication, together with the cost of implementing the recommendations, the perception that it was principally an aesthetic plan, and the desire for quick reconstruction of the devastated parts of the city, prevented the plan's promoters from taking advantage of the replanning opportunity provided by the earthquake. Almost none of the plan's recommendations were followed in reconstructing the city.

It was both ironic and appropriate that criticism of William Penn's gridiron street system provided the impetus for replanning in Philadelphia—ironic because the City of Brotherly Love was one of the most carefully planned of colonial cities and appropriate because its rectangular grid influenced the adoption of the grid system in so many other American cities. Criticism of Philadelphia's street system came to a head in 1902, when the City Park Association released a report that, as one newspaper put it, "roasted Penn

[59] Quoted in Scheffauer, "San Francisco Rebuilt," p. 8.
[60] The San Francisco Plan was forward-looking in its proposal for a chain of parklike squares in the less expensive sections of the city; see Hines, *Burnham of Chicago*, pp. 186-88.

on the gridiron." At about the same time, a private organization, the Fairmount Park Association, released a report recommending a number of City Beautiful–style improvements. Among these was a proposal for constructing Fairmount Parkway as a radial thoroughfare connecting City Hall and Fairmount Park, thereby creating the first break in the city's rectangular street system. Also recommended was the construction of a public building group at the entrance of Fairmount Park and the acquisition of new park land. Whereas these proposals were concerned with public facilities, an attempt was made at approximately the same time to control private development: Philadelphia secured legislation from the state empowering it to make "excess condemnations." With this authority, the city could condemn more land than it needed in making public improvements and then sell the excess land, with restrictions; this power would enable the city to control private development around public facilities and to appropriate, as a profit for the city, a part of the increase in property values resulting from the construction of public facilities. Although Pennsylvania courts later ruled this authority unconstitutional, the law stimulated the adoption of similar legislation in other states.[61]

Planning in Boston followed the clichéd pattern of designer-business collaboration. It was the Boston Society of Architects that took the initiative, preparing a tentative planning document that was published in conjunction with the Chamber of Commerce, the Real Estate Exchange, the Metropolitan Improvement League, the Stock Exchange, the Merchants' Association, the Board of Fire Underwriters, and the Master Builders' Association. These groups secured legislation from the state allowing them to appoint a five-member commission to study the plans of the city and to examine the needs of shipping and land traffic, the scope of building and recreation, and the opportunities for enhancing the city's beauty. The improvement ideas treated in the Society of Architects' forty-page plan report were not endorsed by the society; officially, they were intended only to demonstrate that planning solutions to local problems were in reach. Nevertheless, its proposals are indicative of what these architects and their business collaborators had in mind for the city.[62]

The most striking suggestion in the Boston plan report, and the

[61] Crawford, "Recent City Planning in Philadelphia," pp. 1537-42, quotation, p. 1537.
[62] Arthur Shurtleff, "The Practice of Replanning: Suggestions from Boston," p. 1529.

one most in keeping with City Beautiful precepts, was for a public building group on an island to be created in the middle of the Charles River. The building group would "acquire dignity through a certain aloofness," it was suggested. Evincing a desire to create a sense of awe and reverence toward government, the report described the island building group as follows: "Such an island, with high stone embankments, crowned by balustrades broken by statues, with domes and towers of public buildings, civil and ecclesiastical, rising above a circle of trees, the whole reflected in the still water that surrounded it, would be almost unique in the line of civic beauty, whether in the Old World, or the New." Yet there were also suggestions concerning the efficiency of the city's transportation system, no doubt reflecting the interests of the participating business groups. Noting that the city lacked an adequate means of crosstown transportation, the plan proposed a system of inner and outer thoroughfares to improve peripheral circulation and connect otherwise isolated parts of the city. To improve dockage, it was recommended that railroad lines be extended to the harbor's edge, facilitating both the speedier transshipment of goods and the movement of passengers from ship to train. Interestingly, Charles Robinson sought to characterize these seemingly practical-minded transportation recommendations in aesthetic terms. He wrote that, although "the point of view is the commercial and utilitarian," they were "beautiful in their aggregate effect" in that they substituted system, order, and harmony for "the haphazard, the unrelated and the flimsy."[63]

In both Baltimore and New York, the initiative for planning came from the Municipal Art Society. Baltimore's art society, inspired by the work of the McMillan Commission in nearby Washington, commissioned the Olmsted Brothers in 1902 to explore the possibility of reserving park land on the outskirts of the city. The resulting report was therefore primarily a park report: it made familiar recommendations for building a series of parkways that would encircle the city and for setting aside land for future parks. Of greater interest, however, was the recommendation for controlling future private development. The report called for the appointment of a special commission, armed with the power of eminent domain, to restrict development in Green Spring Valley on the city's perimeter; this area was to be preserved for recreational use as well as for its potential to supply water. The proposal proved

[63] Plan report quoted in Arthur Shurtleff, "Practice of Replanning," p. 1530; Robinson, "Ambitions of Three Cities," p. 346.

too far in advance of prevailing attitudes concerning property rights, however, and was disregarded.[64]

The 1907 plan of the New York City Improvement Commission was, in effect, an elaboration of a set of earlier recommendations made by the Municipal Art Society in collaboration with various groups, including the Merchants' Association, the Board of Trade and Transportation, the Manufacturers' Association, the American Society of Civil Engineers, the Architectural League of New York, the National Society of Mural Painters, and the National Society of Sculptors.[65] In recommending the construction of broad thoroughfares, improvements in the park system, and a public building group, the New York plan was like other City Beautiful efforts. Yet, while it was mainly an aesthetic plan, the recommendations regarding the street system were concerned with economy and convenience as well as with better integrating the city's boroughs.[66] Also, the plan addressed the property question by recommending that the city be granted authority for "excess condemnations." With this power, it noted, the cost of local improvements "could be greatly reduced," and, following the model of British cities, it would be possible to "secure architectural effects" and "remedy unsanitary conditions." Furthermore, the plan pointed toward the future in citing the need for a "comprehensive plan" that would "anticipate the future growth of the city . . . [and] be so designed that all of its parts shall be consistent, the one with the other, and form a homogeneous whole." It was anticipated that such a plan would involve a whole range of government activities, from the layout of parks, streets, and highways to the designation of appropriate house numbers and the location of statues and monuments.[67] And yet the report of the New York City Improvement Commission did little to bring about the implementation of these recommendations, due to the lack of official support for planning and the naiveté of commission members about how easily the placement of public facilities could be extracted from the control of real estate interests.[68]

[64] See Scott, *American City Planning*, pp. 60-61; and Robinson, "New Dreams," pp. 418-20.

[65] For the background of the plan, see Frederick Lamb, "New York City Improvement Report," pp. 1532-36.

[66] See Kantor, "The City Beautiful in New York," pp. 164-65.

[67] Quoted in Frederick Lamb, "New York City Improvement Report," pp. 1535, 1533.

[68] On the failure of the commission's report, see Croly, "Civic Improvements:

The plan report of this era that most directly addressed the property question was that adopted in St. Louis in 1907. And interestingly, this report was prepared not by professional designers but by a citizens group with broad participation from the city's business and professional community. The effort was organized by the St. Louis Civic League, which appointed committees to develop recommendations in five substantive areas. The committee members, representing a broad segment of the city's business and professional class, included merchants, bankers, state officials, educators, and design professionals. And while the plan was like other City Beautiful undertakings in its private origins and its focus on street improvements, parks, and public buildings, it was explicit about the connection between development problems and the market system. In its opening pages, the plan report attributed St. Louis's haphazard growth and inadequate public facilities to land speculation and unregulated private development. "Real Estate speculators and property owners have been allowed to follow their own caprices and self-interest," it declared. Thus, instead of having "a city with convenient and commodious thoroughfares, plenty of open spaces and squares, and a harmonious grouping of public buildings, we have narrow streets, few breathing spaces, and a general absence in the business portion of the city, of those features which make a city attractive." Furthermore, the report asserted that "the average citizen is helpless in face of this riot of conflicting and selfish interest—the direct results of a lack of plan and insufficient regulation."[69]

The St. Louis plan report broke ground in another area as well: it called for a civic center or its equivalent in every neighborhood. The center could be any private or public institution or facility having as its object "the mental, moral, or physical improvement of the neighborhood," such as a public or parochial school, a public playground, a social settlement, or even a firehouse. The idea was to nurture neighborhood communities by providing a focus for community life and, more than that, to "realize the unity of our city life by bringing together the different sections of the city." In effect, then, this proposal was like other City Beautiful projects in its attempt to stimulate civic loyalty through physical planning. In this case, however, the strategy was to contribute to the for-

The Case of New York," pp. 347-52, especially p. 352, and Kantor, "City Beautiful in New York," pp. 166-71.

   [69] Civic League of Saint Louis, *A City Plan for Saint Louis*, pp. 10-11, 14.

mation of community at the neighborhood level, with the hope of incorporating neighborhoods rather than individuals into the larger community.[70]

INTERPRETING THE CITY BEAUTIFUL

To interpret the City Beautiful, one must understand the political meaning of the quest for urban beautification. The emphasis upon aesthetics arose from the interests of two groups—the architects and art professionals who dominated the movement and those in the business class who provided support for it. Regarding the former, the City Beautiful orientation was, on the one hand, an autonomous expression of the background and training of the design professionals who led the movement. They defined the ideal of the movement in their own terms, in terms that came naturally to them, given their preparation and experience, and that reflected their autonomy from other occupational and social groups. On the other hand, these design professionals defined the ideal of the City Beautiful, and of city planning in general, in terms that guaranteed their ability to dominate the movement. This definition was a product of their competition with kindred professionals, notably with engineers, who emphasized economy and utility rather than art.

The architect-planners of the City Beautiful held up the ideal of city beautification as an overarching goal, subsuming other goals and objectives, such as utility and sanitation. Beauty in urban design was presented as more important than, or as naturally leading to, these other ends. Burnham maintained that through the pursuit of beauty one gained an appreciation of the "reciprocal relations of a whole," leading him to conclude that "what is logical is also beautiful." Likewise, architect J. F. Harder wrote, "Utility is economy, but artistic utility is greater economy." There was, moreover, an express awareness of the implications of these pursuits for the status of the architect. "Somebody that knows has got to show the way to the City Beautiful," wrote one Boston architect in the *American Architect*. "The architects are of the *cognoscenti*; if they cannot, no one can." Correspondingly, architect John M. Carrère, one of the designers of the Cleveland building group, cited the "great waste of artistic opportunity" that arose from "the fact that the engineer's point of view and not the artchitect's has pre-

[70] Ibid., p. 37.

161

vailed" in municipal development. Compared with the holistic perspective of the architect, the engineer's viewpoint was "one-sided" and "narrow."[71]

But the City Beautiful also articulated with the needs and interests of the business class. First, this was because the proponents and practitioners of this approach were themselves *of* the business class. The architects who led the movement were experienced in designing homes and commercial structures for the wealthy, and they were often persons of wealth themselves—which is no doubt why their business supporters accorded them so much autonomy of action. As the most outstanding example, Burnham was both an architect for the wealthy and a member of Chicago's upper crust himself, making him a wise choice for director of the Fair and principal planner for other City Beautiful projects. Second and more important, these neophyte planners depended on the support of the business class, or at least some members of that class, to achieve their urban ideal. Only by incorporating the interests of business into their planning ideal would it be possible to achieve their goals as planners—the one was a means to the other.

The City Beautiful benefited the business class in several respects. First, it provided economic rewards, although these were mostly particularistic benefits, such as those received by the owners of land adjacent to improvement projects. These were limited economic benefits, like the ones arising from the building of public parks—the kind of rewards Haussmann had drawn attention to in his rebuilding of Paris. Second, the City Beautiful provided political-ideological benefits, and these benefits were probably more important in stimulating business support for the movement than were the economic rewards. Part of these political-ideological benefits was the power of beautification projects, combined with the ideology of the movement, to divert attention from more threatening reform agendas, such as the attacks on housing conditions and population congestion. Little will be said of this here, since the following chapter examines how formal city planning became divorced from housing reform and the attack on population congestion. Of greater importance was the City Beautiful's role in creating a physical civic ideal promoting respect for country, American culture, and capitalism.

[71] Burnham, "White City and Capital City," pp. 619-20; Harder, "City's Plan," p. 30; Kilham, "Boston's New Opportunities," p. 22; Carrère, "The Beautifying of Cities," pp. 283-84.

The icons of the movement—its civic centers, public building groups, equestrian statues, and grand boulevards—were the physical embodiments of an attempt to organize what Antonio Gramsci called "class hegemony": the presentation of the interests of one group or class as the motor force for the universal expansion of the community or nation.[72] This effort to dress up the city with European-derived ornamentation represented an attempt to fashion a link in the public mind between contemporary cities, or at least their public cores, and the great cities of the past. It was a way of glorifying capital's control of the city, past and future, because in accepting the City Beautiful ideal and celebrating its icons, local citizens were being asked, behind their backs as it were, to accept the leadership of the group that made these works possible. This formula for organizing class hegemony at the local level required an expansion of the state's role in providing collective facilities. Unlike the parks discussed in the previous chapter, however, these facilities were not offered as a substitute for private forms of consumption organized through the market; they were more nearly pure public goods. Moreover, it was as objects of sight and aesthetic enjoyment that they acquired their political significance.[73]

As collective facilities, City Beautiful works were a response to collective needs. Yet they did not respond to all groups the same, and they did not meet all needs equally. These works fulfilled the designers' need for professional status; they made it possible for architects to dominate the early planning movement. Simultaneously, urban beautification and its supportive ideology fulfilled capital's need for a legitimating civic ideal; it was this response that made City Beautiful planning politically possible. Yet urban beautification also answered the need of the larger population for relief from the drab, disorderly, and blighted conditions of the city. It was this response to a broad public need that made City Beautiful works effective in organizing business hegemony.

As Gramsci wrote, however, hegemony must be based upon economics. Even if it is organized at an aesthetic or ethical level, to be an effective guide to action it must be based upon the economic

[72] See Gramsci, *Prison Notebooks*, p. 182.

[73] Manuel Castells theorizes about how collective facilities provided by the state contribute to the reproduction of labor power and, thus, to the maintenance of the class character of society, yet he does not comment on how facilities of an ornamental sort—facilities "consumed" by the enjoyment of their visual effects—contribute to this result; see Castells, *Urban Question*, pp. 429-36.

facts of life of a particular society and address itself to the economic needs of groups within that society.[74] This was the weakness and ultimately the reason for the downfall of the City Beautiful. It failed because it was insufficiently attentive to the economic needs of its supporting class; in particular, it did not address capital's need for a more economic and efficient organization of land use and transportation. The dawning of this recognition will be recounted in another chapter. It can be said here, however, that this failing was a reflection of both planners' autonomy from their business supporters and the process of historical experimentation, there being no guarantee that the policies most in accord with capital's needs will be formulated and adopted. In particular, there is no guarantee that they will be adopted in the first instance.[75]

There was, however, another important sense in which the City Beautiful failed to face up to economic facts or, better, to political-economic facts: it was insufficiently responsive to the property contradiction. It failed to respond in a manner that could "work," in the sense of achieving its own goals, to the contradiction between the social character of land and the fact that it was under private ownership and control. Social critic Herbert Croly, discussing the 1907 report of the New York City Improvement Commission, said it best.

> At present the local owners of real estate are always the most stubborn opponents of improvements in the public interest which in any way impair their chances of reaping their unearned reward from the growth of the city. It is their opposition which has prevented the adoption of the Burnham plan in San Francisco, and it will be found in the long run that the radical and comprehensive improvement of our large cities in convenience and good looks will be effected only, as it were, over the dead body of the great American real estate speculator. The interest of the real estate speculator demands congestion and concentration of business and population, which enormously increases real estate values along particular lines and at particular points, while the interest of the whole people in a beautiful and convenient city demands the distribution of population and business in the most liberal manner and according to an organic plan. The local interest of the individual

---

[74] *Prison Notebooks*, p. 161.
[75] On the theoretical point, see Wright, *Class, Crisis and the State*, p. 179.

owner of real estate in his particular property outweighs the public interest in a good general lay-out. The conclusion is, consequently, that before the visions of the municipal art reformers can ever be carried out, two vital changes in American municipal government will be necessary. Their powers will have to be increased in several different respects, and these powers will have to be exercised in a manner which makes the individual owner of real estate the public servant instead of the public master.

Croly was not alone among his contemporaries in citing the problem of unregulated private development. As previously noted, Henry McFarland, president of the Commissioners of the District of Columbia, faulted the McMillan Plan for not addressing the effects of private sector construction. And Montgomery Schuyler, the leading architectural critic of the day, wrote that, "in the interest of beauty," the supervision of the McMillan Commission should be extended to private as well as public buildings. "Unless the individual builder can be restrained and coerced to a conformity which no architectural artist would find irksome, we simply cannot have in Washington what otherwise we may very reasonably hope to have, 'the most beautiful capital city in the world.' "[76]

The inadequacies of the City Beautiful as a response to the property contradiction were not entirely the fault of the architect-planners who led the movement; they were constrained in what they could do by the need to make planning effective. As the saying goes, they could not make history just as they chose. The fundamental source of the problem lay with the organization of society—with the fact that the institution of private property limited the capacity of these architect-planners to incorporate social needs into the town building process, even when the social or collective needs in question were those of the city's business class.

The City Beautiful was also an inadequate response to the capitalist-democracy contradiction. The movement contributed to the development of the independent plan commission not by its positive example but by the failure of private planning to stimulate voluntary compliance. Thus, it was an inadequate response to the capitalist-democracy contradiction in that (once again) it was incapable of achieving its own ends. Architect John Carrère described this problem when he wrote that the task of enhancing the

[76] Croly, "Civic Improvements," p. 352; Schuyler, "The Art of City-Making," pp. 22-23.

165

beauty of our cities was made "difficult and at times so very dis-
couraging" by our reliance on democratic institutions; it meant,
he said, that men were continually moving in and out of office,
policies were constantly being changed, and great schemes of municipal improvement "no sooner thought of and partly worked
out" than they were upset by a change in administration.[77] Private
planning had been the City Beautiful's response to the tension between the City Beautiful ideal and the exigencies of democratic
government—because it kept the control of planning in the right
hands. But the experience of City Beautiful planning demonstrated a need for the coercive powers, moral sanction, and financing of government to make planning effective. The task, therefore,
was to institutionalize planning so as to take advantage of these
government powers while maintaining private control of planning. As illustrated in the following chapters, further developments in planning addressed this problem, but not without posing
the capitalist-democracy contradiction anew.

[77] Carrère, "Beautifying of Cities," p. 277.

SIX

Roads Not Taken

THE CITY BEAUTIFUL was not the only approach to city planning in the first decade of this century. There were three other examples of purposeful intervention in the urban development process in this period. One was the attack on urban population congestion, another was the American Garden City movement, and a third was the building of company towns by private business corporations. Each of these was a response to the property contradiction as it manifested itself in the problem of urban population concentration. As such, each involved an assertion of social needs against the private purposes governing the city building process. In particular, social needs were being asserted against the land speculators, developers, and builders—those whom Lamarche includes under the term "property capital"—responsible for the building of the urban physical environment.[1] And in the building of company towns like those at Pullman, Illinois and Gary, Indiana, the "social need" being invoked—for housing free from the tax of land speculation—was asserted by and corresponded with the interest of capitalist employers.

The three planning efforts examined in this chapter all took place in the context of burgeoning urban population growth, labor surpluses due to continuing high rates of immigration, and increasing competition for urban space for residential, commercial, manufacturing, and warehouse purposes. These pressures stimulated an interest in urban deconcentration that was shared by a number of urban groups, yet each meant something different by it.[2] For suburban land speculators, it meant extending transporta-

[1] For Lamarche's use of the term "property capital," see Lamarche, "Property Development," pp. 90-93.

[2] In attempting to understand the social and historical context of the attack on population congestion, I benefited from Richard A. Walker's excellent dissertation, "The Suburban Solution: Urban Geography and Urban Reform in the Capitalist Development of the United States." I see the attack on population congestion as being more broadly based than Walker does, however. In my view, workers and capitalists both had an interest in urban deconcentration, if not in the same program for accomplishing this aim. The different proposals for dispersing factories and worker residences discussed in this chapter reflected this divergence of interest.

tion and utilities to outlying suburban land. To manufacturers, it meant relocating factories and worker residences to rural or semi-rural areas, away from the expensive land and radicalizing environment of the city. And to workers and their spokesmen, it meant finding relief from overcrowded and insalubrious housing. Nevertheless, the fact that these groups shared a broad interest in lessening congestion made it possible for early "planners" to try to construct alliances of interest around the congestion issue.

Yet none of these planning efforts was in the end successful. They all failed, with qualifications that will be noted, to provide a programmatic basis for the development of formal city planning. This "failure" was not a failure of analysis; it was not that they incorrectly perceived the social or collective needs that might usefully be incorporated into city building. It was rather that they failed to respond to the property contradiction in a manner that accorded with prevailing power relations. It was in this sense that they charted "roads not taken."

The Attack on Urban Population Congestion

The campaign against population congestion can be said to have begun in New York City with the Exhibition on Population Congestion in March 1908. This exhibition, irreverently called the "Congestion Show" by its organizers, was sponsored by a newly created organization, the New York Committee on Congestion of Population (CCP), which had been formed by leaders and representatives of thirty-seven organizations active in the social welfare field in New York. Among the founders of the organization were Florence Kelly, secretary of the National Consumer's League; Mary Simkhovitch of Greenwich Village Settlement House; Lillian D. Wald, head of the Nurses Settlement and Home Nursing Service; Reverend Gaylord S. White of Union Theological Seminary and Union Settlement; and Dr. Herman C. Bumpus, director of the American Museum of Natural History. These individuals and groups had come together, in the words of Mrs. Simkhovitch, chairman of the CCP, "in their conviction that back of all the evils of city life lay the dominant evil of congestion of population." They had come to recognize that their multifarious efforts in combating bad housing, insufficient schools, the dearth of parks and playgrounds, juvenile crime, and tuberculosis and other health problems only dealt with the *effects* of congestion; what was needed was an attack on congestion itself. Accordingly, they argued for decentralization of factories and worker residences and, so that congestion would not recur, increased government control of land use and housing. As revealed at the Congestion Show, increased government control was to be achieved by increasing the tax on land in relation to buildings, adopting a districting or "zone system" for regulating land use and buildings, and embarking upon a program of municipal land purchases.[3]

The campaign against population congestion cannot be adequately discussed without first introducing Benjamin C. Marsh. When the CCP was formed, it named Benjamin Marsh, thirty years old at the time, as its first secretary. It was Marsh who organized the Congestion Show, after the model of the many housing exhibitions organized by Lawrence Veiller. Before joining the CCP, Marsh had served briefly as assistant state secretary of the Iowa YMCA and as secretary of the Pennsylvania Society to Protect Children from Cruelty. The son of Congregationalist missionaries, he spent much of his early childhood in Bulgaria, where he observed firsthand the power of his parents' innate humanism and sense of compassion, if not necessarily their religion, to win converts. He graduated from Grinnell College in Iowa, going from there to the Iowa YMCA post; spent a year studying economics, sociology, and history at the University of Chicago; worked for two years raising money for foreign missions, becoming familiar with living and working conditions in the urban Northeast through his many speaking engagements; and then accepted a scholarship for graduate study, at the University of Pennsylvania, on the subject of homeless men. There, he became a student of the progressive-minded economist, Simon Patten. It was while he was a graduate student at Pennsylvania that Marsh was elected secretary of the Pennsylvania Society to Protect Children from Cruelty, a lobbying position in which he demonstrated the outspokenness and flair for publicity that continued to mark his career. Marsh left that post because his advocacy of improved housing offended owners of slum housing who were on the society's board.[4]

Marsh did not complete his doctorate in economics at Pennsylvania; he observed later that doing so would have signified "mental acquiescence in an outworn economic system." As the newly named secretary of the CCP, he traveled to Europe in the summer

<hr />

[3] Martin, "The Exhibit of Congestion Interpreted," pp. 27-39, quotation, p. 33; also Marsh, *Lobbyist for the People: A Record of Fifty Years*, pp. 17-19.

[4] Marsh, *Lobbyist*, chap. 1.

of 1907 to gather material on housing and city planning from Germany, Britain, France, and elsewhere. The year after he organized the Congestion Show, he repeated this trip. From his travels in Europe, he acquired many of the ideas he sought to apply in his lobbying and propaganda efforts. He was especially impressed with the methods used by German cities to regulate land use and control urban growth. Frankfurt, for example, had adopted a "zone system" that divided the city into separate zones, each with distinct regulations governing the height, bulk, and use of buildings within that zone. In addition, Frankfurt, like most other German cities, owned much of the land on its outskirts, thus enabling it to control peripheral development through its right of ownership and to prevent speculators from making unearned gains.

Marsh's observations on the progress of city planning in Europe were set forth in a book, *An Introduction to City Planning: Democracy's Challenge to the American City*, privately published by him in 1909. Beginning with the admonition that "A City without a Plan is Like a Ship without a Rudder," Marsh's text urged American cities to control their development by adopting the German zone system and purchasing municipal land. In addition to analyzing the problem of population congestion and reviewing planning progress in Europe, the book contained a chapter, written by architect George B. Ford, on the technical aspects of city planning. The appearance of this text coincided with the organization by Marsh of a second exhibition, known as the "City Plan Exhibition," which was placed on display in conjunction with the first national conference on city planning, likewise organized by Marsh and the CCP.[5]

It was the earlier Congestion Show, however, that first brought Marsh and the CCP to prominence. This exhibition of maps, charts, models, and photographs, and an accompanying series of talks by persons active in social work and municipal reform, sought to describe the housing and living conditions of the urban poor, identify the causes of population congestion, and propose possible solutions. From accounts at the time, the exhibition was apparently as startling in its depiction of the conditions of the poor as in the far-reaching solutions it proposed. One especially vivid display, described as "horrifying to a person with sympathetic imagination," was a life-size model of a tenement sweatshop in which a family of seven lived and worked in a twelve-by-twelve

---

[5] Ibid., quotation, p. 6.

foot area. This display was financed by the Italian government and organized by the Neighborhood Workers Association. An adjacent display made clear that one sixth of the Italian families investigated by the workers association lived and worked in such dehumanizing conditions. Small children, the exhibit showed, suffered especially in these conditions; while the death rate for children under five in the city as a whole was 51 per thousand, the figures for the areas of greatest Italian concentration were 82, 87, and 92 per thousand. In Manhattan as a whole, the average population density was 150.4 persons per acre, as compared with 2.4 persons per acre in Queens and 1.9 in Richmond. Moreover, within Manhattan there were eleven blocks with a density of 1,200 persons per acre; if Delaware were similarly crowded, the display noted, it could contain the population of the entire world.[6]

As for the causes of population congestion, the Congestion Show sought to demonstrate that the economic growth of New York City and its status as the principal port of entry for European immigrants were contributing factors. But the organizers of the exhibition went further in unraveling the complex chain of cause and effect. Several displays showed that concentrated land ownership, high rents, and an imperfect tax system compounded the congestion problem while constraining the city's ability to respond. "Thus," as reviewer John Martin wrote, "the contrast was made vivid—oppressive rents, narrow quarters, bestial overcrowding on the one side; unimaginable land values, imperial fortunes, bountiful harvests reaped without sowing on the other side."[7]

Although the exhibit's proposed solutions coincided in that they all dealt with the congestion problem, they demonstrated different perspectives on the problem and, correspondingly, the different interests that came together in the attack on population congestion. Some proposals sought to cope with the effects of population congestion; one, for example, suggested cooperatively owned tenements underwritten by government loans and modeled on cooperative housing in Germany as a way of improving housing for the poorer classes. Yet most of the recommendations were concerned with reducing population congestion. Edward T. Hartman, secretary of the Massachusetts Civic League, argued that part of the population of the congested district (in Benjamin

6 "Exhibit of Congestion," pp. 27-28.
7 Ibid., p. 30.

Marsh's paraphrase) "must literally be dug up by its roots and transplanted into areas developed in such a way as to make slums impossible." New York's City Club, an organization of reform-minded business and professional leaders, called for measures to rationalize the system of land use and population distribution. They proposed that the city be mapped for different land uses, with factories located along important transportation routes and worker districts adjacent to the factories. A number of speakers and displays called for moving factories to the edge of the city, and for improving mass transportation and lowering transit fares so workers would not have to live so close to where they worked. In addition, the Bureau of Municipal Research proposed improving methods of data collection and government administration, and there were also proposals for adopting the German "zone system," and for ratifying tax measures that would discourage speculators from withholding land from development.[8]

Not surprisingly, the Congestion Show did not produce immediate results. Marsh wrote later that the exhibition "was a distinct success from every point of view—except producing action to remedy the condition shown."[9] Yet he and the CCP continued their propaganda efforts. Several smaller exhibits were held in Brooklyn and at the National Conference on Charities and Corrections; in 1908, Marsh published his *Introduction to City Planning*; and the following year he and the CCP organized the first national conference on city planning, of which more will be said later. Finally, in 1910, there was an official response to the congestion problem in New York City. Two commissions were appointed to study the problem: New York Mayor William Jay Gaynor, a Tammany Democrat, established a Commission on Congestion of Population and Governor Charles Evans Hughes created a complementary body, the Commission on Distribution of Population. Benjamin Marsh was named secretary of both bodies, thereby linking the two together.

The report of the state commission chiefly addressed how population could be redirected from urban to rural areas. In this connection, it recommended more government control of factory locations, state aid for resettling people in rural areas, more publicity on agricultural opportunities within the state, improved

[8] Marsh, "The Congestion Exhibit in Brooklyn," p. 211; Martin, "Exhibit of Congestion," pp. 30-39.
[9] Marsh, *Lobbyist*, p. 18.

agricultural training in rural schools, and shifting the tax burden from labor products to land values.[10]

According to Marsh, the commission established by Mayor Gaynor was promoted by real estate and loaning interests. They hoped that, if conservative members were appointed, the commission would propose remedies less threatening than the land use regulations and transferral of taxes from buildings to land values being advocated by the CCP.[11] And indeed, only two of the commission's nineteen members had any expert knowledge of planning—Jacob Cantor, a former Manhattan Borough president and early planning advocate, and Professor Frank Goodnow of Columbia University (later president of Johns Hopkins University). Ten of the appointees were aldermen, and the remainder were mostly from the real estate trade.[12] Yet the commission's 270-page report, completed after eleven months of investigation, made considerable headway in addressing the congestion problem, progress which no doubt reflected Marsh's involvement. The report's chief recommendations were (1) stricter regulation of tenement construction to ensure better living conditions, (2) extended public ownership of transportation, (3) the creation of freight belt lines, (4) higher income taxes, (5) a land increment tax, (6) a widows' pension, and (7) a reduction in the tax rate on buildings to half that on land. On the question of city planning, the report declared that "the failure to provide a City plan determining the way in which various sections of the City are to be developed is also largely responsible for the congestion through intensive use of land." Intensive congestion was "perfectly natural," the commission wrote, because "private interest" rather than the "public welfare" had been allowed to control the development of Manhattan and the other boroughs.[13]

It was the mayoral commission's proposal for increasing land taxes in relation to that on buildings that engendered the most controversy. The idea was that, by shifting the tax burden to land values, land speculators would be forced to develop their property, thereby increasing the stock of housing and reducing congestion. Moreover, the city would be able to appropriate, from the tax on

[10] On the report of the state commission, see ibid., p. 19, and "Farm and City and Factory," pp. 896-98.

[11] *Lobbyist*, p. 22.

[12] See Kantor, "Benjamin C. Marsh and the Fight Over Population Congestion," p. 425.

[13] Quoted, ibid.

speculators, part of the "unearned" increment in land values resulting from the city's expansion. This recommendation bore fruit in a bill before the state legislature calling for a city referendum on transferring the tax burden from buildings to land values. And the ensuing battle attested to the strength of the city's real estate lobby. Lined up in support of the bill were the CCP and a newly formed homeowner group, the Society to Lower Rents and Reduce Taxes on Homes. On the opposite side were the real estate interests that specialized in land speculation, including the president of the New York Real Estate Board, and the lending interests, led by the comptroller of the Metropolitan Life Insurance Company. Despite an aggressive campaign in which Marsh spoke in every assembly district in New York State, in some as often as ten times, the real estate and lending interests prevailed. The measure was killed in committee by Majority Leader Al Smith, although Smith had earlier supported the bill. (Marsh surmised that Smith's turnabout was due to pressure from the Catholic Church, which was a large landowner in the city.) In commenting on a speech by Governor Hughes at the Congestion Exhibition, Marsh summed up the lesson of this experience. Hughes had observed that it was just being recognized how the tax power of the state could be used to remedy social injustice, leading Marsh to remark, "Unfortunately some wealthy people did realize just what the State could do in this way and, being the State, they saw to it that the State did not in any way interfere with their legalized rackets."[14]

Although Marsh was familiar with Henry George's work and was influenced by his ideas on land taxation, he was not a doctrinaire "single-taxer." Unlike Cleveland reformer Frederic C. Howe, for instance, Marsh did not advocate a "single tax" on land.[15] He was concerned that such a tax would exempt too many other forms of wealth; he also worried that the tax would burden workers who owned their own homes, and that landlords would merely shift the tax to tenants.[16] Instead, Marsh favored a differentiated tax on land and buildings, taxing land values more heavily, and a special tax on increases in land values so that the community could share in the profit resulting from its own growth. Marsh argued for these measures on the ground that "land values are cre-

[14] *Lobbyist*, pp. 20-22, quotation, p. 18.

[15] For Howe's view on land taxation, see Frederic Howe, "Land Values and Congestion," pp. 1067-68.

[16] "Taxation and the Improvement of Living Conditions in American Cities," pp. 605, 609.

ated chiefly by the labor and industry of the entire population." He also maintained, drawing from the experience of German cities, that these measures would create additional housing, lower rents, reduce congestion, and generate additional tax revenue to meet other social needs. The land question was the essence of the housing problem for Marsh, but he did not regard land taxation as a panacea, despite having written a book on the subject in 1911.[17] In his view, city planning involved five essential functions: (1) regulating factory locations and ensuring adequate facilities for freight transportation; (2) zoning land use to regulate the height and bulk of buildings and the density of population; (3) providing adequate public transportation; (4) building and maintaining adequate streets, open spaces, and recreational facilities; and (5) exercising the power of "excess condemnation" in connection with public improvements.[18]

The interests that called forth the attack on population congestion were not those of one economic or social group. Workers had an interest in reducing population congestion, since they were the ones who lived in congested districts. Business, or at least some segments of business, also had an interest in lessening congestion. Although it was workers' interest in particular that Benjamin Marsh articulated, he attempted to create an alliance with the more enlightened segments of business on the congestion issue. However, business interest in congestion focused primarily on the central area of the city. This was a period of increasing competition on the part of retailing, banking, and various other functions for space in the central areas—areas that were dominated by manufacturing. This competition, together with the congestion in these districts, stimulated an interest in dispersing industry to the suburbs and creating a more efficient overall system of land use and transportation.[19] This interest was reflected in a recommendation made by the elite-dominated Reform Club at the 1908 Congestion Show in New York City. It called for locating factories along the waterfront (with intervening parks) and along selected transportation routes on Long Island, building tenement districts adjacent to the factories so workers could walk to work, and reserving central Manhattan for office buildings, theatres, and the

[17] *Taxation of Land Values in American Cities: The Next Step in Eliminating Poverty*, pp. ix-xv, quotation, p. ix.

[18] "City Planning in Justice to the Working Population," p. 1515.

[19] On this point, see Richard Walker, "Suburban Solution," p. 323.

like.[20] On the issue of dispersing industry and deconcentrating worker districts, there were some grounds for an alliance between workers and their employers. The movement of industry to the suburbs was viewed in some cases in this period as a socially responsible act. For example, the reform-minded journal, *The Survey*, praised the decision of Doubleday, Page and Company to move its printing plant employing eight hundred workers from East Sixteenth Street in New York to the suburb of Garden City, Long Island.[21] Yet, in the absence of some form of public control, relocations of this sort would occur only when they made business sense to individual firms.

The problems and possibilities of a worker-business alliance on the congestion issue are suggested by the relationship of Marsh and millionaire financier Henry Morgenthau. As the owner of large suburban tracts, Morgenthau had an interest in promoting suburbanization. Yet he was owner of enough land and knowledgeable enough about land speculation and the real estate market to recognize the need for some overall regulation of development. An early supporter of city planning, he served for a time as the honorary president of the CCP. In that capacity, he and Marsh worked together briefly—until their differences on the congestion issue drove them apart. When Morgenthau became aware of the sentiment building for the land tax being advocated by Marsh, he asked Marsh to cease his advocacy of the tax, threatening to resign from the CCP and withdraw his financial support if Marsh did not comply. This tax, it should be noted, was aimed precisely at speculators like Morgenthau who owned large tracts of suburban land and withheld them from development while awaiting increases in their value. Predictably, Marsh refused to comply with Morgenthau's request, and the financier not only made good his threat, but also kicked the CCP out of the building where he had given them free office space.[22] This experience was repeated when reformer and Columbia University Professor Frank Goodnow asked Standard Oil treasurer Charles Pratt whether he would appear before the CCP. Pratt declined, informing Goodnow, "I don't believe you know how radical that man Marsh is, or you wouldn't have anything to do with him." Goodnow reported the conversation to

[20] Martin, "Exhibit of Congestion," p. 32.
[21] "From City to Country," pp. 898-99.
[22] Marsh, *Lobbyist*, p. 13.

Marsh, adding, "I support you, but I suppose you can't expect people to contribute to the cutting of their financial throats."[23]

Part of the antipathy of business toward Marsh no doubt stemmed from his personal style. By all accounts, he was an outspoken man with a flair for publicity. A case in point was his widely reported description of New York's City Club as a "home for fallen men." This remark, which led to Marsh's expulsion from the club, was occasioned by the decision of the club's transportation committee to endorse a bid by August Belmont and Theodore Shonts, both club members, to acquire a city transit franchise. Marsh, who favored municipal ownership of the city's transit system, believed the endorsement was influenced by the men's membership in the club.[24] Yet it was not only Marsh's flair for publicity that engendered business hostility; it was also the targets he chose. Marsh saw the congestion problem confronting workers and the urban poor as an outgrowth of the way land was owned and controlled. Only by incorporating social needs into urban development, whether through tax policy or municipal land ownership, could the congestion problem be meaningfully addressed, he believed. This way of viewing the problem put him at odds with people like Henry Morgenthau, who opposed planning interventions that limited their profits or prerogatives without providing compensating benefits. Recognizing this resistance, Robert de Forest warned Marsh when the two men first met, "If you touch the land problem in New York, you probably won't last here two years."[25] And, revealing where he stood, de Forest himself refused to work with Marsh on the CCP. He wrote Jacob Riis that he had serious doubts about Marsh's "practical judgement" and did not look for "practical results from a Commission, the leadership of which rested in some of our aldermen and Mr. Marsh."[26]

Marsh understood the political-economic conditions that gave rise to the demand for urban planning. In an article entitled "City Planning in Justice to the Working Population," he presented an analysis similar to that of Manuel Castells. He observed that the process of capitalist development led to the proletarianization of the work force and the concentration of workers in space, and that this situation spawned demands for state intervention to provide facilities for collective consumption in support of the working

[23] Ibid., p. 24.
[24] Ibid., pp. 24-26.
[25] Ibid., p. 35.
[26] Quoted in Kantor, "Benjamin Marsh," p. 426.

class. Yet there was this critical difference in the thinking of the two men: where Castells's analysis is framed in terms of capital's need to "reproduce labour power," Marsh's was based on an assertion of workers' rights.[27] What Castells's analysis obscures and Marsh's helps to reveal is that the attack on congestion had, at least potentially, a multi-class basis. Workers had an interest in reducing congestion, too; the problem was that defining the congestion problem around their interests was politically disadvantageous. The flaw in Marsh's efforts was that he sought to advance the housing and environmental needs of the working-class poor by shaming the rich into providing support, in effect asking them to "contribute to the cutting of their own financial throats," as Frank Goodnow had put it.[28] The contradiction in this strategy was not of Marsh's making, however. It arose, on the one hand, from the inequality of power in American society that made appealing to the wealthy a surer means of winning support for his approach to planning and, on the other, from the workplace orientation of the American labor movement that deterred it from addressing workers' needs in the living place. If, as Leonardo Benevolo argues, city planning in Europe became increasingly conservative following the defeat of the revolutions of 1848, the same result obtained in the United States only here it owed as much to default as to defeat.[29] Marsh believed that the struggle of the working population had to be waged in the workplace as well as in the living place and regarded the ownership and control of land as the central issue in the latter arena. He urged farm, labor, and consumer organizations to take up the struggle in both these realms, believing as he did that these organizations, by virtue of their membership, had a responsibility to promote political and economic change.

In 1912, Marsh departed from the field of city planning, observing that "land speculators and bankers had captured the city plan-

[27] Marsh, "City Planning," pp. 1514-15; Castells, *Urban Question*, pp. 456-62.

[28] When Carola Woerishoffer, a wealthy heiress and supporter of Marsh, made a large financial contribution to the CCP, Marsh promised her (in his words) "to use the money she gave the Congestion Committee to try to end the system which gave her her wealth" (*Lobbyist*, p. 34). Marsh also related his experience in requesting a financial contribution from J. P. Morgan. When he informed Morgan of the purpose of his visit, the financier and industrialist abruptly rose to leave, commenting as he went, "I have always been more interested in improving my own condition than that of other people." Marsh responded, "Mr. Morgan, I have always understood that to be the case" (*Lobbyist*, p. 36).

[29] On how urban planning became separated from progressive social forces in Europe, see Benevolo, *The Origins of Modern Town Planning*, pp. 105-47.

ning movement."[30] He did not retire from public life, however. Following two years as a war correspondent in the Balkan War, he returned to New York City to work with the Farmer's National Council and, beginning in 1918, with the People's Reconstruction League. He later organized the People's Lobby, a national organization based in Washington, D.C., that boasted over twenty thousand members and had as its presidents such persons as John Dewey and Colston Warne (who later organized the Consumer's Union). Through this organization, Marsh promoted, up until the 1950s, a variety of reform causes, from depression relief to social control of industry.[31]

Marsh's concern with decentralizing jobs, manufacturing, and urban residences eventually was incorporated into formal city planning, although not on the terms Marsh advocated and not until the 1950s. In the second decade of this century, as discussed in the following chapter, city planning addressed itself to creating a more rational and efficient distribution of factories, commercial zones, worker districts, and high-class residential areas. It was not until the 1950s, however, that city planning actually became concerned with suburbanization; this concern coincided with federal support for both suburban home building and the development of suburban infrastructure (for example, highways and water and sewerage systems). And the focus here was on coordinating public infrastructural investments with one another and with private development, rather than on regulating private development in the interest of the housing and environmental needs of the working class and urban poor. This suburban planning was thus a far cry from the program of land taxes and municipal land purchases urged by Marsh and others to control private development and promote urban deconcentration. Yet there had been an earlier attempt to achieve a suburban solution to the congestion problem in the form of the Garden City concept.

Garden Cities and Suburbs

The Garden City movement, which originated in England, was also a response to the problem of population congestion, one with its own idealized concept of the city. At the center of the Garden City idea was an attempt to deconcentrate the city—to remove

[30] *Lobbyist*, p. 28.

[31] On the activities of the People's Lobby and Marsh's efforts after leaving New York City, see Marsh, *Lobbyist*, and Kantor, "Benjamin Marsh," p. 428.

persons and employment from the crowded quarters of the city and locate them in planned communities in the countryside with special provisions to ensure easy access to nature. This idea was not entirely new, but rather the descendant of European thought extending at least as far back as Saint-Simon, his follower Charles Fourier, Jeremy Bentham, and Robert Owen, all of whom envisaged alternatives to the overcrowded cities of the early industrial period. Unlike the park movement, the Garden City movement (at least in its original incarnation) did not seek environmental reform apart from a change in the system of ownership and control of land and housing. It promoted collective ownership and control of town land as well as cooperative ownership of housing—although the collective principle was not extended with equal force to the factory system. From its beginnings in England, the Garden City movement spread throughout much of Europe and to the United States and Canada. Yet, as the Garden City idea spread, it became dissociated from the concept of collective control of land and housing, often signifying little more than environmentally conscious, low-density suburban housing.

The most immediate intellectual inspiration for the Garden City movement was the publication by Ebenezer Howard, an English court stenographer, of a short monograph, *Tomorrow: the Real Path to Social Reform*, in 1898. Reissued in 1902 as *Garden Cities of Tomorrow*, Howard's book called for the founding of self-contained "garden cities" based on common land ownership and a marriage of the best features of town and country life. The idea was not merely to create a showcase model community as a critique of existing cities, but to lay the basis for a new type of urban form. It was hoped that, by its constant repetition, this urban form could alter the pattern of urbanization in England and the rest of the urbanized world. Howard envisaged the founding of carefully planned communities separated from each other by belts of agricultural land—one of the hallmarks of the original Garden City idea. Other essential elements of the Garden City idea were a limit on the population of the town (thirty-two thousand was suggested as the upper limit); insistence on sanitary, commodious, and artistic building in accordance with an overall plan; and community ownership of town land so that the community could reap the benefits of its own growth.[32]

---

[32] Howard, *Garden Cities of Tomorrow*; the best source on Howard and his connection with the Garden City movement in England is Dugald MacFadyen, *Sir Ebenezer Howard and the Town Planning Movement*.

Howard's Garden Cities were to be as economically self-sufficient as possible. Factories were to be located at the edge of the town, adjacent to rail facilities but away from residential areas, and commercial shops were to be set around a central town common. Howard wanted to limit the number of shops in hopes of making them more profitable and enabling the city to extract more revenue in land rent. Town residents could vote to allow additional shops, however, if they were dissatisfied with existing businesses, thereby providing shopowners with an incentive to give good service. A ward system similar to that of eighteenth-century Savannah was to be followed in laying out the residential section of the town. Residential areas were to be arranged in coherent neighborhoods, each centering around a public school, and the population density of each neighborhood was to be limited. The houses of the town also were to be preplanned: they were to be of different sizes to suit the needs of different income groups, and all the lots were to provide access to nature as well as space for a garden. Through these and other measures, Howard hoped to avoid the spread of the city into the countryside, the depopulation of rural areas, the growth of slums, the increase in land values without corresponding benefits to the community, and the denial of the benefits of city life to rural residents (and vice versa).

Howard's ideas were not entirely the product of his own imagination. As a young man, he had spent ten years in the United States and may have been familiar with the term "garden city" from its use to describe a model estate built on Long Island in the 1860s. He also witnessed one of Chicago's great fires, which may have inspired him to try to find an alternative to the densely crowded cities of the day. But it was principally from Europe that Howard gained his practical and intellectual inspiration. His great accomplishment was his "unique synthesis" of former proposals, many of which evolved from the political turmoil of 1848, and the "astonishing simplicity and range of detail that made in one stroke seemingly idealized and impractical schemes realizable within the contemporary political and social context." In his *Utopia*, written in 1515, Thomas More had proposed the laying out of communities with a surrounding belt of agricultural land. And in the first half of the nineteenth century, Saint-Simon, Jeremy Bentham, Charles Fourier, and Robert Owen all proposed the founding of new communities that blended aspects of the urban and rural. Yet Howard, who was not a learned man, did not acknowledge the influence of these earlier thinkers, although he did acknowledge the imprint of ideas from his more immediate historical milieu, such as Edward Bellamy's proposed socialist commonwealth (*Looking Backward*), 1888; economist Alfred Marshall's ideas on resettling slum dwellers away from congested factory cities (1844); and Herbert Spencer's writings on the pursuit of equality through the redistribution of income and the state's duty to protect the spiritual and physical health of its citizens (*Social Statics*, 1851).[33] Howard's thinking also was influenced by existing "model" communities in England. Two of them, Bournville and Port Sunlight, were particularly important; both were organized by business corporations as extensions of their manufacturing operations.

Bournville was built by chocolate manufacturer George Cadbury.[34] Initially he was only seeking to expand his operations and found it cheaper to build on land outside Birmingham. Yet Bournville eventually became a full-scale exercise in town planning, with Cadbury determined to prove that a model community could be made to pay. Only half the male residents worked for Cadbury, however; the others commuted to jobs in Birmingham. The town was built around a village green and consisted of rows of small cottages surrounded by gardens. There was also a large playground, and land was reserved for park purposes. Because he believed in the pacifying powers of nature and also wanted to avoid overcrowding, Cadbury required that every house have a garden. In addition, gardening classes were provided for male residents of the town. And just in case this dosage of nature did not deter men from drink, the sale of liquor was forbidden.

Interestingly, Cadbury discovered that achieving his urban ideal required overcoming fragmented land ownership. Although some cottage sites were sold when the project got under way in 1879, Cadbury soon realized that to make the town self-financing and to control its expansion centralized land ownership was essential. For a while, Cadbury held the land himself, but eventually own-

[33] Quotation from Batchelor, "The Origin of the Garden City Concept of Urban Form," p. 185. On the sources of Howard's ideas, see, in addition, Osborn, "The Garden City Movement: Reaffirmation of the Validity of Ebenezer Howard's Idea," pp. 43-54; Buder, "Ebenezer Howard: The Genesis of a Town Planning Movement," pp. 390-98; and Petersen, "The Ideological Origins of Britain's New Towns," pp. 160-70.

[34] On Bournville, see Ashworth, *The Genesis of Modern British Town Planning: A Study in Economic and Social History of the Nineteenth and Twentieth Centuries*, pp. 132-33, and Trueblood, "The Bournville Village Experiment: A Twentieth Century Attempt at Housing the Workers," pp. 449-58.

ership was ceded to the trustees of the town. Rental income from the land was used to finance town improvements, making the town reasonably self-sufficient economically.

In the same period, the companion town of Port Sunlight was built by W. H. Lever, the soap manufacturer. It was erected on the outskirts of Liverpool as a new site for the company's soap works and a residential village for employees. All of the male residents were employed in the soap works, making it a one-factory town. Described as an attractive community, Port Sunlight provided access to nature (although gardens were not compulsory), and, by 1904, the town included two schools, a men's social club, an open-air swimming bath and theatre, a technical institute, Sunday schools, and a church. As in Bournville, there was centralized control of town land, although the land was not ceded to the inhabitants of the town. Instead, the village was run by a department of the firm, and for many years the tenants could air their complaints only to the firm's estate managers. Moreover, Port Sunlight did not grow as Bournville did, whether because it was only indirectly profitable to the firm, or because workers objected to the firm's paternalism. Twenty years after its founding, it provided only enough housing for half the firm's employees.[35]

In the view of Benjamin Marsh and most other critics, Bournville was clearly superior to Port Sunlight as a model industrial community. Marsh credited Cadbury's Bournville with genuinely seeking to "ameliorate the condition of the working class," while Port Sunlight, he believed, was founded on "the desire to increase the efficiency of the workers." Yet it should be remembered that neither venture was an exercise in philanthropy—both were intended to be profitable for their organizers. If Cadbury appeared more solicitous of his workers' interests than Lever did, his social control objectives—manifested in his requiring a garden and prohibiting the sale of liquor—were also more in evidence. As reported in the United States, Cadbury maintained that his efforts had been "recompensed a hundredfold," adding that "nothing pays a manufacturer better than to go into the country." For his part, Lever declared that the greatest attraction of relocating to the suburbs was the enormous reduction in the value of land. He also held that planned communities like Port Sunlight produced a "physically superior, contented, happy people." Here he echoed the King of Siam, who, upon visiting Port Sunlight, called it "one of the

[35] On Port Sunlight, see Ashworth, *British Town Planning*, pp. 133-34.

most important of the world's factories." Its workers, the King declared, "should be the best workers anywhere" inasmuch as "cheerful homes make cheerful workers." Indeed, comparative studies indicated that workers in Bournville and Port Sunlight were physically superior to those in conventional cities.[36]

By contrast, Ebenezer Howard's Garden City concept does not appear to have been motivated by commercial interest. Howard's motives were more nearly sociological and humanitarian, although this was not true of all those who sought to apply his ideas. He believed that the cities of the day had done their work: "They were the best which a society largely based on selfishness and rapacity could construct, but they are in the nature of things entirely unadapted for a society in which the social side of our nature is demanding a larger share of recognition."[37] Above all, Howard sought to experiment in "new wealth forms"; he wanted to increase the effectiveness of the productive forces of society and nature and to create a more equitable and just distribution of economic reward.[38] It was this concern that led him to propose collective ownership of land, which underpinned many of his other proposals. Yet Howard was not a consistent advocate of collective ownership. Although he had earlier favored collective ownership of all the means of production, by the time he wrote *Garden Cities* he had decided that public ownership of business activity was not an essential element of his model. His social philosophy, which he called "social individualism," was to create a "social city" based on collective land ownership, leaving it up to residents whether to go further in the direction of socialized ownership.[39] These ideas would have been merely those of another utopian thinker had they not led to the founding of two model communities, Letchworth and Welwyn.

Letchworth was launched in 1904 and Welwyn in 1920, both communities within an hour's commute from London. They were successful in that they became going concerns, although their practical success came at the expense of Howard's more radical

[36] Marsh quotation, in Marsh, *Introduction to City Planning*, pp. 118, 120; Cadbury, Lever, and King of Siam quotations, in Diggs, "The Garden City Movement," pp. 628, 627. On the comparison between workers in speculatively built towns and those in Bournville and Port Sunlight, see Marsh, *Introduction to City Planning*, p. 118.

[37] *Garden Cities*, p. 133.

[38] MacFadyen, *Ebenezer Howard*, p. 31.

[39] See Buder, "Ebenezer Howard," pp. 391-93.

proposals. The problem, in brief, was that the reliance on private capital to finance these communities, and the consequent need to reassure and indulge stockholders, worked against Howard's collectivist principles. Letchworth was founded with an initial sum of three hundred thousand pounds. That amount was raised by a limited dividend company, Garden Cities Limited, formed by the English Garden Cities Association. Except for the limitation on dividends (5 percent), the building company was organized along orthodox lines; most of its directors were successful businessmen, half of them industrialists. This proved to be a difficult structure through which to raise capital, however: the project was continually hampered by a shortage of capital, and it was ten years before a dividend (of 1 percent) was paid.[40] As a result, stockholders were, in effect, given control of the community as a way of reassuring them about their investments. This action was, of course, contrary to Howard's idea that title to the community would be held by trustees representing the residents, and that the residents themselves would manage the town through an elected council. Howard had also proposed a system of periodic rent revisions to prevent individuals from acquiring an "unearned increment." But the desire to attract industry led to long-term leases with no provision for adjustments.

As an exercise in physical planning, Letchworth proved more successful. It demonstrated the attractiveness of environmentally conscious low-density development. Yet densities were higher than Howard had recommended, there were fewer gardens, and the actual layout bore only slight resemblance to Howard's diagram.[41] In terms of its effect on subsequent town planning, however, the actual success of Letchworth measured against Howard's ideals is less important than how its "success" was perceived and interpreted by planners and reformers at the time.

The promotional activities of the English Garden Cities Association were sympathetically described in one American reform journal as a beneficial exercise in social control and a means of protection against socialism. The article went on to explain that the English association was founded upon a recognition that the realms of "workplace" and residential "environment" were the principal sources of both worker radicalism and the problems of the city. The Garden City remedy was a "partnership" between la-

[40] See Ashworth, *British Town Planning*, p. 143.
[41] See Buder, "Ebenezer Howard," pp. 395-96.

bor and capital, one that "the more intelligent of the employing class perceive is the only hope for their own future." Capitalists would be forced to give up some freedom of action in recognition that this was what a "contented industrialism" required, and workers would be contented with their lot in view of the advantages of living in a Garden City.[42] In another American journal, the Garden City was described as a replacement for socialism, presumably an equivalent one, which demonstrated the possibility of creating cities that were responsive to society's collective needs (Howard's "social cities") "without waiting for socialism or any political revolution."[43] Another American reviewer saw the Garden City as an example of how the decentralization of industry could be planned for and facilitated. "If the development of the movement of decentralization was left to chance, as the prime movement of centralization under the factory system was left," he stated, "we might anticipate with some confidence the growth of evils not less serious than those which the short-sighted indifference of our predecessors compelled us to cope with today."[44] The English Garden Cities were also regarded as a demonstration that, to produce good and attractive homes, a change in the principles governing land development was needed. George B. Hooker, secretary of Chicago's City Club, wrote in the *Journal of the American Institute of Architects* that the "essential element" of the English Garden Cities was "their idealism expressed on the one side in their superior physical aspects as community homes, and on the other side in their violation of so-called business principles." Achieving improved housing on the model of the Garden City, Hooker declared, would require a "revolution in land policy" entailing unified rather than fragmented ownership of land, exclusion of speculation, limitations on population densities, and turning unearned increments in land values to community use.[45]

But there were others who minimized the importance of collective ownership in the Garden City concept. Chief among these, significantly, was Lawrence Veiller, secretary of the NHA. On the one hand, Veiller saw the Garden City as a means of achieving social and political control objectives. In an article reviewing the ex-

[42] Quoted in Diggs, "Garden City Movement," pp. 631-32.
[43] Miller, "What England Can Teach Us About Garden Cities," p. 534.
[44] Melville, "Garden Cities," p. 68.
[45] Hooker, "Garden Cities," pp. 88, 90; for other American perspectives on the Garden City, see Brown, "Progress of the Garden City Movement in England," pp. 459-60, and Pratt, "Garden Cities in Europe," pp. 503-10.

perience of the English Garden Cities, he quoted at length from a speech to the NHA by English Ambassador James Bryce. Speaking on "The Menace of Great Cities," Ambassador Bryce had warned that overgrown cities were "liable to become great dangers in a political sense, because the more men are crowded in great masses the more easily they become excited, the more they are swept away by words, and the more they form what might be called a revolutionary temper." Veiller expressed agreement, citing "industrial disturbances" as the greatest menace of large cities. At the same time, Veiller sought to adapt Howard's Garden City concept to American conditions by robbing it of its collectivist content. Community ownership of land, he wrote, "is in no sense essential to [Howard's] scheme. . . . [T]he fundamental idea is just as sound, just as easily applied without this feature, as with it."[46]

American interest in the Garden City idea led to the founding in 1906 of the Garden Cities Association of America. The announced creed of the association was that "the very best thing that can be given a workingman is steady work with a good home in a country community." With its directorship of churchmen and business leaders, the association boasted at its founding that it was "the most far reaching progressive movement in New York, and at the same time the safest business investment."[47] It did not, however, propose to sponsor the development of model villages, as its English counterpart had done. Instead, suggesting the limit of its progressive orientation, it intended to persuade large corporations to undertake and be individually responsible for the construction of Garden City–style developments, subject to the advice and approval of the association. The association was to form joint committees with each company, and the companies were to limit their dividends to 5 percent, submit their plans for the association's approval, and sell town land only to prospective residents. W. D. P. Bliss, secretary of the association, observed that the Garden City model was apt to be more difficult to implant in the United States than in England. He feared that it would be harder to induce American employers and workers to move to the country, and that limiting profits to 5 percent would be more difficult since profit rates were generally higher in the United States. Moreover, the Garden City idea was alloyed in this country with speculative interests.

[46] "Are Great Cities a Menace? The Garden City as a Way Out," pp. 178, 175, 181; Veiller maintained (p. 181) that Howard agreed that collective control of land was not essential to his ideal.

[47] "The Garden Cities Association of America," p. 286.

Bliss noted that the capital interested in the movement was mostly "Long Island capital"—Long Island being the last remaining undeveloped borough of New York City. The problem was not simply that speculative interests were seeking to appropriate the Garden City idea. As Bliss pointed out, Long Island was desirable for manufacturing as well as residential purposes, and it also represented a difficult railroad proposition. It was serviced by only one railroad, the Long Island Railway, whose fares were higher than those of other railroads because it did not carry freight and had to make all its earnings from passenger fares. The Long Island Railway had an obvious interest in the residential development of Long Island, and, indicative of the "Long Island capital" involved in the movement, the railroad's president was the first vice-president of the Garden Cities Association of America.[48]

Although, as will be discussed in the next section, a number of towns were established by industrial corporations during this period, none followed Howard's Garden City model. However, the Garden City idea was influential in the building of middle- and upper-class suburbs. The best example was Forest Hills Gardens, built in 1911 by the Russell Sage Foundation. Forest Hills was an attractive community of Tudor-style homes and spacious open areas, located in the Queens section of New York City and based on a plan by Frederick Olmsted, Jr. The development was similar to the Garden City idea in that it was located away from New York's built-up core, there was adequate space for gardens, and the houses were designed to "encourage life out of doors."[49] Forest Hills also demonstrated how community amenities such as open areas and playgrounds could be incorporated into the plan of development when land ownership was centralized, although the Sage Foundation sold lots and houses to individual buyers without provision for continued collective control. Grosvenor Atterbury, architect for the project, declared that the Garden City was "primarily a means of protection against our modern land speculators." Yet the benefits of this protection went to those who needed it least. The town was built for middle- and upper-middle-income residents, since that was the only way to make the project profitable and, thus, a practical model for others to follow. Atterbury wrote in defense of the project that it was "essential to the finan-

[48] "The Movement in America," p. 252; Bliss, "The Garden Cities Association in America," pp. 268-69.
[49] See Samuel Howe, "Forest Hills Gardens," p. 154.

cial success of the enterprise that the size and quality of the houses be suited to the value of the property upon which they are placed."[50] The effect of this idea in the case of Queens, where land values were already escalating due to speculation, was that no low-income housing would be built. For its part, the Russell Sage Foundation acknowledged that the homes in Forest Hills were beyond the financial reach of the unfortunate classes whom Howard had hoped to assist. The foundation rationalized this development on the grounds that it was sponsoring other projects for the benefit of the poor, although these never materialized.[51]

Other proclaimed "Garden Cities" built in the early twentieth century included Shaker Heights in Cleveland, an upper class suburb; Torrance, California, an industrial suburb named after its founder, Jared S. Torrance; and the two model suburbs built by the Regional Plan Association—Sunnyside, in the Queens section of New York City, and the better-known example of Radburn, New Jersey. These communities addressed to the need for urban deconcentration, but, with the exception of Torrance, they provided a suburban solution only for people who were better off and could afford it. Moreover, accommodating the Garden City idea to American conditions meant stripping it of its association with collective ownership and control of land. Although centralized control of land, achieved through single ownership, was necessary to incorporate collective amenities into the development of these communities, none practiced collective control after homes and lots were sold. By the 1920s, the Garden City concept in the United States had lost any association with collective control of land or the housing of workers and the poor; it signified little more than environmentally conscious, low-density developments for those able to afford a surburban haven.[52] Where we do see atten-

[50] "Forest Hills Gardens," p. 565.

[51] See Scott, *American City Planning*, pp. 90-91.

[52] During the New Deal era, Roosevelt brain truster Rexford Tugwell promoted "greenbelt towns," partly modeled on Howard's Garden City concept, through the offices of the Resettlement Administration. This effort was steeped in controversy from the beginning: Roosevelt approved eight projects, Congress cut the number to five, one was eliminated by opposition from a local housing commission, and another was stopped by a court injunction. The three greenbelt towns that were built—Greenbelt at Berwyn, Maryland; Greenhills near Cincinnati; and Greendale outside Milwaukee—were hampered by limited funding and were never as large as planned. Moreover, they were continually fought by real estate interests and denounced as "communist towns"; see Glaab and Brown, *History of Urban America*, pp. 263-71.

tion to worker housing, however, was in the building of planned
industrial communities.

INDUSTRIAL TOWN PLANNING

A number of planned industrial towns were built by large business
corporations in the late nineteenth and early twentieth centuries.
Pullman, Illinois is the best known of these, although there were
a number of others, including Gary, Indiana and Homestead,
Pennsylvania. Most were on a smaller scale than Pullman, however. These towns were established for a variety of reasons: to find
cheap land on which to build new factories, to be near raw materials, to shape the sociocultural environment of the workforce,
and to remove workers from the radicalizing influence of cities
with large concentrations of workers. Journalist Graham R. Taylor, commenting on the latter impulse, wrote of one urban factory
superintendent who despaired that the sight of strikers parading
past his plant caused a fever to spread among his employees. "He
thought that if the plants were moved to the suburbs, the workingmen could not be so frequently inoculated [sic] with infection,"
wrote Taylor.[53]

The ends that induced these firms to establish new towns—
their desire to control the social and political environment of their
workforce, for example—led in many cases to their becoming
landlords as well as employers. Additionally, they wanted to avoid
the tax that land speculation and speculatively built housing imposed upon the community. Land speculation increased worker
housing costs, which translated into higher wage demands; if they
could hold down housing costs, they reasoned, they could keep
wages down as well. Yet this control over housing costs and workers' residential environment came at a price. In speculatively built
towns, struggle within the workplace and the living place was bi-
furcated: in one domain, workers were pitted against their capitalist employers and, in the other, against landlords and "property
capital." In proprietary company towns, however, this bifurcation
of struggle was destroyed. Here, the employer was also the landlord and housing developer, creating a politically volatile situation
in which workers' frustrations and complaints concerning wages
and working conditions and housing and rent could all be focused
on a single employer-landlord.

[53] *Satellite Cities: A Study of Industrial Suburbs*, pp. 23-25.

The "model" village of Pullman, Illinois clearly demonstrated the dangers to capital of combining the roles of employer and land-lord.[54] Influential both as a model of paternalism and because of its eventual failure, Pullman was built to contain a giant new factory for the manufacture of Pullman sleeping cars and to establish a residential community for the factory's employees. As originally laid out, it consisted of row upon row of two- to five-family build-ings; an area of large, three-story tenements; and a grouping of de-tached and semi-detached homes, all organized in a rectangular grid. At the town's center was a giant building covering a whole block; in it were a theatre, library, and other cultural facilities in-tended for the uplift of town residents. The central area of town also contained a church—built on American Protestant lines, though intended for the use of all the town's denominations—a school, a stable, and a grand hotel. The latter was the only place in Pullman where liquor could be purchased. One of the most attrac-tive features of the town was the park located on the Calumet lakefront: it was built to accommodate a variety of sports and was encircled by a scenic parkway intended for Sunday drives.

"In ways of material comforts and beautiful surroundings Pull-man probably offered to the majority of its residents quite as much as they were in a position to enjoy, and in many cases, even more," asserted Harvard professor Richard T. Ely, who later wrote a trenchant critique of the town.[55] For its founder and proprietor, George Pullman, the town was both a profit-seeking venture and an exercise in practical philanthropy. As a commercial enterprise, the town was expected to be an economical site for Pullman's sleeping car works—efficiently laid out, located on cheap land with good rail and water links, and housing a captive labor force. Moreover, the whole operation, including the residential housing, was calculated to pay a 6-percent return. Pullman believed that by using mass construction techniques and taking advantage of cen-tralized land ownership—thus avoiding the tax imposed by land speculation—it was possible to build decent and affordable worker housing, provided sound business practices were followed. The se-cret to all this, the basis of the "Pullman system," as Pullman was fond of noting, was that "[w]e are landlord and employers. That is all there is of it."[56] By joining these roles, Pullman hoped to pro-

---

[54] On the history of Pullman, see Buder, *Pullman*.
[55] Quoted, ibid., p. 73.
[56] Quoted in Richard C. Wade's foreward, ibid., p. vii.

duce a "superior type of American workingman."[57] This was Pullman's exercise in practical philanthropy—practical because it would pay an immediate 6-percent return and provide the basis for further profit-making. As Pullman historian Stanley Buder has written: "The physical planning of the town was for social ends. Not only were the needs of the inhabitants to be anticipated and met, but they were to be directed and shaped." Through his control of the town, Pullman hoped to engender "habits of respectability among his employees," by which he meant "propriety and good manners," cleanliness and neatness of appearance, industriousness and sobriety, and self-improvement through education and savings.[58] And as subsequent events made clear, he also expected loyalty to the company and deference to managerial authority.

As a profit-seeking venture, the village of Pullman was never successful. Although George Pullman sought to give a contrary impression, the rate of return on investment never exceeded 4.5 percent (in the two years before a strike erupted in 1894, it was 3.82 percent).[59] Moreover, Pullman's desire to prove the merit of his model town prevented him from always employing "sound business methods." Although the Pullman Company maintained that it had no special obligation to its employees, during the business recession from 1883 to mid-1886, Pullman tried to keep his men employed by taking contracts at a loss, realizing how disastrous closing the shops would be for his model town. And when the strike was called in 1894, Pullman found himself unable to evict residents for nonpayment of rent, meaning, in effect, that the company subsidized a strike against itself.[60]

If the town was unsuccessful as a profit-making venture, it was also unsuccessful from the standpoint of social control, for it did not produce labor peace—far from it. The Pullman strike of 1894 lasted four months and led to a nationwide service boycott of Pullman cars by members of Eugene Debs's fledgling American Railroad Union. Although the strike was eventually broken and the union destroyed, the violence and disruption caused by the strike and the worker bitterness it spawned gave the lie to Pullman's belief that the interests of labor and capital could be harmonized within the Pullman system. Nor was the worker radicalism occa-

[57] Ibid., p. 61.
[58] Ibid., pp. 70, 61.
[59] Ibid., p. 91.
[60] Ibid., pp. 138-39.

sioned by the strike a temporary phenomenon. After the town of Pullman was absorbed by Chicago, it became a banner ward for the Socialist Party whose candidates regularly polled 12 to 18 percent of the vote as late as 1915; and the ward produced Chicago's first Socialist alderman.[61] The strike also helped turn Eugene Debs to the cause of socialism.

Although many social reformers were initially supportive of Pullman, most had turned against the community before the strike. Richard T. Ely's opinion that the Pullman style was an exercise in "benevolent, well-wishing feudalism" appears to have predominated in the reform community, even before the events of 1894.[62] The strike was more important for what it taught capitalists; for them, it was an object lesson in the dangers of combining the roles of landlord and employer. Legally, the fate of Pullman as a proprietary town was sealed by an 1898 ruling of the Illinois Supreme Court. In a suit brought by the Illinois attorney general, the court ruled that the Pullman Company was not chartered to engage in the real estate business and would have to divest itself of its real estate holdings. More important, however, was the report of the commission established by President Grover Cleveland to study the cause of the strike. The commission concluded that the strike had been caused by the company's policy of reducing wages during the business recession of 1894 while holding rents constant. The company objected to this tracing of events, pointing out that only one-third of its employees rented homes from the company; as Buder has written, however, this counter argument missed the essential point. "To the workers it was common sense that, since the company dispensed wages with its right hand and collected with its left, the two must be coordinated to leave the residents something to live on."[63] It was this "common sense" that impressed upon manufacturers the value of keeping separate ownership and control of the workplace and living place.

In a sad irony, the failure of Pullman, Illinois caused subsequent company towns to be less responsive to the housing and community resource needs of worker-residents. The organizers of company towns were fearful of becoming home builders or landlords, and of providing community facilities that might make them appear paternalistic, both of which the Pullman strike had shown to

[61] Graham Taylor, *Satellite Cities*, pp. 63-64.
[62] "Pullman: A Social Study," p. 465.
[63] *Pullman*, p. 161.

be dangerous policies. This fear was evident, for example, in the founding of Gary, Indiana by the U.S. Steel Corporation in 1906.[64] Named after the company's chairman, Elbert H. (Judge) Gary, the town was to be the site of a giant new steelworks, replacing the many scattered works acquired by J. P. Morgan in 1901 when he purchased Andrew Carnegie's steel interests and combined them with his own in one of the largest business mergers in American history. Although the town of Gary was billed as an "industrial utopia" by its founders, it was a typical company town, built to house workers from the company's steel plant rather than as a model industrial town.[65] To avoid the mistakes of Pullman, U.S. Steel officials did not want to become either home builders or landlords. Yet, because they were not content to leave the organization of the town to speculative builders, they ended up becoming both.

Like most company towns, Gary was designed by company engineers who were unfamiliar with town planning principles and used "rule of thumb" planning techniques.[66] The town was laid out in a rigid gridiron, and the placement of trees along residential streets and the reservation of land for two parks were the extent of efforts to make the town pleasant and attractive. In his study of industrial suburbs, Graham Taylor contrasted the care taken by the company in planning its steelworks with the lack of concern it demonstrated for making the town convenient and attractive for its inhabitants.

> The placing of the blast furnaces was dictated by the speed of a neighboring locomotive on a curving switch track. Instead of setting the stacks parallel or at right angles to the tracks, "they were placed at an angle of twenty-two degrees, allowing a 200-foot radius for the entering switch." By such careful computations it was sought to avoid the moment wasted, to save the smallest fraction of a degree of heat which might otherwise be regained. So much for transporting metal. But a workman who lives a mile away from the mill gate has needlessly to crisscross the checker-board streets of the town, for a distance easily calculable by the old formula that the square

[64] On the founding of Gary, see Mohl and Betten, "The Failure of Industrial City Planning: Gary, Indiana, 1906-1910," pp. 203-15.

[65] The quoted term is from Fuller, "An Industrial Utopia: Building Gary, Indiana to Order," p. 1482, quoted in Mohl and Betten, "Gary, Indiana," p. 203.

[66] Mohl and Betten, "Gary, Indiana," p. 203.

of the hypotenuse of a right-angled triangle is equal to the sum of the squares of the other two sides.[67]

To avoid becoming a home builder or landlord, U.S. Steel set up a wholly owned subsidiary, the Gary Land Company, which was to organize the town into building and house lots, install improvements such as streets and sidewalks, and offer the lots for sale. Yet the company was wary of leaving the town's development entirely to market forces. To prevent land speculation, a proviso was attached to lot sales requiring that the land be built upon in eighteen months. The lots were slow to sell, however, since only higher-paid employees could afford to purchase lots and build houses, especially in the stipulated time period. Thus, the Gary Land Company built homes on the lots, and when it became evident that most workers could not afford these company-built homes, the company began building barracks-style rental units, becoming in effect a landlord, although it never sought to house all its employees. Many of the company's lowest-paid workers, most of whom were recent immigrants, ended up in speculatively built housing at the edge of the city, in an area known as "Hunkyville" because of its large immigrant population. The result was that two Garys were built: one planned by the company as an appendage of its steelworks, with minimal attention given to workers' residential needs, the other, much worse, built by speculators and shysters with no objective save speculative gain.[68]

The problem of providing housing for the lowest-paid workers continued to dog industrial town builders. The fact that adequate housing could not be built at a price workers could afford was embarrassing testimony to the value of workers' wages. Where workers were forced to fend for themselves, the result was typically the erection of a shantytown, usually on the outskirts of the city and constituting housing of the worst description. And where company housing was erected for the lowest-paid workers, it was typically of the barracks variety. Thus, we find Taylor describing Ensley, Alabama, a mill town built by the Tennessee Coal, Iron and Railroad Company on the outskirts of Birmingham, as an "industrial barracks." On the other side of Birmingham, almost hidden by the steel company's blast furnace, was the cotton mill village of Avondale. There, 600 employees made their home in 130 "unpainted down-at-the-heel company houses" owned by a for-

[67] *Satellite Cities*, p. 8.
[68] Mohl and Betten, "Gary, Indiana," pp. 206-13.

mer governor of the state. "A more depressing neighborhood it would be difficult to find anywhere," Taylor said of this village of mud streets and two-room houses without modern conveniences.[69]

As Pullman demonstrated, there was a danger to manufacturers in becoming both landlord and employer. Yet, as the building of Gary showed, the exigencies of creating an industrial town from scratch often gave the company little choice but to become a home builder and landlord. Moreover, employers were evidently aware of the value of preventing speculatively built housing, since this policy enabled the company to hold down housing costs and reduce wage pressures. In a 1905 study of industrial housing and model communities, an English author counted fifteen planned communities in the United States. Most of these were industrial towns built by factory owners, and some had been established as early as the 1850s (all were built before Pullman).[70] In most instances, the housing was built by the company and rented to employees, giving the company control over town development through its ownership of buildings and land. One interesting case was Leclaire, Missouri, built by H. O. Nelson, owner of a large painting and plumbing business. Here, the company erected and sold housing but, to prevent speculation, reserved the right to repurchase at "cost price" the home of anyone who wanted to leave the community or dispose of his property.[71] Reflecting the social control objectives of industrial town builders, in almost every community noted by this English observer the company forbade the sale of liquor within the town.

There were exceptions to the mean conditions typifying most industrial towns. Taylor discussed one, the town of Fairfield, Alabama.[72] Lying just beyond Ensley, it was built by the Tennessee Coal, Iron and Railroad Company following the company's absorption by U.S. Steel. Whereas, at Gary, U.S. Steel set up its own real estate subsidiary, in Fairfield a local real estate company was used to organize the town. This firm in turn employed the services of George H. Miller, a Boston landscape architect and town planner whose familiarity with town design principles was apparent in Fairfield's curvilinear streets and broad house lots, its districting

[69] *Satellite Cities*, pp. 237, 234-35.

[70] Meakin, *Model Factories and Villages: Ideal Conditions of Labour and Housing*, pp. 382-416.

[71] Ibid., pp. 382-85.

[72] *Satellite Cities*, pp. 237-58.

scheme for regulating land use, and its projected civic center and central park, all of which set Fairfield in "radiant contrast" (in Taylor's words) to nearby Avondale and Ensley.[73] Yet Fairfield was the exception that proved the rule. The interest in aesthetically pleasing town planning remained cut off from industrial town building. And, conversely, the concern with worker housing that was forced upon industrial town builders by the nature of their undertaking remained separate from formal town planning.

LESSONS OF ROADS NOT TAKEN

The three planning efforts discussed in this chapter were responses to different aspects of the congestion problem, but none of them succeeded in becoming part of the mainstream of American town building and city planning. Benjamin Marsh and the CCP sought to reduce congestion in the living place for the working population, the American Garden City movement to pioneer a congestion-free model of urban development, and industrial town builders to build new plants and towns on cheap land away from the radicalizing influence of large concentrations of workers. In responding to these different faces of the congestion problem, each group sought to assert social needs and collective interests against the private interests governing the town building process. This endeavor led to their placing limits on land speculation and to attempts to displace the property capitalist in urban development. These planning efforts were therefore similar to earlier responses to the property contradiction, such as the regulation of tenement houses, park building, and aesthetic planning. Unlike the park and City Beautiful movements, however, these planning efforts did not become part of the programmatic basis of formal city planning—because they did not adequately correspond with the interests of the city's business class.

The building of company towns did not become an alternative basis of urban development and was resorted to only infrequently after the failure of Pullman, Illinois because combining the roles of landlord/developer and employer threatened employers' ability to control labor. Similarly, the American Garden City movement did not achieve the practical consequences of its English counterpart, and neither effort realized Ebenezer Howard's ideal of community control of town development, because they could not

---

[73] Ibid., p. 239.

break the hegemony of property capital's control of land and housing. They could not achieve both adequate capitalization and community control. Finally, the effort of Marsh and the CCP to control congestion in the interest of the working population did not provide a thematic basis for the development of formal city planning, because their attack on land speculators, in the absence of appreciable benefits for the larger business community, made this program politically ineffective. The implication, then, is that those responses to the property contradiction that "work" and are incorporated into town building and city planning are those that are either compatible with the interests of property capital or, if not, correspond with the interest of a broad section of the business community. In the following chapter, we see the adoption of an approach to city planning that superseded the City Beautiful orientation, and that better corresponded with the needs of business, albeit without resolving either the property contradiction or the capitalist-democracy contradiction.

SEVEN

Planning the City Practical

DESPITE the efforts of Benjamin Marsh and others to focus attention on the problem of population congestion, the aesthetic orientation remained dominant in city planning through the first decade of the twentieth century. So many plans for city beautification were prepared by architects and landscape architects working for private civic and business groups that the term city planning became partially stereotyped by this association: city planning came to be seen as a project of private civic and business organizations, carried out by architects and landscape architects and aimed at improving the physical appearance of the city. In addition to the City Beautiful ventures discussed in Chapter 5, planning projects of one sort or another were undertaken before 1909 in Chicago, Oakland, Los Angeles, San Jose, San Diego, Colorado Springs, Detroit, Providence and New Haven, as well as in a number of smaller cities and towns. Frederick Ford, an early leader of the planning movement, commented that most of these plans were "made from the aesthetic viewpoint," although he also observed a growing attention to hygienic and economic concerns.[1] It was this interest in the "practical side" of urban development that eventually spelled the demise of the City Beautiful.

This chapter examines how City Beautiful planning was superseded by an approach to planning that took as its ideological model the City Practical. This new orientation sought to create a more economical and efficient system of land use and transportation—more economical and efficient, that is, in terms of the needs of the emerging business system. It will be shown how the aesthetic orientation was found wanting, how the City Practical approach came to dominate city planning, and how even this approach was prevented from achieving its aims.

The City Practical provided a response to both the contradictions that have structured the history of urban planning. It responded to the property contradiction—the contradiction between the private ownership and control of land and the social

---

[1] "The Scope of City Planning in the United States," p. 71.

needs that land must serve—by asserting a social need, not for a more visually attractive city, but for a more economical and efficient system of land use and transportation. It was a concern for economy and efficiency in the urban environment that corresponded with the introduction of Taylorism in the realm of work. Here we see the emergence of one of the aspects of urban planning analytically defined in Chapter 1: planning to provide for those elements of the built environment (for example, bridges, harbors, streets, and transit systems) that are used by capitalists as "means of production." These public facilities, although collectively owned and produced by the state, are as important to the system of private production as are privately produced and appropriated inputs. Contemporary planning theorist Edmond Preteceille refers to these immobilized fixed-capital investments as "urban use values." In his view, the state must not only produce the urban use values needed by the system of private production; planners and the state must also provide for the coordination of these facilities in space, creating what he terms "new, complex use values."[2] With the rise of the City Practical orientation, we encounter efforts to secure Preteceille's "complex use values." The need for state intervention to provide for the production and maintenance of these urban use values, and to ensure their coordination in space, was asserted as a social need against the private purposes governing the town building process.

Making possible this intervention and the accompanying coordinative role of government required that institutional arrangements be devised. The most important of these adaptations associated with the City Practical were land use zoning and the independent plan commission. These institutional arrangements provided a way of regulating or balancing between the asserted need for a more economical and efficient system of land use and transportation and the private rights and purposes of those who owned and developed urban land. Yet they were also a response to the capitalist-democracy contradiction. In the City Practical era, planning became a governmental activity; there was an evolution from the private planning of the City Beautiful and a transcendence of the private origins of most City Practical projects. This expansion of government activity carried with it the prospect of democratizing the control of urban development, of submitting the city building process to the democratic control of property owners

2 "Urban Planning," p. 70.

and non-property owners alike. As we shall see, transportation planning, land use zoning, and the independent plan commission provided a way of guarding against this danger—or what would have been a danger—to capital. These innovations made it possible to partially governmentalize the control of urban development while insulating the planning mechanism from public involvement, thereby preventing the control of urban development from being democratized. These practices and institutional arrangements were thus expressions of and ways of coping with, of holding in balance, both the property contradiction and the capitalist-democracy contradiction. Yet, as we shall see, these contradictions were far from being resolved; they appeared again in new problems, engendering new conflict and requiring further institutional adaptations.

TRANSITIONAL DEVELOPMENTS

The year 1909 represented a turning point in the history of planning. In that year, the United States Supreme Court upheld the constitutionality of the height zone established in Boston. In Wisconsin, legislation was adopted authorizing large- and medium-sized cities to appoint city planning commissions, following the lead of Hartford, which established the nation's first city planning commission in 1907. At Harvard, the first city planning course to be offered at an American university was taught, while at the University of Liverpool, the world's first academic department of city planning was organized. It was also in 1909 that Benjamin Marsh published his *Introduction to City Planning*, urging American cities to adopt the German "zone system" and to engage in municipal land purchases to control peripheral development. The most important developments in 1909, however, were the convening of the first national conference on city planning (NCCP) and the publication of Daniel Burnham's Chicago Plan.

The latter two events signaled a change in the substantive scope and dominant orientation of city planning. The speeches and papers delivered at the first national city planning conference provided ample evidence of the growing disenchantment with the aesthetic approach to planning. The conference participants also showed an interest in expanding the scope of planning to include matters of land use and transportation, as well as housing and sanitary conditions in the city's slum. The Burnham Plan, in addition to offering the standard litany of City Beautiful proposals, recommended improvements in the city's street and transportation system aimed at making the city more convenient and efficient. Also included were recommendations pertaining to the city's private rail system. The Burnham Plan thus signified an interest in creating a more practical and efficient system of land use and transportation and a desire to include private facilities within the scope of planning.

First National Conference on City Planning

This first national conference on city planning, held in Washington, D.C., was organized by the Committee on Congestion of Population under the leadership of Benjamin Marsh. Reflecting the interest of its organizers, the meeting was officially known as the "Conference on City Planning and the Congestion Problem." It coincided with the CCP's "City Plan Exhibition" in Washington and was organized by Marsh on the model of the earlier "Congestion Show." Through Marsh's skillful promotional efforts, the conference gained the backing of Washington officialdom. House Speaker Joe Cannon was in attendance, and the Senate District Committee held hearings on city planning and housing in conjunction with the conference and published the conference proceedings as a committee document.

Almost to the man, the speakers at the conference were critical of the City Beautiful orientation in planning. And this was not because the conferecs were unrepresentative of the planning movement. Although Daniel Burnham was absent, most of the leading figures in city planning were there, including Frederick Olmsted, Jr., Charles Robinson, John Nolen, Frederick Ford, and George B. Ford. The conferees were probably not surprised to hear Marsh proclaim that city planning was "fundamentally a health and, hence, an economic proposition."[3] But they were perhaps more interested in hearing New York landscape architect Robert A. Pope's speech in which he decried the aesthetic orientation in planning. Pope contended that the assumption that the "first duty of city planning is to beautify" had led to the expenditure of vast sums for ornamental public works benefiting the "wealthy and leisure classes, who of all society need these advantages the least." Reversing the logic of City Beautiful planning, he declared, "City planning for social and economic ends will logically result in a

---

[3] "Economic Aspects of City Planning," p. 105.

genuinely and completely beautiful city."[4] Similarly, Frederick Ford, Hartford city engineer and secretary of the Hartford Planning Commission, observed that the aesthetic orientation could no longer be sustained in light of the "civic awakening" to the need for "some well-defined policy looking well into the future," which would prevent the unwise expenditure of local public works funds.[5]

In calling for a reorientation of planning, the conferees advocated that planning address itself to two distinct needs. One was for a more economical and efficient organization of land use and transportation, which led to proposals for land use zoning and improvements in the city's street and transportation system. The other was to relieve population congestion and improve housing and living conditions in the city's slum. As noted above, this second concern was represented in the official title of the conference, although reference to "congestion" was dropped from the title after the second conference. Frederick Olmsted, Jr., explained this change in his address at the 1911 conference by stating that the congestion problem was integral to city planning and hence did not require separate mention.[6] Yet the facts suggested otherwise. In the years following 1909, concern for housing and sanitary conditions in the city's slum, which is what Benjamin Marsh meant by the "congestion problem," became more and more separated from formal city planning, leading to an exodus from the organized planning movement of social workers and social reformers like Marsh. Organizationally, this division of responsibility was symbolized by the founding in 1910 of the National Housing Association as a separate organization for housing reformers.

The turning away from focusing explicitly on the congestion problem demonstrated the wide appeal of a program aimed at improving the economy and efficiency of the city's system of land use and transportation. It also indicated that the congestion problem meant different things to different people. Henry Morgenthau, the millionaire financier who served for a time as honorary president of the CCP, was one of those speaking against the aesthetic orientation at the first planning conference. He urged a focus on the congestion problem, but not for the same reasons as Marsh. The congestion problem needed to be attacked, he said, be-

[4] "What is Needed in City Planning?" pp. 75-76.
[5] "City Planning," p. 71.
[6] "Reply on Behalf of the City Planning Conference," p. 4.

cause it bred "physical disease, moral depravity, discontent, and socialism." Moreover, as a suburban land speculator, Morgenthau saw population congestion as a problem requiring the establishment of height zones, the separation of manufacturing and residential areas, and the provision of transit facilities "to move your population away from the center of cities," all of which comported with his interests as a speculator.[7] In viewing the congestion problem in this way, Morgenthau could find common cause with those who advocated planning to achieve economy and efficiency in the division of land use and in the street and transportation system.

In conjunction with their efforts to reorient city planning, the conferees at the first planning conference urged greater public control over private development. Speaker after speaker promoted the "zone system" used in German cities to regulate the height and bulk of buildings and to control the pattern of land use. Frederick Olmsted, Jr., devoted his entire speech to the progress of city planning in Europe. In addition to advocating the German zone system, he called on American cities to engage in municipal land purchases as German cities had done—both to control peripheral development and to enable the city to profit from its own expansion.[8] Likewise, Hartford City Engineer Frederick Ford was insistent on the need for more government control of private development. "The conditions which now exist point conclusively to the necessity of more restrictive regulations concerning the occupancy and use of private property," Ford told his fellow planners. Accordingly, he called for land use zoning, advance planning for the location of streets and other public facilities, and "suitable restrictions" on the use of private property in new areas.[9]

No one at the first planning conference spoke against the adoption of zoning. On the one hand, this consensus signified a desire to submit urban development to some measure of collective control rather than continuing to rely on an unregulated market system. On the other, it attested to the adaptability of zoning to a variety of purposes. Land use zoning appealed to social reformers like Marsh as a means of limiting population density in the city's slum, and to speculators and developers like Morgenthau as a way of protecting property values by preventing incompatible uses of land. And it appealed to a variety of planners because it could be

[7] Morgenthau, "A National Constructive Programme for City Planning," pp. 59-60.
[8] "The Scope and Results of City Planning in Europe," pp. 63-70.
[9] "City Planning," p. 72.

used as an instrument of plan implementation; in this regard, ample notice was given to the Supreme Court's decision upholding the constitutionality of Boston's height zones.

Yet, demonstrating how some forms of government intervention commanded more support than others, the conferees disagreed on government's role in housing. Benjamin Marsh favored a larger government role but stopped short of advocating government-built housing. Speaking before the Senate District Committee in connection with the first planning conference, he called for a study of the feasibility of constructing government housing in Washington, citing the finding of the U.S. Homes Commission that the capital had a shortage of decent and affordable housing for low-paid government workers. But he did not go further because he feared, based on his examination of public housing in Liverpool, that government-subsidized housing would be used by employers as a pretext for reducing wages. As he told members of the District Committee, employers might say to their workers: " 'Very Well; if you can get good housing for half what it is worth, and the Government "pays the freight" we will pay you that much lower wages.' " Marsh called for higher wages rather than public housing as the best way to improve worker housing, thereby indicating his understanding of the connection between issues in the workplace and those in the living place.[10] By contrast, conference participant Andrew W. Crawford, who was associate city solicitor of Philadelphia, argued against including housing matters in city planning. He believed that if the definition of city planning was broad enough to include a concern for housing, it might as well include "all the physical aspects of the . . . city."[11] Although Crawford saw this broad scope as a danger, it was precisely what other conference participants had in mind.

At this first city planning conference, attention was also given to the institutional form and intellectual substance of planning— to its character as a method of policy formulation. For Frederick Ford, the intellectual task of city planning was to harmonize the relationship between municipal functions and avoid "lopsided, disorderly, and unsymmetrical development."[12] He urged the appointment of bodies to oversee municipal development, using as an institutional model the Hartford Plan Commission, of which

[10] "Statement of Mr. Benjamin Clarke Marsh," p. 10.
[11] "Discussion of the Papers of Mr. Olmsted and Mr. Ford," p. 82.
[12] "City Planning," p. 73.

he was secretary. The membership of this commission, as described by Ford, consisted of the heads of municipal departments with public works responsibilities, city council representatives, and private citizens appointed by the mayor to long, staggered terms. The formal powers of the Hartford Plan Commission were somewhat restricted, however. It had the power only to review public works proposals for their conformance with city planning, as well as limited authority to condemn excess land around public facilities. Moreover, the technical staff consisted only of Ford, who, as city engineer, was named permanent secretary of the commission.

There were others at the first conference who still believed in private planning. One was Munson Havens, secretary of the Cleveland Chamber of Commerce, who presented the Chamber-sponsored Cleveland Group Plan as a model for other cities to follow. Yet Havens' preference for private planning was based not so much on an aversion to government planning per se, as on a fear of the existing local officialdom. He argued that until businessmen and professionals began running for office and taking charge of local affairs, "the initiative for great public improvements must come from without rather than from within the minds of city officials."[13]

The major ingredients of the City Practical were thus in evidence at the first city planning conference. There was an awareness of the need to reorient city planning toward such practical matters as the economy and efficiency of the city's division of land use and of its street and transit system. This emphasis on economy and efficiency was presented as a new norm for planning intervention, displacing the earlier aesthetic orientation and posing a challenge to the concern for housing and congestion in the city's slum. By 1909, land use zoning and the independent plan commission already had been seized upon as institutional responses to the property contradiction, as means of striking a balance between the asserted social need for economy and efficiency in the system of land use and transportation on the one side and the private control of property on the other. Correspondingly, the formation of the independent plan commission as a partial-step toward government planning—partial because the control of planning was still in private hands—indicated an emerging response to the capitalist-democracy contradiction. Yet, as we shall see, the critical failure of

13 "Remarks," p. 84.

the City Practical, its failure to provide an adequate base for sustaining support for and implementing planning, can be traced to its equivocal responses to these contradictions. In Daniel Burnham's 1909 Chicago Plan, we see how the City Practical orientation developed and was applied in a particular case, and how it was stimulated by the involvement of members of Chicago's business community.

The Chicago Plan

Daniel Burnham's Chicago Plan represented the apogee of the City Beautiful. Consistent with the designer's injunction to "Make no Little Plans," the plan covered a region stretching from Kenosha, Wisconsin to the north to Michigan City, Indiana to the south.[14] Within this area of four thousand square miles, Burnham proposed two systems: a network of highways organized radially and concentrically around Chicago as the hub of the region, and an outer chain of forest preserves and parkways, together with twenty-five miles of lakeshore development to be created by landfill. In its proposals for a lakefront park, a scenic lakefront drive, a system of broad boulevards, and a downtown civic center, the plan held to the traditions of the City Beautiful, creating a city for "merchant princes" befitting its locus of support.[15]

Yet, attesting to the limitations of business-designer collaborations, the plan failed to address health and housing conditions in the city's slums. Only one paragraph, inserted in the middle of a discussion of needed street improvements, was devoted to the problem of slum housing. And here Burnham's proposals were a combination of the ideas of Haussmann and Veiller. The "remedy" for the slum was "the same as has been resorted to the world over": first, the "cutting of broad thoroughfares through the unwholesome district" (credit Haussmann), and second, "the establishment and remorseless enforcement of sanitary regulations which shall ensure adequate air-space for the dwellers in crowded areas" (credit Veiller).[16]

It was in the area of transportation that the Burnham Plan broke with the traditions of the City Beautiful, and it was here as well that it showed the influence of members of Chicago's Commercial

[14] The quotation is from a speech by Daniel Burnham, quoted in Burnham and Bennett, *Plan of Chicago*, p. v.

[15] The quoted phrase is from Scott, *American City Planning*, p. 108.

[16] Burnham and Bennett, *Plan of Chicago*, p. 108.

Club, sponsors of the plan. Going beyond proposals for broad thoroughfares, radial boulevards, and improved grade crossings—the typical fare of City Beautiful plans—it called for a regional system of highways centering on Chicago; a system of freight handling for land and water transportation; the consolidation of railroad facilities; and the creation of elevated, surface, and subway loops around an enlarged business district. These recommendations were aimed at making Chicago's center a more attractive and efficient hub of business activity. Improved access to the central business district was to be provided by the system of regional highways and the proposed intercity train system. At the same time, freight handling facilities were to be moved to the outskirts of the city in an effort to bring about the "ultimate removal of the wholesale and heavy business interests from the downtown district."[17] These proposals owed to the influence of the Commercial Club and certain of its members and committees. The recommendation for a central clearing and warehouse yard in the southwestern part of the city grew from the work of the club's Committee on Railway Terminals, and the proposal for consolidating rail passenger service outside the central business area was based on an earlier plan by Frederic A. Delano, president of the Wabash Railroad and secretary of the Commercial Club's General Planning Committee.[18]

As significant as these specific proposals was the view of the city that inspired them. The city was conceived of in the report as "a center of industry and traffic."[19] This conception corresponded nicely with the emerging interest in rationalizing the system of land use and transportation, demonstrating the movement away from the City Beautiful ideal. Yet it was also important as a statement of political ideology: it presented a unitary concept of the city as a place of business, enabling businessmen to put forward their interest in rationalizing the system of land use and transportation for purposes of business and commerce as the truest expression of the city's collective interest.

The Burnham Plan was also important for the planning experience it gave to Burnham's business collaborators. Sitting with Frederic Delano on the Commercial Club's General Planning Committee were Charles H. Wacker, a wealthy merchant, and

[17] Graham R. Taylor, "The New Chicago," p. 1556.
[18] See Robert Walker, *Planning Function*, p. 17, and Scott, *American City Planning*, p. 105.
[19] Burnham and Bennett, *Plan of Chicago*, p. 4.

Charles D. Norton, an insurance executive. Wacker became permanent secretary of the Chicago Plan Commission, which was formed upon completion of the Burnham Plan. In that capacity, he served as a skillful and effective campaigner on behalf of the Burnham Plan for the next twenty years. Norton, whose faith in planning was demonstrated by his success in persuading fellow Amherst College alumni to prepare a plan for that institution, moved to New York City; there, as a director of the Russell Sage Foundation, he became the driving force behind the 1929 Regional Plan for New York and its Environs. Delano also moved to New York, where he was recruited by Norton to serve as a director of the Russell Sage Foundation; the two then worked together in promoting the Sage-sponsored New York Regional Plan. In the 1930s, Delano was appointed by his nephew, Franklin Delano Roosevelt, to head the Natural Resources Planning Board, the New Deal's most significant experiment in national planning for public works and natural resource management.[20]

Besides helping to change the orientation of city planning, the Chicago Plan was instrumental in formulating a response to the capitalist-democracy contradiction. It served as a model of how the planning function could become partially incorporated into local government without thereby being democratized. Although the plan began as a private effort, its sponsors soon recognized the need for government support. It was particularly the moral sanction of government that was needed—to aid the promoters of the plan in presenting it as the embodiment of the community interest. Greater control over private development was not deemed necessary, first, because most of the plan's recommendations focused on public sector development, creating a need for improved government coordination but not for new authority. Second, where the plan did have an impact on private development, its recommendations were to be achieved through voluntary action—so the planners and sponsors hoped. The private sector recommendations centered on the consolidation and relocation of rail freight and passenger service, which, the plan report asserted, could be achieved through the "hearty cooperation" of the railroads, without government intervention.[21] Beyond this there was a belief on Burnham's part that "if the plan is really good it will commend it-

---

[20] On the role of Norton and Delano in promoting the Sage-sponsored New York Regional Plan, see Scott, *American City Planning*, pp. 198-204.

[21] Burnham and Bennett, *Plan of Chicago*, p. 139.

self to the progressive spirit of the times, and sooner or later it will be carried out."[22]

To gain government sanction and assistance, the Commercial Club recommended that an official city plan commission be created to engage in propaganda efforts on behalf of the plan. Chicago Mayor Fred Busse agreed and, with the consent of the city council, appointed a city plan commission, thereby transforming the planning effort from a private to a public, or at least semipublic, activity. The Chicago Plan Commission was unlike other plan commissions in its large size—it consisted of 328 of Chicago's "leading citizens." To make the commission manageable, a 27-member executive committee was formed, with those who had promoted the plan from the beginning in control. As noted above, Charles Wacker was named permanent secretary. To fill the position of managing director, he recruited Walter D. Moody, a brilliant public relations man who was working as secretary of the Chicago Association of Commerce (Chicago's Chamber of Commerce). Although the city did not officially adopt the Burnham Plan at this time, the commission adopted a creed that read, in part, "We are to make the Plan of Chicago our ideal and keep it before us—dare to recognize it—and to believe in it and build for it."[23]

The propaganda campaign orchestrated by Wacker and Moody is unrivaled in the annals of American city planning. The campaign was made possible through the largess of the Commercial Club and its members. The organization spent more than two hundred thousand dollars over twenty years to promote the plan, in addition to the one hundred thousand dollars spent on the initial development of the plan. One of the Chicago Plan Commission's first steps was the publication of a ninety-page booklet entitled "Chicago's Greatest Issue—A City Plan," which explained the plan in simple, concise prose. Addressed to the "Owners of Chicago," the pamphlet was distributed to all property owners in the city and to everyone paying over twenty-five dollars per month in rent. In addition, a slide show was prepared, at a cost of fifteen thousand dollars, for members to use in their presentations to groups throughout the city; in the first seven years, over four hundred such presentations were made. A two-reel "moving picture" contrasting existing conditions in Chicago with the grand future envisaged in the Chicago Plan was prepared. Chicago's

---

[22] Ibid., p. 2.
[23] See Wacker, "Gaining Public Support for a City Planning Movement," p. 227.

ministers were asked to preach a service on the humanitarian aspects of the plan, and a document entitled "Seed Thoughts for Sermons" was produced for their use. But the crowning accomplishment of Moody's brilliant campaign was the preparation of a school text extolling the virtues of the plan. Known as *Wacker's Manual*, although written by Moody, the text was adopted into the eighth grade curriculum in 1912 and was used in Chicago schools for over a decade.[24]

As with much future planning, the Chicago Plan Commission did not encourage citizen participation in the planning process; nor did it assume that future modifications of the plan would be necessary. The plan was instead treated as a civic bible: it was presented as a holistic document, produced by talented experts, that would surely be harmed if alterations by nonexperts were allowed. Expressing this view, Wacker stated that a planner's motto should be "First know you're right, and then go ahead." The Burnham plan was presented to the city "without hesitation," he declared, "because we knew our plan was right." He saw the planner's task as one of harmonizing the interests of various classes into a concrete plan and presenting it to the community as the expression of its collective interest. "Above all things," he argued, the city planner "must be able to show conclusively that the plan advocated is a plan not for a class but for all the people, and a plan not for a section, but for the entire city."[25]

Wacker had a somewhat less glorified view of the planner's role than did the authors of the Chicago Plan report. Chapter 2 of the report presents a history of the founding of "great cities" such as Rome, Athens, Venice, and Paris. The story told is how these cities emerged from the will, intelligence, and vision of great men—men presumably like Burnham and his collaborators. The authors appear wishful of the centralized authority that made possible the planning of these great cities. Crediting Haussmann with the "highest success" in replanning Paris, they observe that his planning task "corresponds with the work which must be done for Chicago." They suggest a parallel between the leadership of Napoleon and the role of Chicago businessmen: much as Napoleon gave free reign to Haussmann in the replanning of Paris, Chicago businessmen had a habit of entrusting great work "to those best fitted

[24] See Robert Walker, *Planning Function*, pp. 235-41; Walker's account is taken from an unpublished manuscript by Clifford J. Hynning, "The Planning of Metropolitan Chicago" (1937).

[25] Wacker, "Gaining Public Support," pp. 226, 231, 224.

to undertake it." Moreover, citizens would have to trust this leadership if their city was to achieve greatness. The chief reason some cities exercised such power over the imagination, the plan report contended, was the "intense loyalty on the part of the great body of citizens . . . which led them to strive to enhance the prestige and dignity of their city."[26] Parisians, it was asserted, "have always supported those who aimed to make their city grand and beautiful." Chicagoans presumably were to take their cue.

It took a combination of nerve, zeal, and great skill in public relations for Wacker, Moody, and their collaborators to present the Burnham-Commercial Club Plan as a plan "not for a class but for all the people." For it was a plan prepared by the civic arm of the wealthy elite, and it focused on their needs to the exclusion of Chicago's tenement poor. Yet, to the credit of their promotional ability, they were able to gain public support, or at least politically influential support, for carrying out key elements of the plan. The implementation of the plan began where the interest of its sponsors lay—with the recommendations concerning downtown streets and transportation.

The first street construction carried out in conjunction with the plan was the widening of Twelfth Street from the "Ghetto" (as it was termed in the plan) to the lakefront, a project approved by a large majority in a 1912 city referendum. This was an important part of the larger street project, since it provided the south baseline for the street system's central quadrangle. Street construction was also part of Burnham's program for improving slum areas—by driving thoroughfares through them. Following the Twelfth Street project, the Chicago Plan Commission secured authority for widening and extending Michigan Avenue. Although half the sixteen-million dollar cost of this project was assessed against neighboring property owners, it was later estimated that the increased property values stimulated by the project were over twelve times the amount of the assessment.[27] The plan commission also helped convince the Illinois Central Railroad to relinquish its riparian rights along the south lakeshore, making possible the erection of the Field Museum at the foot of Twelfth Street and the construction of lakefront parkland.

[26] See Burnham and Bennett, *Plan of Chicago*, pp. 18, 4, 18, 22; I was made more aware of the political implications of Burnham and Bennett's historical analysis by reading Wollner, "Daniel Burnham and the Tradition of the City Builder in Chicago: Technique, Ambition and City Planning," especially pp. 278-79.

[27] Thomas Adams, *Outline of Town and City Planning*, p. 203.

In seeking to build public support for the Burnham Plan, its sponsors found it useful to emphasize the plan's practical aspects. Discovering that the people of Chicago were, in the words of Charles Wacker, "preeminently practical," the Chicago Plan Commission attempted to demonstrate "that instead of 'Chicago Beautiful,' the Plan of Chicago could better be described by the phrase 'Chicago Practical.' "[28] This effort to emphasize the plan's practical aspects corresponded with changes in the field of planning that fostered a closer relationship between planners and the city's business community. Architect Arnold W. Brunner, who collaborated with Olmsted on the 1911 Rochester Plan, provided one of the best explanations for this changed orientation. "The City Beautiful failed—failed because it began at the wrong end," he declared at the 1912 planning conference. "Since utility and beauty go hand in hand, let us insist on utility. Since we have in mind a combination of science and art, let us emphasize science."[29] George B. Ford, a leader in the search for a "scientific" approach to planning, went further. "City planning," he observed at the 1913 conference, "is rapidly becoming as definite a science as pure engineering." If the task of planning is approached scientifically, carefully analyzing local conditions and ranking needed actions in terms of their urgency, he maintained, "one soon discovers that in almost every case there is one and only one, logical and convincing solution of the problems involved."[30]

Brunner and Ford's interest in scientific planning was no doubt influenced by the publication in 1911 of Frederick Taylor's *Principles of Scientific Management*. Taylor had shown how industrial efficiency could be improved through the application of "scientific management" aimed at eliminating wasted time and motion, leading municipal reformers to ask whether the same could not be done in the field of municipal administration. Ford and other proponents of scientific planning sought to extend the reach of scientific management by applying it to the pattern of land use and the layout of streets and transportation. The appeal of the efficiency norm associated with scientific management and scientific planning was that it seemed to transcend class interests. Yet, as Samuel Haber observes, *efficiency* had many meanings, not all of them unrelated to class interests. For example, it referred to a per-

[28] Wacker, "Gaining Public Support," p. 238.
[29] "The Meaning of City Planning," p. 24.
[30] "The City Scientific," p. 31.

sonal attribute—an efficient person was an effective person—carrying with it all sorts of latent class associations and meanings. It had an engineering meaning, referring to the relationship between inputs and outputs, and it had an economic meaning, describing the relationship between investment and profits. But *efficiency* was also applied to relationships between people, signifying "social harmony and the leadership of the 'competent.' "[31] In this latter application, the efficiency norm and the complementary concept of scientific management provided a way of reconciling democracy with the role of the expert, social harmony with social control, and planning with the market system.

The critical question remained "efficiency for whom?" George Ford answered this question in the preface to a 1917 survey of city planning conducted by the AIA. Commenting on the large number of aesthetically oriented plans that had been drawn up, he observed that city planning had been retarded by the emphasis on beautification. Speaking for the AIA's Committee on Town Planning, he declared that the committee "insisted with vigor that all city planning should start on a foundation of economic practicableness and good business; that it must be something which will appeal to the businessman, and to the manufacturer as sane and reasonable."[32]

The search for a new approach to planning and, simultaneously, for strengthened support for planning within the business community, did not go unrewarded. In a speech at the 1917 planning conference, business leader J. Horace McFarland, president of the American Civic Association, applauded the emerging efficiency orientation. Invoking the economic meaning of efficiency, he declared that city planning's aim was to "cause one dollar to do the work of two dollars or more." Businessmen and landowners needed a means of organizing the system of land use and transportation in their collective interest, and this effort to plan need not entail an abridgement of property rights, he maintained. Land use zoning, if applied with "forethought and wisdom," could "assure continuing [property] values" and prevent "wasting many millions of dollars through the business and residence movements arising from lack of plan." In McFarland's view, this was "com-

[31] Haber, *Efficiency and Uplift: Scientific Management in the Progressive Era, 1890-1920*, p. x; on the quest for efficiency among municipal reformers, see also Fox, *Better City Government*.

[32] Committee on Town Planning of the American Institute of Architects, *City Planning Progress in the United States*, p. iii.

mon sense applied to the common interest," the same business-minded common sense as "that which a wise citizen uses in building a home or store."[33]

McFarland was saying that individual property owners could not rely on the market system to ensure the conditions required to maintain and enhance the value of their property. The market system and fragmented land ownership prevented property owners from applying the same common sense and foresight to organizing the pattern of land use and transportation that they applied to building houses, stores, and factories. While all landowners had an interest in preventing land uses that diminished the value of their property, there was no way of protecting that interest against offending landowners, save through government. Accordingly, McFarland believed that government planning and regulation were required to impose external control on recalcitrant landowners in the interest of the property values of the many.

Transportation planning and land use zoning were two important areas in which there developed a realization of the need for government planning of the urban infrastructure. In both areas, we see how businessmen and property owners, aided by planners, came to recognize the benefits of some form of collective control organized through the state. We also see how the efficiency norm was used to justify this intervention on the grounds that it was in the collective interest.

Transportation Planning

Unlike the planning of private transit facilities, the interest in street planning was not entirely new. Colonial town planners regarded the street plan as the essential element of the town plan. And proposals for radial boulevards and scenic parkways were defining features of City Beautiful plans. In the City Practical era, however, the interest in street planning was more systematic. The emphasis was on creating an efficient overall street system rather than on incorporating scenic parkways and radial boulevards into the existing street pattern. This endeavor led to a rejection of standard street designs, including not only the rectangular grid, but also the baroque-style radial design, both of which were regarded as too formulaic. "The day has gone by for the unqualified

---

[33] "The Relation of City Planning to Business," pp. 156, 161, 157.

employment of definite systems," wrote planner John Nolen.[34] The idea instead was to adapt the street plan to the requirements of the city—to the configuration of the land, the flow of traffic, and the nature of the city's activities. This orientation corresponded with a conception of the city as "a depot and a distributing apparatus," in the words of an advocate of an engineering approach to planning.[35] The new interest in transportation planning was also different in that it extended to private rail facilities, whereas City Beautiful plans dealt with transportation only in terms of streets.

The Chicago Plan of 1909 broke new ground in its attention to street and transit facilities, a concern prompted by the involvement of members of Chicago's Commercial Club. In the same year, a plan was prepared for metropolitan Boston that provided a comprehensive study of the relationship of railroads, terminals, and docks to the city plan. These subjects, along with a study of the city's street system, occupied two hundred pages of the plan report, whereas only fifteen pages were devoted to a proposed civic center.[36] The 1911 Plan for Dallas, prepared by George Kessler for the Dallas Park Board, included recommendations on levees, a belt railroad, a union station, freight terminals, and grade crossings, in addition to more traditional proposals for a civic center, parks and playgrounds, and a system of parkways and boulevards. In like fashion, the 1911 Rochester Plan prepared by Olmsted and architect Arnold Brunner made recommendations concerning a railroad station, the river and canal, street transportation, railroad consolidation, and bridges.[37]

The interest in transportation planning was reflected in the topics of discussion at national planning conferences. Every conference but one between 1910 and 1920 included a major address on transit and transportation. Half the discussion at the 1910 conference was devoted to "The Circulation of Passengers and Freight in Relation to the City Plan"; approximately one-third of the 1917 conference dealt with traffic and transportation improvements, with another third devoted to land use zoning; and almost half of the 1920 conference was spent on such topics as trunk highways, the unification of railroad lines, and the "urban auto problem." Some of the transportation-related topics discussed at other con-

---

[34] "Types of City Plans," p. 214.
[35] Koester, "American City Planning—Part I," p. 142.
[36] Flavel Shurtleff, "Six Years of City Planning in the United States," pp. 34-35.
[37] See Robert Walker, *Planning Function*, pp. 19-20.

ferences were: "Street Widths and their Subdivision" (1911), "The Provision for Future Rapid Transit" (1914), "Street Systems Including Transit Problems" (1916), "Waterways and City Planning" (1918), and "The Steam Railroad in Relation to the City Plan" (1919).

Recognition of the problems created by fragmented ownership of the city's rail system is evident in the comments of George Hooker, secretary of the Chicago City Club. The City Club was an organization of civic-minded business and professional leaders, and Hooker's comments presumably reflected the views of these groups. Like Horace McFarland, he was conscious of the irrationalities that sprang from divided private ownership of collective facilities such as rail transit. He complained that it was easier to move vertically in the elevators of Chicago's skyscrapers than to travel the same distance by rail in the city's business district. This, as Hooker pointed out, was because the elevator moved between different floors of a building owned by the same person or corporation, whereas rail transit coursed between the "separate buildings on a street, all owned by different individuals or companies, with no common agent save a city government unaccustomed to municipal undertakings."[38] As a remedy, he proposed the consolidation of freight handling services, interline transfers on commuter railways, and crosstown rail service connecting the rail lines radiating from Chicago's Loop. Yet he failed to suggest a method of coordination that would overcome the irrationalities arising from divided ownership of the city's buildings and rail lines.

LAND USE ZONING

Land use zoning was another area in which the problem of divided ownership was confronted. With the rise of zoning came the recognition that some form of government regulation was needed to cope with this problem and the development of a particular institutional mechanism for providing such regulation. Numerous proposals for land use zoning were made at the first national planning conference, most of them modeled on the German land districting system. That scheme, as first adopted in Frankfurt in 1891, entailed dividing the city into distinct zones with different regulations governing the height, bulk, and use of buildings in

[38] Hooker, "Congestion and its Causes in Chicago," pp. 42-57, quotation, p. 46.

each zone. The German zone system was regarded by many in the planning and urban reform community in the years before World War I as a positive model of reform.[39] A significant attempt to promote the German system was a speech given by B. Antrim Haldeman, assistant engineer of Philadelphia's Board of Survey, at the 1912 planning conference; his talk was later described by a planning association president as having "blazed the trail" for zoning.[40]

Haldeman argued that the meaning and social function of land had been so altered by urbanization and industrialization that an assertion of the community interest against the rights of private landowners was needed if the social fabric of society was to be preserved. A land districting scheme like that of Germany offered many potential public benefits, he maintained. It would enable local authorities to predetermine what public facilities should be built in a given area and prevent costly alterations to accommodate changes in private land use. It could be used to limit construction of barracks-style tenements and stimulate the building of low-cost single-family homes, thereby facilitating working class home ownership. And it would permit the city to restrict the location of industrial establishments, thus preventing them from intruding upon residential areas and simplifying industrial transportation. Yet, in spite of these benefits, Haldeman feared powerful private interests would thwart the adoption of zoning. Landowners would see it as an abridgement of property rights. Builders and real estate operators would regard it as an imposition that limited their profits. And other "large interests not directly concerned in the development of land" would oppose it as an "invasion of vested rights."[41] These fears were only partially justified by subsequent events, however. Some real estate interests did indeed fight the adoption of zoning. Zoning statutes were contested in the courts until, in 1926, the Supreme Court finally upheld the concept of zoning in *Euclid* v. *Ambler*. But many of those whom Haldeman had expected to oppose zoning turned out to be its greatest advocates.

Although in most cities the zoning movement was led by home-

[39] See Mullin, "American Perceptions of German City Planning at the Turn of the Century," pp. 5-15.

[40] Haldeman, "The Control of Municipal Development by the 'Zone System' and its Application in the United States," pp. 173-87; the quotation is from Buttenheim, "President's Address: Looking Backward and Pressing Onward," p. 2.

[41] Haldeman, "Control of Municipal Development," p. 186.

owners who were concerned about commercial and manufacturing establishments intruding into their neighborhoods, zoning was also seized upon by residents of high-status neighborhoods as a protection against the influx of lower-status groups. In fact, that is how zoning began. While New York City is generally credited with adopting, in 1916, the first zoning ordinance covering an entire city, San Francisco had already adopted a rudimentary form of zoning in the 1880s. San Francisco's ordinance had an obvious, if obliquely stated, intent: it restricted Chinese laundries to a particular area of the city in an attempt to keep the Chinese out of white areas.[42] In New York, by contrast, it was Fifth Avenue merchants complaining about the encroachment of the garment district that generated official interest in zoning.

In 1907, leading Fifth Avenue merchants formed the Fifth Avenue Association to develop and maintain the character of the avenue. Of particular concern to this group was the spread of the garment district—with its Italian and Russian immigrant employees—which found in the loft buildings of the lower avenue and the area's public transportation links an ideal location. After several years of agitation on this issue, the association enlisted the support of Manhattan Borough President George McAneny, who appointed a seven-member Fifth Avenue Commission; five of these members belonged to the association. In 1912, the commission recommended a building height limitation of 125 feet for buildings on Fifth Avenue and 300 feet for buildings to the east and west. As Seymour I. Toll explains, behind this physical planning requirement was a hope that further garment loft buildings would be discouraged, and that the industry would remove itself to areas having no such restrictions.[43] McAneny forwarded the commission's recommendation to the Board of Estimate, which appointed a Heights of Buildings Commission to examine the matter more closely.

In contributing to the cause of height control, McAneny was re-

---

[42] This ordinance was overturned by a federal court. However, the neighboring city of Modesto escaped the constraint of the state constitution and the Fourteenth Amendment by creating two zones, one permitting laundries and the other excluding them; see Warner, *Urban Wilderness*, p. 28. In neighboring Los Angeles between 1905 and 1915, ordinances were adopted establishing three districts, one basically residential, another for industry, and a third for residential purposes and a limited selection of industries (Warner, p. 29).

[43] See Toll, *Zoned America*, p. 146; my account of the development of New York's zoning ordinance is drawn largely from Toll.

sponding not only to the parochial interests of Fifth Avenue merchants, but also to a smaller group, led by Edward Bassett, which was concerned about congestion in the skyscraper area of lower Manhattan. Bassett, who helped to shape the legal institution of zoning, had been involved in developing New York's subway system and feared from that experience that extending the subway system to the downtown area would spawn more tall buildings and bring with it further congestion if height controls were not adopted. Bassett was appointed to the Heights of Buildings Commission, along with reformer types such as attorney Abram Elkus, Lawson Purdy (later president of the National Municipal League), and houser Lawrence Veiller, as well as an architect and four others directly connected with the real estate industry. Following a number of informal meetings with businessmen, the commission released a report six months after its founding in which it not only promulgated height limitations for upper Fifth Avenue and lower Manhattan, but also issued a policy statement regarding a city-wide system of height regulations and land use controls. The maximum height on upper Fifth Avenue was to be 125 feet, the same as that proposed by the Fifth Avenue Commission, although this limit was tied to a standard of one and one-half times the street width. Factories were to be excluded from the upper avenue. Building heights in lower Manhattan were to be limited to twice the street width, but not less than 100 or more than 300 feet. And it was proposed that the rest of the city "should be divided into districts and the restrictions for each district worked out with reference to the peculiar needs and requirements of the particular district."[44] The recommendations in this report formed the basis for the comprehensive zoning scheme that New York City adopted in 1916.

As explained by commission member Purdy, the purpose of the New York zoning system was to "enhance the value of the land of the city and conserve the value of the buildings." Purdy, whose ideas were a combination of those of Henry George and Herbert Spencer, maintained that regulating land use to prevent objectionable neighborhood effects was a way of protecting property rights. "Every property owner," he wrote, "has a right from the state to be protected by the state from the encroachment of his neighbor upon his light, upon his air, and upon his access to the streets, just as much as he has a right to be protected from the intrusion of his

[44] Quoted, ibid., p. 163.

neighbor's building upon his own land."[45] Recognizing that land, because it is not transportable, is inherently subject to neighborhood effects or externalities, the architects of New York's zoning system sought to protect owners from the deleterious effects of changes in land use. The character of development in an area must be guaranteed to protect existing landowners, as well as to make home ownership more attractive, they held. "Unless the general character of [a residential area] is fixed for a considerable period of years," the 1913 report observed, "no one can afford to build a home."[46]

A more urgent reason for promoting land use regulation, however, was the changes occurring in the city's high-class retail district. This concern was well illustrated by a full-page advertisement in the March 5, 1916, issue of the *New York Times*. Signed by thirteen of the city's leading retailers and endorsed by fifty-four merchants, manufacturers, banks, hotels, clubs, and real estate owners, the advertisement asked:

> Shall we save New York?—Shall we save it from unnatural and unnecessary crowding, from depopulated sections, from being a city unbeautiful, from high rents, from excessive and illy [sic] distributed taxation? We can save it from all of these, so far at least as they are caused by one specified industrial evil—the erection of factories in the residential and famous retail sector.[47]

Signers of the ad declared that they would give preference in making purchases to firms whose manufacturing plants were located outside a specified zone of high-class shops, hotels, and fine residences; this policy would go into effect in a little over one year, to give offending manufacturers time to relocate. These threatened economic sanctions proved effective. Several weeks after this ad was printed, another ad appeared, this one signed by 75 percent of the members of the Cloak, Suit and Shirt Manufacturers' Association, in which they agreed to remove themselves from the Fifth Avenue area. As Toll observes, this private initiative was more effective in preserving the Avenue's high-class retail district than was the comprehensive zoning ordinance that followed on its heels, for the conservative form of zoning adopted in New York

[45] "Districting and Zoning of Cities," p. 174.
[46] Quoted in Lewis, *The Planning of the Modern City: A Review of the Principles Governing City Planning*, p. 349.
[47] Quoted, ibid., p. 354.

City and elsewhere in the United States only guaranteed the existing character of an area, whereas Fifth Avenue property owners forced a return to the status quo ante.[48]

New York City adopted its comprehensive zoning ordinance in 1916. Fears that zoning would be harmful to property interests were allayed by the active support given the ordinance by mercantile, real estate, and banking interests, and by specific provisions of the ordinance. The most worrisome issue for property interests was how the ordinance would treat "non-conforming uses"— those existing uses that did not conform with the use classification for its area, such as a factory in an area designated residential. Seeking to assure property owners that zoning, in the words of Edward Bassett, "looked to the future" and sought to "stabilize and protect lawful investment and not to injure assessed valuations or existing uses," the New York City ordinance allowed nonconforming uses existing at the time of the 1916 resolution to be continued.[49] As a further, procedural guarantee for property owners, a Zoning Board of Appeals was created to serve as a safety-valve institution. In addition, dissatisfied petitioners could bring suit in the civil courts. An institutional procedure was thus created for balancing between property owners' need for a method of regulating land use to preserve the economic value of land, a need they believed corresponded with a public interest in ordered development, and the desire to protect individual property owners from over-zealous regulation.

There followed a tidal wave of zoning ordinances in the next decade. Although some states sought to invoke their eminent domain authority as the legal basis for zoning, most relied on their inherent police powers. This was the approach recommended by Secretary Herbert H. Hoover's Department of Commerce, which in 1924 published a Standard Zoning Enabling Act for states to follow. By 1925, Secretary Hoover could report that 19 states had adopted the standard act wholly or in part; and by the end of the year there were 425 zoned municipalities, accounting for half the nation's urban population (although some cities adopted zoning in name only).[50] While constitutional challenges were mounted in a number of states, most courts gave sweeping approval to the zoning principle. The Minnesota Supreme Court authored an exem-

[48] Toll, *Zoned America*, p. 178.

[49] Quoted, ibid., pp. 182-83.

[50] Herbert H. Hoover, "Foreword," in U.S. Department of Commerce, *A Standard State Zoning Enabling Act*, p. iii.

plary statement on how the progress of urbanization made this restriction of property rights necessary. It declared:

> A restriction, which years ago would have been intolerable, and would have been thought an unconstitutional restriction of the owner's use of his property is accepted now without a thought that it invades a private right. As social relations become more complex restrictions on individual rights become more common. With the crowding of the population in cities there is an active insistence upon the establishment of residential districts from which annoying occupations and buildings undesirable to the community are excluded.[51]

While some property interests did indeed oppose zoning, appreciation of how zoning could be used to maintain property values was maturing among more enlightened real estate and lending interests. As evidence of this appreciation, a mortgage banker speaking on "Zoning from the Viewpoint of the Lender on Real Estate Mortgages" at the 1920 planning conference described zoning as the "greatest stabilizer of real estate values ever conceived." He speculated that the "lender on mortgage is more vitally interested in zoning than any other one class, with the possible exception of the individual owner of real estate."[52] If zoning proved itself as a means of stabilizing real estate values, however, it was not similarly effective in limiting population congestion and generating housing improvements in the city's slum. But, this failure reflected on the forces that came to dominate zoning, not on the potential of zoning as a policy tool. As zoning ordinances spread across the United States in the 1920s, most cities over-zoned for industrial and commercial uses, which provided higher tax revenues. Industrial and commercial establishments were prohibited only from locating in middle- and upper-class neighborhoods. Moreover, the universal practice was to permit "higher" residential uses in areas zoned for "lower" uses, which meant commercial and manufacturing concerns were permitted in working-class neighborhoods. The view of labor's representative in the Oregon House of Representatives on the adoption of a zoning enabling law is instructive. In opposing the ordinance, the representative declared, "You rich men live in protected and privately restricted

[51] Quoted in Flavel Shurtleff, "City and Regional Planning Since 1876," p. 59.
[52] Ulmer, "Zoning from the Viewpoint of the Lender on Real Estate Mortgages," p. 133.

home neighborhoods and let all the stables and public garages and other dirty businesses intrude into any block of the workers' home neighborhoods, to spoil all that they work and live for."[53]

That zoning was used to maintain property values and the character of development in high-class retail and residential neighborhoods and not to address the housing and congestion problem in the city's poorer districts attested to the unequal power of the constituencies served by these uses. The planning community encouraged and defended this property-serving use of zoning, because it was a way of making planning effective. These, then, were the simple facts: using zoning to protect property values and maintain the character of an area (that is, its economic function and racial/ethnic character) was a way of gaining politically effective support for planning, whereas promoting zoning as a means of attacking housing and congestion problems was not. This reading of the political scene is captured in George Ford's statement that what was needed was an approach to planning "which will appeal to the businessman, and to the manufacturer as sane and reasonable."[54]

The planning community responded to the alternative uses of zoning and to their different constituencies, by elaborating a justification for the use of zoning to maintain property values and preserve the character of an area. This justification took two forms: one argument was about the need for an economical and efficient organization of land use, the other was about the naturalness of separating races and classes. The latter argument was sometimes made obliquely, as when planners complained about allowing apartment houses to intrude into neighborhoods of single-family homes. Flavel Shurtleff, who was secretary of the NCCP, maintained that if apartment buildings were allowed to spread indiscriminately over the town, "the quality of the town as a residence place would be cheapened."[55] In other cases, this argument was made more explicitly. Planner Frank Koester identified as one of the first tasks of planning "the segregation in suitable districts of the different classes of the population."[56] Similarly, Robert H. Whitten, who chaired New York's City Plan Committee and participated in developing the city's zoning ordinance, ac-

[53] Quoted in Cheney, "Zoning in Practice," p. 164.
[54] Committee on Town Planning of the American Institute of Architects, *City Planning Progress*, p. iii.
[55] "City and Regional Planning," p. 59.
[56] "American City Planning," p. 145.

knowledged that zoning contributed to the segregation of economic classes but asserted this was neither "anti-social" nor "anti-democratic." "A reasonable segregation is normal, inevitable and desirable and cannot be greatly affected, one way or the other, by zoning," he asserted.[57] Whitten also clearly articulated the economy and efficiency argument, writing that the task of city planning and zoning was to organize the urban built environment so as to "facilitate an increasing concentration and specialization of function without interference, friction or waste either on the economic or on the human side."[58] This justification of zoning in terms of the public interest also was articulated by public officials, notably by Commerce Secretary Hoover, who wrote to a president of the NCCP, "The fact is constantly brought before me as Secretary of Commerce that lack of city planning and zoning constantly hampers commerce and industry in their basic function of serving mankind."[59]

INDEPENDENT PLAN COMMISSIONS

The other important institutional adaptation of the City Practical era was the independent plan commission. It was a response to the need for government to implement planning, but it was only a partial step toward government planning. As modeled on the 1907 Hartford Plan Commission and the Standard City Planning Enabling Act promulgated by the United States Department of Commerce in 1928, the independent plan commission consisted of government officials serving ex officio (usually the mayor and public works heads), together with unpaid citizen members appointed by the mayor to long, staggered terms. As such, the independent plan commission was a mini-legislature for planning purposes, one part a government institution and one part an institution of civil society. In its separation from the institutions of local government and its reliance on lay members, it continued the tradition of the semi-independent park commission. The reasons for creating this hybrid public-private institution, moreover, were the same as those behind the formation of the earlier park commission. The independent plan commission was able to gain some of the powers and financing of local government while maintaining a degree of autonomy from local elected officials, and from the

[57] "Zoning and Living Conditions," p. 28.
[58] Ibid.
[59] Quoted in Bettman, *City and Regional Planning Papers*, p. 176.

machinations of local politics. Planning sponsors found this institutional arrangement desirable because of their distrust of local politics and their belief that elected officials, public works heads, and the like were too mired in the narrow and mundane aspects of municipal administration to possess the comprehensive vision needed for good planning; that, at least, is how they defended their preference for the independent plan commission. More to the point, this institutional arrangement was appealing because, as noted above, it allowed planning sponsors to partly governmentalize the planning function, thereby gaining public legitimacy and some governmental powers and financing while maintaining their control of planning. Another rationale was that what the independent plan commission sacrificed in government authority by being an autonomous body rather than an operating agency of municipal government was compensated for by the influence and prestige of its citizen members. As one proponent wrote, the plan commission should be "composed of citizens of influence" to move public opinion in the direction of policies favoring planning.[60] In the end, however, this institutional arrangement failed to make city planning effective, since local officials were reluctant to grant broad powers to plan commissions or give much heed to planning that remained outside their control.

The powers of the 1907 Hartford Plan Commission had been largely advisory. It had the power to review public works proposals for their conformance with city planning and limited authority for condemning excess land around public facilities. The U.S. Commerce Department's model city planning enabling act called for a significantly larger grant of power, however. It declared that the task of the plan commission was to "make and adopt a master plan for the physical development of the municipality" (no mention was made of social planning, for example, for housing and population congestion).[61] After a plan was adopted, the commission was to review public works proposals for their conformance with the plan; if a proposal did not conform, the model act enabled the commission to block the project unless it was overridden by a two-thirds vote of the city council. Although opposed by city councilmen, enabling laws providing for such powers were adopted in a number of states, including California and New York.[62] Yet the re-

[60] Magee, "The Organization and Functions of a City Plan Commission," p. 80; Magee was mayor of Pittsburgh at the time.

[61] U.S. Department of Commerce, *A Standard City Planning Enabling Act*, pp. 13-14.

[62] Robert Walker, *Planning Function*, p. 146.

sistance to actually appointing plan commissions with these powers led some supporters of the two-thirds requirement to rethink
the idea. For example, two model enabling acts were detailed in
Volume VII of the "Harvard City Planning Studies": one, drafted
by Alfred Bettman, retained the two-thirds requirement; the
other, by Edward Bassett and Frank B. Williams, rejected it. In explaining their stance against the requirement, Bassett and Williams wrote, "Experience seems to show that if planning commissions are given too great powers, councils will not appoint
them."[63] Bettman, who sat with Bassett on the Commerce Department advisory commission that prepared the standard enabling act, said the plan commission's role should be advisory, yet
he defended the two-thirds requirement as necessary to ensure
careful consideration of planning problems.[64]

Appointment of the Hartford Plan Commission stimulated the
creation of similar bodies in other cities. Planning conference secretary Flavel Shurtleff reported in 1913 that eighteen cities had established plan commissions, although at that time a larger number—thirty-four cities—had "comprehensive" plans.[65] It was
1914, however, before a plan commission was given mandatory review power; in that year, Cleveland adopted an ordinance stipu-
lating that no public works project could be initiated "until and
unless such plan, design or location shall have been submitted to
and approved by the [Plan] Commission."[66] The Cleveland commission could not block nonconforming projects, however. As
more and more plan commissions were appointed, the lay-board
form continued to predominate, although as early as 1913 a
speaker at the national planning conference complained of the independent commission's "undeveloped relation to the other
forces engaged in the management of the public business."[67] In
1923, Flavel Shurtleff counted 185 cities with official plan commissions, although, reversing the earlier relationship, less than
half had actual plans.[68] The number of city plan commissions continued to increase—according to a survey by the National Resources Committee, by 1937 there were 933.[69]

[63] Quoted, ibid.
[64] Bettman, "The Planning Commission: Its Functions and Method" (1935), pp.
27, 29-30.
[65] "The Progress of City Planning," pp. 19-20.
[66] Quoted in Flavel Shurtleff, "Six Years of City Planning," p. 37.
[67] Magee, "Organization and Functions," pp. 73-74.
[68] Cited in Kimball, *Manual of Information on City Planning and Zoning*, p. 14.
[69] Robert Walker, *Planning Function*, p. 133 n. 2.

The increase in plan commissions was a misleading indicator of the planning being done, however. Many of the plan commissions existed in name only, the original interest in planning having died out, and there were many more plan commissions than actual plans. In the view of Robert A. Walker, an advocate of incorporating the planning function into the municipal executive, the independent plan commission, with its predominately lay membership, was an impediment to planning. The problem with the lay-board organization was that it generated conflict between plan commissioners and elected officials, thereby weakening the latter's support for planning. This conflict arose from planning sponsors' mistrust of politicians and the local political process, which led them to create a semiautonomous body for planning that they sought to defend on the ersatz grounds that it would separate politics from planning. Reflecting this effort to create a separate mini-legislature for planning, one influential text stated that the plan commission should be composed of "representative citizens."[70] In like manner, the Commerce Department's standard enabling act declared that commissioners should be removable within their term of office only for "inefficiency, neglect of duty, or malfeasance in office." As explained in a footnote, this requirement was to prevent the mayor from punishing a plan commissioner for recommending something "not in harmony with his political desires"—a remark that reflected the authors' view of the local political process.[71] It is little wonder, therefore, that politicians were reluctant to grant broad powers to plan commission members or to heed their planning.

In the 1930s, Robert Walker studied the two key arguments for granting the independent commission special powers: (1) such commissions were above "politics" and (2) their members possessed a special competence for planning and could be relied upon to take a long-term view. Walker's conclusions are presumably relevant for understanding the role of plan commissions in an earlier period. He maintained that neither of these arguments was valid. Although appointments to plan commissions were made by elected officials and, to that extent, were subject to political influence, he did not believe that commissioners were influenced much by elected officials. Rather, he detected a bias arising from the fact that certain occupational groups were disproportionately

[70] Kimball, *Manual on City Planning*, p. 6.
[71] *Standard City Planning Enabling Act*, p. 11 n. 21.

represented on planning boards. Based on a study of 208 citizen plan commissioners in 31 large cities, he found that businessmen comprised the largest group (35 percent, predominately in the "executive and owner group"), followed by realtors (15.4 percent), lawyers (11.1 percent), architects (10.1 percent), and engineers (7.7 percent). One consequence of this representation, Walker believed, was a bias in favor of the conservative outlook of upper-income business groups. Other consequences were that realty and construction interests were overrepresented and lower income groups were without voice "except through the good offices of altruistic members." There were also few members from social welfare organizations, a lack he attributed to the planning movement's failure to address the social aspects of planning.[72]

Walker found no evidence for the proposition that lay members possessed a special competence for planning. In fact, he found the opposite. From his interviews and observations, he concluded that lay commissioners typically were too involved in their own business affairs to acquire the necessary understanding of planning; this lack of involvement also resulted in poorly attended commission meetings and excessive reliance on the commission chairman and planning engineer.[73] Early in the life of a plan commission, lay members might have been energetic and committed, but this vigor too often disappeared as new members were appointed and the original spasm of interest in planning died out. Thus, the features that originally made the lay-board organization attractive to planning sponsors—it gave them government backing while enabling them to maintain control of planning—rendered it ineffective in securing and sustaining official support for planning.

THE CITY PRACTICAL INTERPRETED

At one level, the problem of the City Practical arose from the capitalist-democracy contradiction: how to achieve a modicum of collective control of urban development in the interest of capital without subjecting that control to the claims and considerations of non-capitalist groups. The response was to partially governmentalize the planning function but not to democratize it—to acquire for planning the imprimatur of government and some government powers and financing, but to ensure that it remained

[72] *Planning Function*, pp. 147-55.
[73] Ibid., pp. 155-56.

sufficiently independent from popularly elected institutions to avoid democratic pressures. Such was the rationale behind the adoption of the independent plan commission. Yet, as we have seen, this solution was itself contradictory, for elected officials were unwilling to empower and heed the call of a plan commission when they were institutionally excluded from the commission's affairs. This conflict between elected officials and plan commissioners made manifest a deeper conflict between the popularly elected basis of local government and the attempt to acquire government power for private purposes. Here, because of the formally democratic basis of local government, the promoters of planning did not entirely get their way.

At another level, the problem of the City Practical arose from the property contradiction. Fragmented private control of transportation and land use failed to meet important collective needs of both workers and capitalists. For workers, the problem was primarily one of population congestion and insalubrious housing; for capitalists, it was the inefficiency of the system of transportation and land use for purposes of business and commerce, as well as the threat to property values and to the character of development arising from incompatible uses of land. These problems indicated the need for some means of imposing collective interests on the pattern of public as well as private development. And, as we have seen, it was the collective interests of capitalists and property owners that were given emphasis in the development of City Practical planning; appealing to their interests was deemed the surest way to build support for planning, and it corresponded better with what planning advocates took to be the public interest. Yet the forms of control adopted stood as a threat to the autonomous control of property, especially for property capitalists who performed the role within the market system of planning and equipping space (albeit who did so through the accretion of many individual acts rather than on the basis of an overall plan, except where concentrated ownership made some degree of coordinated development possible). And, on the other side, the continued existence of a privately owned and controlled built environment and the interests, pressures, and political resources arising from it severely restricted these limited attempts at collective control of buildings, transportation, and land use. Thus, the search continued for a directive system capable of satisfying, or more effectively balancing between, capital's collective need for a rational and efficient urban built environment and particular capitalists' need for autonomy of control to protect and enhance the value of their property.

For their part, persons in the planning community continued to promote purposeful planning carried out by experts as part of a continuous process. In a 1913 address, Frederick Olmsted, Jr. characterized planning not as the preparation of a static master plan but as a "live thing"—"a growing and gradually changing aggregation of accepted ideas or projects for physical changes in the city, all consistent with each other, and each surviving, by virtue of its own inherent merit and by virtue of its harmonizing with the rest."[74] Similarly, Alfred Bettman defined planning as "the adjustment and coordination of all the types of development and uses within the territory of the city, so that each may reach its own high grade of efficiency and promote rather than impair the other, and so that the community may gain the benefits of an harmonious, adjusted, and coordinated development."[75] In both statements, planning is conceived of as a continuous process requiring the involvement of technical experts or "planners." But the adoption of such an approach was encumbered, first, because of the threat that any real, effective planning posed to property rights and especially to property capital, and second, because a planning process requiring the continuing involvement of planners limited the role of politicians, whose support was necessary for the adoption of such an approach.

The relationship forged between city planners and their business patrons in the 1920s was, therefore, an ambiguous, even contradictory one. With the failure of the City Beautiful to generate a broad enough base of support for planning, planners searched for an alternative, more practical approach—in the words of George Ford, one that would appeal to the businessman and manufacturer as "sane and reasonable." Such an approach, it was thought, was the best way to ensure that planning became valued, respected, and effective. At the urging, initially, of businessmen themselves, most notably in the development of the Commercial Club-Burnham Plan for Chicago, the emphasis in planning turned to fashioning a more efficient system of streets and transportation, an interest later extended to the pattern of land use. Although aesthetic, civic-center type plans continued to be produced into the 1920s, the orientation of planning changed. Planning focused increasingly on the practical arrangement of the physical city, embracing such elements as streets, transit, railroads, waterways, and terminals; parks and playgrounds; the grouping of public buildings; and

[74] "A City Planning Program," p. 5.
[75] "City Planning Legislation," p. 432.

the creation of city districts to regulate the height, area, and use of buildings. With this change in orientation, planners formulated a unitary concept of the city as a "depot and distributing apparatus" and, in support of this concept, a legitimating ideology that presented interventions aimed at improving the economy and efficiency of the physical city for purposes of business and commerce as being in the collective interest of urban residents. Furthermore, as the orientation of planning changed, the occupational base of the planning community changed as well. Out went social reformers like Benjamin Marsh, architects and landscape architects assumed a reduced role, and in came engineers (specialists in efficiency) and attorneys (specialists in property law). When the American City Planning Institute (forerunner of the American Institute of Planning) was created in 1917, there were fourteen landscape architects, thirteen engineers, six attorneys, five architects, four realtors, and two housers among its charter members.[76]

In spite of the fact that planning was reoriented to accommodate the needs of business, neither businessmen nor politicians were prepared to entrust planners with control of the urban built environment. Nevertheless, planners and some enlightened businessmen were promoting within the business community the view that the commercial city required some degree of overall coordination and planning and, therefore, the expertise of planners. And planners clearly needed business support, since, given political realities, that was the best way to make planning effective, and since, given the nature of the capitalist system, rationalizing the commercial city by appealing to the interests of businessmen and property owners seemed the best way of rationalizing the larger city for the good of all. But at the individual level, where class and collective interests are not always, or only seldom, controlling, meaningful city planning was perceived of as a threat to property owners, since it reduced their autonomy of control. Thus, established in the City Practical era of the 1920s was a dynamic of support and opposition between planners and businessmen that continues to be acted out, in realm after realm, today. It is a dynamic that is inherent in capitalism, given the contradiction between the private ownership and control of property and the social needs, including the social needs of capital itself, that private property must serve.

[76] Scott, *American City Planning*, p. 163.

EIGHT

Planning and Contradiction

URBAN PLANNING can be understood as a productive force of society. It is an accumulation of knowledge and techniques that are acquired from the experience of urban living and are applied to the problems of living and working, producing and consuming, and exchanging goods and services in an urban context. So conceived, urban planning is comparable to the productive technology of society: the latter is an accretion of knowledge about how to produce, the former of how to organize the urban built environment consistent with human needs. Just as industrial technology contributes to the development of society's productive power, urban planning can be seen as an attempt to incorporate social needs—interests larger than those of individual urban actors—into the built environment of the city. Yet, consistent with Marx's treatment of productive forces, the development of urban planning cannot be understood on its own terms; it is not self-determining. Just as industrial technology is shaped by relations in the workplace and by the form of ownership of production, urban planning is shaped by social relations within the living place and by the political and economic ordering of society.

In particular, we have seen how urban planning is determined by the method of owning and controlling urban land. In a capitalist society, where land is treated as a commodity to be bought and sold, subdivided and assembled, developed and redeveloped in pursuit of private economic gain, urban planning takes the form of efforts to impose nonmarket controls on urban development. For in a society organized on market principles, efforts to shape the built environment to meet social needs necessarily entail placing limitations on the market. Yet we have seen that urban planning in America has not always had this character. In the colonial era, prior to the emergence of an individualistic land law and conditions for profitable real estate speculation, urban planning had limited involvement with the market system: town building in this early period was organized by centralized authority more than by markets. By contrast, in the nineteenth century, with the emergence of new forms of land ownership, extensive land speculation, and the rapid growth of urban population, local authorities lost control of urban development, and the character of urban planning changed. Urban planning in this era was given a capitalist stamp, was capitalist planning, not merely because of the interests that dominated its use, but because of its preoccupation with the problems arising from treating land as a commodity, that is, in a capitalist manner.

It has been shown that two problems in particular arise from treating urban land as a commodity. One has been termed the property contradiction and the other the capitalist-democracy contradiction. By *contradiction*, I mean, following Godelier, a limit to the possibilities for compatible development of two elements of a system or structure.[1] The property contradiction was defined as a contradiction between the private ownership and control of urban land (and, by extension, of other elements of the urban built environment such as housing) and the social needs that land and its appurtenances must serve. As we have seen, the social needs in question include those of capital as well as labor. The capitalist-democracy contradiction is a contradiction between the need to socialize the control of urban space to create the conditions for maintaining capitalism and the danger to capital of truly socializing, that is, democratizing, the control of the urban built environment. This latter contradiction is premised on the existence of the property contradiction in that it arises from state intervention in response to the property contradiction. For the adoption of nonmarket controls involves, simultaneously, the question of how to organize those controls—of who will control the controls. The capitalist-democracy contradiction also arises from the formally democratic character of the state (represented by universal adult suffrage, contested elections, and the majority rule principle, for example). In its relation to the economic structure of society, it is an "external contradiction"—a contradiction between the requirements for state intervention arising from the logic of the (capitalist) economic system and the formally democratic character of a particular state system.[2] In an authoritarian state directly dominated by capitalists, the need to use government to replace or substitute for the market system would not pose the same risks for capital.

[1] See Lamarche, "Property Development," pp. 90-93.
[2] This concept of external contradiction is from Godelier, "Structure and Contradiction in *Capital*"; see pp. 350-55.

There is, however, a third contradictory relationship that emerges from the historical analysis, although it involves a somewhat different meaning of contradiction. I refer to the relationship of mutual dependency, opposition, and support observed between planners and capitalists/property owners. This contradiction is unlike the others in that it involves a relationship between social actors rather than between elements of social structure. It is similar, however, in that it involves a relationship of mutual dependency and incompatibility. There is a relationship of mutual dependency between planners and capitalists because they need each other to achieve their respective aims. At the same time, there is a relationship of incompatibility because they each require autonomy—planners to address collective needs in the organization of the built environment, capitalists to secure value from their productive assets, including land.

It is because of these three contradictions that urban planning is an imperfect solution to capital's need for some form of collective control of urban development. Conversely, it is only by understanding the nature and structural origins of these contradictions that one can understand the history of urban planning in all its rich complexity, with appreciation for why urban planning in a capitalist society is both necessary and impossible. In the actual history of planning, these contradictions are not experienced separately or sequentially; rather, they run together, although one may be more salient than another at a particular time. Nevertheless, at the risk of being too mechanical, I address these contradictions separately below.

PLANNING AND THE PROPERTY CONTRADICTION

The property contradiction applies to and arises from more than the private ownership of urban *land*. It extends to other privately owned parts of the urban built environment, including housing, transit facilities, and utilities. Yet the problems arising from the private ownership of land are of central importance to an understanding of the history of urban planning, since the way land is developed is pivotal in determining the physical structure of the city. The structuring role of land and the ownership of land have sometimes been overlooked by advocates of a more socially conscious approach to planning, who have attributed city planning's fixation with land and its appurtenances to the entrenched ideology of the planning profession.[3] This view ignores, as Benjamin Marsh did not, the centrality of the land question and the need to confront the private ownership and control of land as the first step in improving the conditions of the city.

As soon as land began to be treated as a commodity and held and developed for speculative gain, planners and town builders began wrestling with various manifestations of the property contradiction. William Penn, for example, was restricted in what he could do in the layout and design of his "greene country towne" by the need to make land in the Pennsylvania colony marketable to investors. And Penn was ultimately driven from Philadelphia because townspeople believed his control of the town was too oriented toward his own speculative gain. The problems arising from the private ownership of land and its appurtenances led either to an expansion of government's role in urban development or to efforts to replace or restrict the role of property capital. In reviewing these experiences, it is important to understand both the reasons for these interventions and how extensive they have been. If urban planning is an attempt to impose social needs on urban development, which social needs, or, more to the point, whose social needs have taken precedence? And, further, what have been the limits to these interventions?

The marxist urban literature reviewed in Chapter 1 seeks to explain the growth of state intervention/urban planning by identifying the reproduction requirements of capitalism that generate an expanded government role in urban development. These reproduction requirements are equated with the objective general interests of the capitalist class. Thus, Castells relates the growth of urban planning to capitalism's need to provide for the reproduction of labor power. This need, according to Castells, has led to the provision by the state of collective forms of consumption (for example, parks) to complement or substitute for private consumption secured through the market system. David Harvey and Edmond Preteceille both relate the growth of state intervention to the inability of the market system to provide for the immobilized fixed-capital investments used by capital as collective means of production; they refer to infrastructural supports such as bridges, harbors, streets, and sewerage networks. Because the market cannot

---

[3] See, for example, Hansen, "Metropolitan Planning and the New Comprehensiveness," pp. 295-302; cf. Vinton, "Has Physical Planning Been Over-Emphasized?" pp. 94-101.

adequately supply these facilities, due to the problem of capturing positive externalities, the state must do so. In addition, Preteceille observes that the state is called upon to provide for the efficient spatial coordination of these infrastructural supports (use values), producing what he terms "new, complex use values." Similarly, François Lamarche relates urban planning to the sphere of circulation and the need to produce a spatial organization that facilitates the circulation of, for example, capital, commodities, and information. These explanations should not be regarded as mutually exclusive, although the authors pointedly emphasize one reproduction requirement over another in seeking to explain the development of planning. Significantly, these explanations share an emphasis on the economic needs of capital; they are relatively insensitive to how capital's political needs or the nature of the state system might affect the character and extent of state planning in a particular society.

Castells's argument, which emphasizes the need for collective forms of consumption to aid in the renewal of labor power, applies best to housing reform and park planning. Whereas the building of company towns demonstrated the connection between industrialism and the provision of worker housing, in conventional speculatively built towns responsibility for worker housing fell on private real estate developers (Lamarche's "property capital"). In promoting the adoption of tenement house laws, the housing reform movement sought to place a limit on housing exploitation; these laws represented an intervention against property capital on the part of other groups in society, including segments of the propertied class. Yet the interest that guided and delimited this intervention was not so much capital's need to reproduce labor power, implying as it does the centrality of capital's economic needs; rather, it was more nearly capital's desire to maintain its political and ideological leadership—its class hegemony—that made restrictive housing legislation possible. This interest is evident in the New York AICP's advocacy of tenement regulations on the grounds that they would curb the spread of radical doctrine among tenement dwellers while aiding in the assimilation of the immigrant poor.

Castells's explanation works better in the case of park planning. The building of parks originally was conceived of as a way of providing a respite from the world of work; park planners sought to alter the environment outside of work to compensate for what was lost within. Thus, Frederick Olmsted, Sr., spoke of parks as a counterpoint to the "enervating pressures" of the workaday world and as a place for "recuperative relaxation." This concept corresponds with Castells's argument that government intervention in urban development is oriented toward the renewal of workers through the provision of facilities for collective consumption. And, indeed, New York City is more tolerable for the city's working-class poor, at least in the summer, because of Central Park. Yet, if Olmsted sought to appeal to this interest in renewal and social amelioration, it was the success of Central Park in enhancing neighboring property values and increasing the city's tax base, and the patronage bonanza of public parks for local political machines, that stimulated the construction of subsequent parks. Moreover, it turned out that the wealthy made more use of parks than the poor, suggesting that it was not entirely enlightened class consciousness that led them to support (or in some cases only to tolerate) the building of public parks. (Indeed, much of New York City's wealthy class had opposed the construction of Central Park, both because of its expense and because they feared it would become a "bear-garden" for the lower classes.) Yet, drawing from Castells's analysis, it would be hard to understand why so many large urban parks were built, and why park proponents so frequently resorted to the amelioration argument, if credence was not given to the renewal explanation.

Within the organized planning movement, Benjamin Marsh's spirited campaign against land speculation, the system of local property taxation, and concentrated land ownership—all of which he believed contributed to population congestion—provided the best expression of worker interests in planning. Without mobilized worker support, however, Marsh was left to argue for these measures by defending worker rights and tugging at the heartstrings of the well-to-do. Conversely, Castells's explanation implies that the state responds to worker needs through some ineluctable process of capitalist development. In comparison with Marsh's effort to dramatize the housing and environmental needs of the poor, the City Beautiful appeared little more than a sham to conceal Lincoln Steffens's "shame of the city." Yet the City Beautiful was nevertheless an interesting attempt to organize local political hegemony. Besides diverting attention from more threatening reform agenda, it sought to stimulate civic loyalty, including acceptance of American culture and capitalism, and, in the process, to generate support for the business sponsors of city beautification. The City Beautiful involved the provision of what, with some license, might be regarded as Castells's facilities for collective consumption. But, once again, the provision of these facilities was tied to capital's need to secure or maintain its political ascendancy and stimulate civic loyalty on the part of the immigrant working class, not to reproducing labor power. Moreover, it was a rarefied form of consumption that was being provided—City Beautiful works were presented as objects of visual relief and enjoyment, not as a substitute for material forms of consumption that the market failed to provide adequately.

The City Beautiful was ultimately found wanting, however, because it failed to address the economic needs of its business-class supporters, specifically their need for a more economical and efficient organization of transportation and land use. It was this "social need" of capital for a more efficient spatial organization to facilitate production and circulation that provided the most effective basis of support for planning. The assertion of this need, as articulated initially by businessmen and then seized upon and promoted by planner-ideologists, corresponds with the analyses of Harvey, Preteceille, and Lamarche, who assert that state intervention is needed for the establishment and spatial coordination of facilities such as roads, harbors, and railways—facilities that are used as collective means of production. Consistent with their analyses, city planning became established and gained respectability when it began responding to this need. By contrast, other approaches to planning that did not accord with the general interest of the business class were rejected as unrealistic or unworkable. Thus, few industrialists resorted to the building of company towns because, by uniting the realms of workplace and community under the control of a common employer-landlord, they might create a potentially explosive situation that would threaten capital's ability to dominate labor. The American Garden City movement failed to break property capital's control of land and housing, the "Garden City" becoming little more than a fancy name for low-density suburban development. And Benjamin Marsh's effort to put the congestion problem at the center of the planning agenda was rejected in favor of an approach more closely tailored to the interests of business.

If the planning movement was unresponsive to the needs of the working class, it nevertheless stimulated an expanded government role in urban development. A larger government role was essential for realizing the political and social control objectives of planning's business supporters, as well as for helping them achieve their economic interest in a more efficient organization of transportation and land use. The housing reform movement accomplished this by asserting the rights of the community (to be free from disease, worker radicalism, and immigrant culture) against the rights of private landowners, the park movement by promoting government land ownership and the provision of facilities for collective consumption. Both these movements were motivated by conservative purposes, yet they signified an awareness that maintaining political and social order required a larger government role in creating the built environment. The City Beautiful movement stimulated government planning by the failure of its exercise in private planning, a lesson that contributed to the development of zoning restrictions and the appointment of independent plan commissions in the City Practical era. The building of company towns and the American Garden City movement were not attempts to promote government intervention, but they sought to limit the role of property capital and to make the urban physical environment responsive to a broader set of needs. The other side of the property contradiction, however, was that these efforts to intervene in the process of urban development, thereby limiting or displacing the role of the property capitalist, did not go as far, nor were they as successful, as their proponents had hoped. The proximate reason for this, the "structural explanation," is that they came up against the limit of the private ownership and control of land and housing.

But we need to be discriminating here. It is, of course, important to understand how urban planning is a product of capitalist urbanization—how the problems confronted by planners arose from the private ownership and speculative development of land, and how solutions to these problems were in turn constrained by this system. Yet more is needed. Understanding why planning did not go further, why there was not more government intervention, requires more than an awareness of the constraint arising from private ownership. Harvey and Castells, seemingly generalizing from the European experience, where planning began earlier and has been more extensive, appear to anticipate more urban planning in the United States than has actually come about. Yet, precisely because of the greater progress of urban planning in Europe, it is important to ask not only why government became involved in urban development in the United States, but also why there has not been *more* government involvement. In Germany, by 1900, most municipal governments had large land holdings that they used to control development on the city's periphery; they also enacted extensive restrictions on the use of private land. England, Germany, Belgium, and France all had "constructive" housing programs by the turn of the century. The fact that these societies tolerated more government intervention, and that, at least in the case of housing policies, these interventions were more responsive to worker interests, suggests that planning interventions are not simply the product of the logic of development of capitalism. Nor, inasmuch as these societies all combine capitalism and democratic governmental arrangements, is the history of planning reducible to the logic of a social formation combining capitalism and formal democracy. Unique historical characteristics and the nature of social movements in different countries also shape the history of planning.

As emphasized in the discussion of housing reform, the absence of worker mobilization on the housing issue, due in part to the wage and hours orientation of the American labor movement, was an important reason why state intervention went no further. This factor, together with the large flow of immigrants who provided a steady stream of replacement workers, weakened capital's interest in providing for the reproduction of existing workers. Because worker pressure on the housing issue was comparatively mild in the United States, capital's ameliorative interest was, correspondingly, more limited. Much the same could be said of the political-ideological interest behind City Beautiful planning; in the absence of attention to capital's need for a more efficient organization of urban space, this interest was not powerful enough to justify an appreciable limitation of property rights.

As for why the planning and zoning of the City Practical era was so late in coming and so comparatively conservative, there are several possible explanations. One is that because American cities developed as capitalist cities, relying on property capital to provide for the organization of housing and urban amenities, property capital has enjoyed more political sway in the United States than in European cities. Also relevant is the absence of a pre-liberal elite with an organic concept of society; without such an elite, it has been more difficult to address collective problems and to stimulate the consciousness and collective effort necessary to realize the common interests of the dominant class. Apart from whether property capital has had a larger political role in the United States than in Europe, the American business class as a whole is no doubt more ideologically wedded to the property system, and more resistant to government intervention even when it might benefit business as a whole, than are its European counterparts. And as David Vogel argues, there may be less state intervention in the United States because the state is more democratic in its formal structure, making state intervention a riskier proposition for capitalists—riskier because the state is more subject to non-capitalist influence.[4]

Other than to observe the absence of significant working-class mobilization on the housing issue and the effect of immigration on capital's interest in reproducing labor power, this study has not examined how the explanations presented above concretely apply to understanding the limits of planning intervention. To do so would require a more focused analysis of the development of planning in particular cities. Yet it is important to recognize the implications of the comparative underdevelopment of planning in the United States. The variation among capitalist societies in both the nature and extent of government's role in organizing the built environment points to the limits of understanding the growth of urban planning on the basis of the logic of development of the capitalist mode of production. This limitation of the marxist urban literature also applies to our understanding of the capitalist-democracy contradiction.

PLANNING AND THE CAPITALIST-DEMOCRACY CONTRADICTION

When we look at planning as a response to the capitalist-democracy contradiction, we are interested in planning as a method of policy formulation, rather than planning as state intervention. Analytically defined, planning in this sense refers to purposive decision making based upon an efficient coordination of means-ends relations. It has been shown how urban planning developed historically as a method of technical decision making, controlled by social and technical elites and separated from institutions of popular control. This was how the planning movement responded to the capitalist-democracy contradiction, taking advantage of the powers and financing of government but preventing the democratization of planning. We find this idea present in-embryo in Lawrence Veiller's view that housing reform should be based on tech-

[4] Vogel, "Why Businessmen Distrust Their State: The Political Consciousness of American Corporate Executives," p. 61.

nical expertise, but it experienced its full flowering in the independent park commission. This institution was, in effect, a mini-government for park purposes, combining the centralized methods of control of the private business corporation with powers and responsibilities that were public in character. The City Beautiful's response to the capitalist-democracy contradiction was to keep planning in private hands, at least in the plan-development stage; this approach gave private elites a voice in some public works but failed to control private development, and it did not provide an adequate base of support for planning. In the zoning board and independent planning commission, the City Practical tradition perfected the earlier model of the park commission, creating quasi-governments for planning dominated by lay-citizen members.

In seeking to understand the development of planning as a method of policy formulation, we have available two bases of interpretation—one in the work of pluralist political scientists and the other in the writing of structuralist marxist Claus Offe. Pluralists have tended to see urban planning as a largely unsuccessful effort by planners, often working with a subsection of the business community, to institutionalize their control over a particular policy area. That groups attempt to gain, and sometimes succeed in gaining, control of particular policy areas through the creation of independent boards and the like, has not gone unremarked by pluralists, although the pluralist view is that such arrangements (like price cartels) are not likely to be long-lived. Further, pluralists have interpreted the failure of planners and their patrons to gain politically effective support for planning while keeping planning insulated from local politics as a demonstration of the superiority of politics/pluralist bargaining as a method of policy formulation.

No facts have been adduced that obviously disconfirm the pluralist understanding of planning. But if the pluralist view is descriptively accurate in its main essentials, it is not analytically adequate. It fails to appreciate how the history of planning has been structured by the two central contradictions treated here. It neglects, first, how the demand for urban planning arises out of the market's method of treating land, and second, how the opposition between planning and politics/pluralist bargaining arises from capital's need for nonmarket control of urban development on the one hand and the danger of democratizing that control on the other. It is only by understanding this Janus-faced reality, this need for government intervention and the concomitant danger of democracy, that one can understand why the conflict between planning and pluralist bargaining so often recurs. Similarly, pluralists' empiricist interpretation fails to account for the paradox that capitalists both need urban planning and, in a formally democratic state, are threatened by it.

Offe helps to relate the development of planning to the contradictory realities of capitalist democracy.[5] He foresees a gravitation toward planning as the preferred method of policy formulation in democratic-capitalist societies—preferred because it is best able to fulfill the sometimes contradictory demands of capitalism and democracy, although it is incapable of completely resolving the tension between them. In his view, the state is caught in a search for a method of policy formulation capable of producing decisions that aid capital accumulation and maintain the health of the economy on the one hand and secure democratic legitimacy on the other. The problem with political bargaining (the method of policy formulation idealized by pluralists) is that it invites the representation of too many points of view and produces chaos and stalemate. Moreover, it is incapable of anticipating threats to the system, in part because capitalists are unaware of these threats themselves. Interestingly, this analysis comes fairly close to the critique of political decision making offered by Frederick Olmsted, Sr., who argued that park matters should be put in the hands of a "small body of select men" who could take hold of them "as a matter of direct, grave, business responsibility."[6] Yet Offe maintains that the political bargaining method is best able to produce decisions bearing democratic legitimacy. The alternative of bureaucracy in which decisions are based on the application of rules to cases is likewise incapable of anticipating threats to accumulation. Moreover, there is no necessary reason for believing that the rules and operating procedures of bureaucracy correspond (or can be made to correspond) with the accumulation requirements of the economy. Bureaucracy, as Weber noted, may be superior for achieving procedural justice in that similar cases are treated the same; but that is no way to run an economy or control economic interventions. By contrast, planning—which Offe terms purposive decision making—is able to anticipate threats to the

---

[5] This presentation of Offe's argument is from his essay, "The Theory of the Capitalist State and the Problem of Policy Formation."

[6] "Public Parks," pp. 26, 31.

system and has an "ends" orientation adaptable to economic problem solving.

In Offe's view, planning has the least capacity for acquiring democratic legitimacy of the three decision processes identified. His assertion that there is a tendency toward the adoption of planning methods rests on a belief that, in the final analysis, the requirements of capital accumulation take precedence over those of democratic legitimacy in the definition of "good" public policy. Yet Offe believes that planning can never be successful. For one, the kind of purposive decision making he associates with planning cannot, under present circumstances, acquire democratic legitimacy. More important, it cannot be successful in achieving its own aims because of the limitation imposed by private ownership of society's productive assets.

Seen through the lens of Offe's analysis, the early history of urban planning encapsulates and reveals the contradictory tendencies of state planning in a capitalist society. With the realization that some form of nonmarket control over urban development was indicated, promoters of planning focused their attention on how to organize those controls. Private planning was attempted first, then quasi-governmental bodies were created, insulated from institutions of popular control and dominated by lay-citizen members. In time, this form of planning was rejected because public officials were unwilling to heed planning over which they had little or no control. The planning function was then incorporated into the municipal executive, which, in the view of some critics, politicized and corrupted planning. Yet even with this development, the rift between planning and politics continued, and often planning itself has seemed not to matter.

This pattern has been repeated, among other places, in the federal government's attempt in the 1960s to promote regional and metropolitan planning. Legislation adopted in 1966 and 1968 mandated the appointment of metropolitan-level planning institutions (regional, multi-county bodies were mandated for nonurban areas). These agencies were to carry out regional/metropolitan planning and check applications for federal public works grants to see that they conformed with (supposedly) existing area-wide planning, a function which made these institutions analogous to the independent plan commission of the beginning of the century. They were also like their institutional predecessors in that, originally, they were to be composed primarily of lay members representing various constituencies within the planning jurisdiction, although the failure of this model to generate official support for planning culminated in a new federal requirement that a majority of the members be local officials. Yet it appears that these regional planning bodies have not had much of an impact, largely because they are too divorced from local government institutions; thus, the experience of the independent plan commission has been repeated.[7] Corresponding with Offe's analysis, James O'Connor argued in the early 1970s that "monopoly capital" was sponsoring a number of reforms in methods of state decision making to enable the state to respond to monopoly capital's needs in a more cost-effective, less inflationary way. O'Connor cited as examples the use of program-planning-budgeting (PPB) techniques and the creation of regional/metropolitan-level planning institutions.[8] Yet Ronald Reagan, who can fairly be described as a pro-business president, has not promoted this regional planning apparatus and has pressed for decentralizing the federal system, the opposite of what O'Connor said monopoly capital needed.

Why, we might ask, has the development of planning institutions not gone further in the United States? As with planning in the form of state intervention, we need to consider not only why the development of planning as a method of policy formulation went as far as it did, but also why it went no further. (It is much like examining the American welfare state; we need to know why it is so big and why it is so much smaller than its European counterparts.) As shown in the preceding chapter, planners like Frederick Olmsted, Jr., were promoting a greater reliance on planning and planners than their business patrons were willing to accept. And what their patrons did accept, namely the lay-dominated independent plan commission, proved ineffective because of its separation from municipal government. The movement to incorporate planning into the municipal executive was not finally successful until the 1950s, when the federal government mandated the appointment of local planning agencies as a condition for municipalities' receiving certain public works grants. Yet there continues to be resistance to planning on the part of local politicians and among those whom Castells and Offe would regard as part of the natural constituency for planning. Thus, we return to the question, why was there so little acceptance of planning in the

[7] I believe Melvin Mogulof's analysis of these so-called A-95 review agencies is still valid; see his *Governing Metropolitan Areas: A Critical Review of Council of Governments and the Federal Role.*

[8] *The Fiscal Crisis of the State,* chap. 3.

period examined? And, by extension, why today is the gravitation toward planning of which Offe writes so slow, ambiguous, and uncertain?

Two factors seem to have played an important role in retarding the development of planning so conceived. One is the formally democratic structure of the American state system. The point is neither that pluralist-democratic decision making has proven to be superior to planning, nor that the democratic idea has won out over the planning idea—the conflict seldom appears in these terms. Rather, it is that politicians who are involved in the system of democratic politics are impelled to pursue their self-interest in ways that accord with the logic of a representative system. When planning provided rewards that politicians could use to maintain their political support, they were quite willing to support it. We see this in the case of park building. Because of the patronage opportunities provided by park construction and maintenance, parks were generally attractive to local politicians, especially to political machines, although elected officials were generally resistant to the creation of independent commissions for park planning. When, on the other hand, an attempt was made to keep elected officals out of planning, as in the appointment of independent plan commissions, politicians, not surprisingly, were reluctant to heed or support it.

This interpretation raises a question concerning Offe's analysis of the contradictory movement toward planning. It should be recalled that he maintains there is a long-term trend toward the adoption of planning methods, because planning is better able to meet the critical need for generating capital accumulation and economic growth, even though planning has a low capacity for generating democratic legitimacy. My interpretation, however, is that it is not so much the requirements of democratic legitimacy that encumber the development of planning. Rather, in the first instance at least, the resistance is from politicians who are embedded in the system of democratic politics and who are reluctant to support planning that they do not control, or that offers no or few political rewards. An implicit point here is that capitalists cannot always trust politicians to serve their interests—not because politicians are unsympathetic, but because the exigencies of democratic politics sometimes push them in other directions.

Nor can capitalists always trust planners to do the right thing— this is the other impediment to the development of planning as a method of policy formulation. The business community might

have been more supportive of planning decision making dominated by technical experts like Olmsted if they were convinced
that these planner-experts would serve their interests. Despite
planners' efforts to accommodate business interests in the City
Practical, businessmen remained unwilling to move further in
granting control of the built environment to planners. The problem was that, for planning to "work," planners had to be relatively
autonomous from their business patrons; to attend to capital's
collective concerns, they had to be free from the influence of particular capitalists. But this quest for autonomy posed a threat to
capitalists, who likewise needed autonomy to achieve their ends
as capitalists. This problem is examined further below.

The Contradictory Relationship between Planners and Capitalists

The relationship between planners and capitalists can be described as a contradictory one, inasmuch as the two groups are
mutually dependent and yet each requires a certain autonomy. It
is a mutually dependent relationship because, given the inequality
of class power in society, planners cannot achieve their aims without the support of capitalists, and capitalists cannot realize their
collective interests in the organization of the built environment
without the direction of planners. And yet each group requires a
certain autonomy—planners to address issues of collective concern in the organization of the built environment, and capitalists
to secure value from the productive assets in their control.

Capitalists' need for regulation and direction to achieve their
common interests is a problem confronted by Poulantzas. Capitalists, as he correctly notes, function more often as individuals than
as members of a class; the liberal ideology of the state and the pressures of market competition isolate capitalists from one another,
much as they isolate workers. The difference, he asserts, is that
the liberal state organizes and represents the interests of capital
while maintaining the political disorganization of the working
class.[9] But Poulantzas explains neither why the state functions in
this way, nor why it would do so when, as he presumes, it is relatively autonomous from the capitalist class and, further, when
capitalists are presumed to be incapable of understanding and acting on their common interests anyway. (He wrote that the state

---

[9] *Political Power and Social Classes*, pp. 275-89.

must be relatively autonomous from capital for the state to serve capital's political interest in maintaining the political demobilization of the working class.) Poulantzas's anthropomorphizing of the state and his failure to explain the source of the state's capitalist rationality were noted in Chapter 1. It should be added that explaining how the state comes to represent the interests of capital is a problem for Marx and Engels as well. Again and again they write in the *Manifesto* that the state secures the general conditions for maintaining capitalism, yet nowhere is the mechanism that produces this result illuminated. Their formulation that the "executive of the modern state is but a committee for managing the *common affairs* of the *whole bourgeoisie*" is a pithy statement, but it raises more questions than it answers.[10] Engels's characterization of the state as an "ideal personification of the total national capitalist" is likewise felicitous phraseology and possibly descriptively accurate, but he does not bring us closer to understanding why the state performs this function.[11]

The answer considered here is that "planners do it"—that if capitalists are prevented by their practice as capitalists from being able to understand and act on their collective class interests, there are others whose practice as "planners," "intellectuals," and the like enables them to perform this function for capital. John Maynard Keynes is credited with the aphorism that "in the long run we're all dead," the point being that few people can act on the basis of long-term interests. Yet there are "planners" and "intellectuals" who are able to conceptualize broad and long-term interests and whose institutional position rewards them for doing so. This observation arises in part from Gramsci's highly suggestive writing on the role of intellectuals in organizing class hegemony. Gramsci holds that every fundamental social class creates one or more strata of "organic" intellectuals that "give it homogeneity and an awareness of its own function not only in the economic but also in the social and political fields."[12] Following Gramsci, urban planners might be regarded as a specialized stratum of intellectual—specialists in identifying, organizing, and legitimating the interests of capital in the sphere of urban development.

This idea is consistent with the view of urban planners found in the marxist urban literature, except that there planners are re-

[10] "Manifesto of the Communist Party," p. 9 (italics mine).
[11] Engels, "Socialism: Utopian and Scientific," p. 104.
[12] *Prison Notebooks*, p. 5.

garded as the more or less self-conscious agents of capital. Planners are not thought to have any significant autonomy from business or interests distinct from or in competition with those of business. They are assumed to have only the autonomy needed to interpret the needs of the system as a whole, leading to a question analogous to that raised by Poulantzas's conception of the state: why would planners exercise their autonomy in ways that contributed to maintaining capitalism? In contrast, the pluralist literature regards planners as a distinct group of actors with their own interests in planning and urban development. Planners are not seen as advancing the interests of other groups, although pluralist theory lacks the necessary concept of objective interest to determine whether planners perform such a function. Planners are conceptualized as another "group" involved in urban development politics, albeit one with an intense level of interest, given that their value commitments, not to mention their jobs, are so much at stake.

In examining the responses to the property contradiction, we discovered that the orientation of urban planning generally corresponded with the interests of business. The question we are led to ask here is one of agency: what accounted for the correspondence between the kind of planning interventions advocated by planners and the interests of business? Was this correspondence an inevitable one, a product of the ineluctable logic of capitalist development? What role was there for voluntarism and indeterminacy—could the history of planning have been different? How autonomous were planners from their business patrons? Why would planners serve the interests of business if they were partially autonomous?

These are obviously difficult questions, but analyzing the transition from the City Beautiful to the City Practical provides some suggestive answers. It has been shown how the City Beautiful was of political and ideological service to business. But we must recall that this planning ideal was largely a product of the background and training of the architects and landscape architects who led the movement. Although these men were of the business class for the most part, they did not conceive of the City Beautiful ideal as an overt attempt to defend class interests or protect capitalism. It makes more sense to say that they were attempting to preserve the ability of architects and landscape architects to dominate the planning movement. Yet what made this movement partly successful—what made it possible to garner business support and carry out beautification projects in a number of cities—was that it corresponded, or could be stretched to correspond, with the political and ideological interests of this sponsor group. And to achieve this success, these planning ideologists had to educate members of the business class about the potential of City Beautiful planning. Yet the voluntarism of planners, their freedom to shape the development of planning, had its limits—as was evidenced by the demise of the City Beautiful.

The succeeding tradition of the City Practical represented an overt attempt to create a city in which business could thrive. Pluralists might regard this modality of planning as the product of an "alliance" between planners and businessmen (or certain segments of business), based on their mutual interests, albeit a strategic and therefore temporary alliance rather than a structurally determined one. But this alliance was hardly a chance occurrence. There was no other group to which planners could turn for effective support, and, on the other side, reliance on the market to organize urban development had already posed problems for some businessmen. Moreover, as with the City Beautiful, it was not a case of planners aligning their occupational and professional interests with an existing articulated interest on the part of business; rather, planning ideologists helped stimulate their business patrons' awareness of the need for a more efficient organization of urban space. To describe the relationship as an alliance based on mutual interests fails to consider how these groups were driven together to achieve their aims, and how planners helped stimulate business awareness of its needs.

The transition to the City Practical attests to both the nature and the limits of planners' independence from business. As an example of the limits of that autonomy, the transition reveals the relationship of mutual dependency and the two-way process of education and communication between planners and businessmen. Planners sought to educate members of the business community about the benefits to be derived from the City Beautiful; the eventual failure of that message to generate an effective base of support for planning indicated to the planning community the need for some other, more practical approach to planning. In some cases, there was more direct communication, as in the role of members of Chicago's Commercial Club in promoting transportation improvements as part of the Burnham Plan. The City Beautiful failed to garner adequate support because it was only a partial expression of business's interest in the ordering of the built environment; this disparity, in turn, was due to the fact that the City Beautiful was too much a product of the background and traditions of architects and landscape architects—that is, it was too much a product of planners' autonomy. There is no guarantee that the most effective solution to the problems of capitalism will emerge historically, or that capitalists will recognize it as such when it is presented to them. But contrary approaches that do not accord, or do not accord adequately, with the interests of capital are greatly disadvantaged and, in the absence of mobilized worker support, are material for the proverbial dustbin of history.

Yet planners' autonomy did not collapse in the face of the failure of the City Beautiful. The transition to the City Practical did not come about overnight; the idea of planning for economy and efficiency took hold slowly, and only after it had been filtered through the existing norms of the planning community. Charles Robinson, the leading ideologist of the City Beautiful, provides a case in point. While still maintaining an interest in urban beautification, he demonstrated in his 1911 plans for Fort Wayne, Indiana and Waterloo, Iowa that he was also interested in prohibiting manufacturing establishments from locating in residential areas, in creating separate industrial districts adjacent to freight terminals, and in limiting building heights in commercial areas as a way of avoiding traffic problems. In Robinson's work, as in the work of other proponents of the City Beautiful, the aesthetic approach was not so much eliminated as it was superseded as the guiding orientation of city planning.

Although planning thought displayed a bias toward the interests of business, it possessed a logic and internal coherence all its own. The history of planning thought cannot be reduced altogether to the evolution of the interests of capital in the ordering of the built environment. In the move away from the City Beautiful, there was a tension between maintaining an orientation to planning that corresponded with the professional interests of architects and landscape architects and the ability of planners to represent the interests of the business community and so gain their political support. And here it was the City Beautiful emphasis that gave way, but not completely, and only after a lengthy period of debate and reeducation within the planning community.

Despite the class bias of their models of planning, the leaders of the planning movement believed in the validity of those models on their own terms; that is what gave planning thought its internal coherence. Yet planners were also searching for effectiveness—in a double sense: they wanted to make the city effective, within the constraints of the existing organization of society, and they wanted to make planning effective. It is in this search for effectiveness that the class bias entered. Attempting to make the city more effective within the constraints of the property system necessarily involved aiding the city's economically dominant class. In failing to question that dominance, and in seeking to mitigate the problems of the city as best they could within the limits of the system of private ownership of land and productive assets, these early planners contributed to the maintenance of that system. This was the structural source of the bias of planning; it arose from the organization of society rather than from the attitudes or class position of members of the planning community. Then, too, the desire to make planning effective caused planners to turn to the business community as their only realistic base of support, given political realities. The instrumental and political source of the bias of planning thus turned on the differential power of business, labor, and other groups to provide support for planning. It was this twin desire for effectiveness that accounts for the correspondence between what planners advocated and what business needed.

Significantly, these observations pertain to an era in which planning was a political movement more than a state function, and in which the character of planning was determined largely outside the state. Planning in this period was initially a private activity; when planners worked for government, it was typically in a consulting capacity. Therefore, the evolution of planning depended upon relationships outside the state, namely on the relationship between the planning movement and business. The situation today, however, is quite different; planning has become a government function and planners, as government employees, have become members of the state system. What planners do today is probably less a product of the traditions and internal history of the planning profession and more a product of planners' role within the state, the relationship between business and the state, the organization of the state, and the state's role in the economy. An examination of contemporary urban planning, or of other forms of state planning, would therefore proceed differently.

METHODOLOGY AND POLITICAL PRACTICE

It has been argued that the history of American urban planning cannot be adequately understood via a deterministic theory that relates the development of planning to the logic of development of

253

the capitalist mode of production, or to the logic of a social formation combining capitalism and democracy. There is too much variation among capitalist societies in the nature and extent of urban planning, and too many disparate factors influencing how these societies respond to the contradictions arising from their political and economic structures, for such a theory to be entirely adequate. Yet the alternative of a pluralist analysis that fails to take account of how planning corresponds with business interests, and that disregards the structural origins of the conflicts that have marked the development of planning, is not adequate either. Nor should we be satisfied with the historical idealist perspective that sees planning history as the progressive development of the "planning idea."

The approach here has been to relate the development of urban planning to contradictions that are structurally rooted, that is, objectively given, existing independent of anyone's consciousness and will. This is where structuralist analysis seems most useful. As Godelier argues, identifying the contradictions that inhere in the structure of a society is necessary before historical analysis can begin.[13] Such theoretical analysis is, however, only a first step. How a society responds to the contradictions arising from its structure is, within some limits, historically variable. Its response depends upon a variety of factors, such as the level of organization and consciousness of the classes in society, the ideology of the dominant class and its penetration into the consciousness of subordinate classes, and the organization of the state system (in particular, the democratic nature of the state). Within this intellectual space, where consciousness, will, and organization all matter, historical analysis is essential.

The focus of this book has been on the planning community, its leaders, their practices and ideas. It has been shown how the ideas and efforts of particular individuals like Lawrence Veiller, Robert de Forest, Frederick Olmsted, Jr. and Sr., Daniel Burnham, and Benjamin Marsh shaped the planning movement's response to the contradictions of capitalist urbanization. One expense of this strategy is that we have observed little overt struggle over the forms and purposes of planning. Undoubtedly, more such conflict would have been included had the focus been on planning in particular cities, although such a focus would have made it difficult to characterize the planning movement as a whole. Yet it is also

---

[13] "Structure and Contradiction in *Capital*," pp. 343-49.

true that there was not much overt struggle over the development of planning, in part because planning was largely an elite undertaking in which conflicts were worked out *in camera*, and in part because, as I have stressed, the workplace orientation of the American labor movement minimized worker mobilization on issues pertaining to the built environment. This is not to say that the working class had no effect on the development of urban planning. The housing reform, park planning, and City Beautiful movements were all attempts to exercise or acquire greater control over the urban proletariat. But in these instances, the working class exercised its effect on the development of planning indirectly, through the efforts of the business class to stave off working-class threats (real or only anticipated) to social and political order.

The problem of methodology is not just of theoretical or analytical interest; it also matters for political practice. The trouble with deterministic theories is that they convince one in advance that this or that development will occur, and that reform movements will necessarily fail. The result is often a fatalistic passivity and/or an irrelevant strategy based upon an erroneous, too unilinear anticipation of the future. Gramsci took note of this political and theoretical error in his criticism of economism, stating that it puts forward in advance "when no concrete fact yet exists to support it" what should be considered in the last analysis only as a hypothesis—that reform movements will necessarily be perverted and serve quite different ends than the mass of their followers expect. "Thus the political struggle is reduced to a series of personal affairs between on the one hand those with the genie in the lamp who know everything and on the other those who are fooled by their own leaders but are so incurably thick that they refuse to believe it."[14] There is a tendency to make a similar error in the way part of the American left views the prospect of state planning—whether it is urban and regional planning or, of more current interest, national economic planning. The nature of this error can be examined in terms of the two central contradictions used in this analysis.

First, there often appears to be a one-sided understanding of the property contradiction, and sometimes a failure to view state planning in a capitalist society as contradictory at all. Deterministic theories about the need for state intervention to resolve or mitigate the problems of capitalism lead one to the conclusion

[14] *Prison Notebooks*, pp. 166-67.

that state planning is an inevitable concomitant of capitalist development. This view fails to recognize that state interventions confront the structural limit of the private ownership and control of property. It also fails to appreciate that, within some limits, the response of the state to the contradictions of capitalism is politically determined, and that there is indeterminacy and room for maneuver here—in short, that space exists for a left politics. In the United States, state intervention and the adoption of nonmarket controls have been slower to develop and less extensive than in other capitalist democracies, indicating the possibility for an expansion of what Ira Katznelson has called the "social democratic surplus"—social democratic reforms in excess of the minimum required for maintaining capitalism.[15]

State intervention that entails the adoption of nonmarket controls is potentially progressive to the extent that it involves the application of social need or social utility criteria in place of the profit criterion. The democratic left should assume neither that significantly expanded state intervention in response to the needs of capital is inevitable, nor that efforts to adopt nonmarket controls will necessarily be perverted and put to the unqualified, noncontradictory use of capital. Part of the task of the left is to liberate society from the dead weight of deference to market principles. The left should not be a force of reaction that, because it cannot carry out its program, ends up defending market capitalism against the expansion of state planning under advanced capitalism.

Realistically, the adoption or nonmarket controls based on social need criteria may necessitate certain alliances with capital. There are grounds for such an alliance in responding to the property contradiction—this book has shown that capitalists cannot rely entirely on the market system and need government intervention to secure their collective interests. But there are less grounds for alliance in the case of the capitalist-democracy contradiction—capital often requires nondemocratic planning, whereas the democratic left does not, or should not. Urban renewal policy provides a case in point. The land-grabbing of real estate developers and large institutions such as hospitals and universities under the cover of urban renewal programs required that urban renewal agencies be insulated from popular pressures. When grass-roots opposition to the urban renewal bulldozer gained political expres-

[15] "Considerations on Social Democracy," p. 87.

sion and federal guidelines were changed to require community participation in urban renewal planning, the federal renewal program was largely ended.[16] This particular class-biased form of renewal could not survive once a semblance of democracy was brought to the decision making process.

Critics of American capitalism should not take for granted Offe's assertion that the requirement of capital accumulation takes precedence over securing democratic legitimacy in the definition of "good" public policy (which for Offe is why technocratic, nondemocratic state planning is advantaged and is probably inevitable). Offe may be describing accurately the tendencies of advanced captialist societies, but these tendencies are not ironclad. It is possible to mobilize support around an alternative concept of the local public interest—one in which democracy is valued over assisting in the creation of private wealth. The task is to build upon society's existing commitment to democracy, extending the principle of democratic decision making to the realm of the built environment. There is no better hope for overcoming the imbalance between private purposes and social need in the organization of our cities.

[16] See Mollenkopf, "The Postwar Politics of Urban Development," pp. 117-52.

Adams, Henry. *The Education of Henry Adams: An Autobiography*. Boston: Houghton Mifflin Co., 1918.

Adams, John Coleman. "What a Great City Might Be—A Lesson from the White City." *New England Magazine* (March 1896): 3-13.

Adams, Thomas. *Outline of Town and City Planning*. New York: Russell Sage Foundation, 1936.

Akagi, Roy H. *The Town Proprietors of the New England Colonies; A Study of their Development, Organization, Activities and Controversies, 1620–1770*. Philadelphia: University of Pennsylvania Press, 1924.

Allensworth, Don. *The Political Realities of Urban Planning*. New York: Praeger, 1975.

Althusser, Louis. "Contradiction and Overdetermination." In Louis Althusser, *For Marx*, translated by Ben Brewster, pp. 89-128. New York: Vintage Books, 1970.

———. "From 'Capital' to Marx's Philosophy." In Louis Althusser and Etienne Balibar, *Reading Capital*, pp. 11-98. London: New Left Books, 1970.

Altshuler, Alan. *The City Planning Process: A Political Analysis*. Ithaca, N.Y.: Cornell University Press, 1965.

Ashworth, William. *The Genesis of Modern British Town Planning: A Study in Economic and Social History of the Nineteenth and Twentieth Centuries*. London: Routledge & Kegan Paul, 1954.

Atterbury, Grosvenor. "Forest Hills Gardens." *The Survey* 25 (January 1911): 565.

"Baltimore Municipal Art Conference." *Municipal Affairs* 3 (December 1899): 706-13.

Banfield, Edward. *Political Influence*. New York: Free Press, 1961.

Banfield, Edward, and Wilson, James Q. *City Politics*. Cambridge: Harvard Univerity Press, 1963.

Bannister, Turpin P. "Oglethorpe's Sources for the Savannah Plan." *Journal of the Society of Architectural Historians* 20 (May 1961): 47-62.

Batchelor, Peter. "The Origin of the Garden City Concept of Urban

Form." *Journal of the Society of Architectural Historians* 28 (October 1969): 184-200.

Bauer, Catherine. *Modern Housing*. Boston: Houghton Mifflin Co., 1934.

Bellows, H. W. "Cities and Parks: With Special Reference to New York's Central Park." *Atlantic Monthly* (April 1861): 416-29.

Bender, Thomas. "The 'Rural' Cemetery Movement: Urban Travail and the Appeal of Nature." *New England Quarterly* 47 (June 1974): 196-211.

Benevolo, Leonardo. *The Origins of Modern Town Planning*. Translated by Judith Landry. Cambridge: MIT Press, 1967.

Bettman, Alfred. *City and Regional Planning Papers*. Edited by Arthur C. Comey. Cambridge: Harvard University Press, 1946.

―――. "City Planning Legislation." In *City Planning*, edited by John Nolen, pp. 431-71. National Municipal League Series. New York: D. Appleton & Co., 1929.

―――. "The Planning Commission: Its Functions and Method" (1935). In Alfred Bettman, *City and Regional Planning Papers*, edited by Arther C. Comey, pp. 23-30. Cambridge: Harvard University Press, 1946.

Birch, Eugenie Ladner. "From Civic Worker to City Planner: Women and Planning, 1890–1980." In *The American Planner: Biographies and Recollections*, edited by Donald A. Krueckeberg, pp. 396-427. New York: Methuen, 1983.

Birch, Eugenie Ladner, and Gardner, Deborah S. "The Seven-Percent Solution: A Review of Philanthropic Housing, 1870–1910." *Journal of Urban History* 7 (August 1981): 403-38.

Blashfield, Edwin H. "A Word for Municipal Art." *Municipal Affairs* 3 (December 1899): 582-93.

Bliss, W. D. P. "The Garden Cities Association in America." *The Garden City* 2 (February 1907): 268-69.

Block, Fred. "The Ruling Class Does Not Rule: Notes on the Marxist Theory of the State." *Socialist Revolution* 33 (May-June 1977): 6-28.

Blodgett, Geoffrey. "Frederick Law Olmsted: Landscape Architecture as Conservative Reform." *Journal of American History* 62 (March 1976): 869-89.

Boyer, M. Christine. *Dreaming the Rational City: The Myth of American City Planning*. Cambridge: MIT Press, 1983.

Boyer, Paul. *Urban Masses and Moral Order in America, 1820–1920*. Cambridge: Harvard University Press, 1978.

Bremner, Robert H. "The Big Flat: History of a New York Tenement House." *American Historical Review* 64 (October 1958): 54-62.

Bridenbaugh, Carl. *Cities in the Wilderness*. New York: Ronald, 1938.

Bridges, Amy. *A City in the Republic: Ante-Bellum New York and the Origins of Machine Politics*. Cambridge: Cambridge University Press, 1984.

————. "Nicos Poulantzas and the Marxist Theory of the State." *Politics & Society* 4 (Winter 1974): 161-90.

Brown, Robert. "Progress of the Garden City Movement in England." *Arena* 40 (1908): 459-60.

Brunner, Arnold W. "The Meaning of City Planning." In *Proceedings of the Fourth National Conference on City Planning*, pp. 22-29. Boston: N.p., 1912.

Buchholz, William. "Acquirement of Kansas City Park and Boulevard System and Its Effect on Real Estate Values." *Proceedings of the Ninth National Conference on City Planning*, pp. 96-105. New York: N.p., 1917.

Buder, Stanley. "Ebenezer Howard: The Genesis of a Town Planning Movement." *Journal of the American Institute of Planners* 35 (November 1969): 390-98.

————. *Pullman: An Experiment in Industrial Order and Community Planning, 1880–1930*. New York: Oxford University Press, 1967.

Burnham, Daniel H. "The Organization of the World's Columbian Exposition." *The Inland Architect and News Record* (August 1893): 5.

————. "White City and Capital City." *Century* 63 (January 1902): 619-20.

Burnham, Daniel H., and Bennett, Edward H. *Plan of Chicago*. Edited by Charles Moore. Da Capo Press Series in Architecture and Decorative Art, vol. 29. Chicago: Commercial Club of Chicago, 1909. Reprint. New York: Da Capo Press, 1970.

Buttenheim, Harold S. "President's Address: Looking Backward and Pressing Onward." *Proceedings of the Thirtieth National Conference on City Planning*, pp. 1-3. Chicago: American Society of Planning Officials, 1939.

Caparn, H. A. "Central Park, New York: A Work of Art." *Landscape Architecture* 2 (July 1912): 167-76.

Caro, Robert. *The Power Broker: Robert Moses and the Fall of New York*. New York: Vintage Books, 1975.

Carrère, John M. "The Beautifying of Cities." *House and Garden* 5 (1904): 276-84.

Castells, Manuel. *The City and the Grass Roots*. Berkeley: University of California Press, 1983.

————. "Theory and Ideology in Urban Sociology." In *Urban Sociology: Critical Essays*, edited by Chris Pickvance, pp. 60-84. London: Tavistock Press, 1976.

————. "Towards a Political Urban Sociology." In *Captive Cities: Studies in the Political Economy of Cities and Regions*, edited by Michael Harloe, pp. 61-78. London: John Wiley & Co., 1977.

————. *The Urban Question*. Cambridge: MIT Press, 1977.

Castells, Manuel, and Godard, François. *Monopoville: L'Entreprise, L'Etat, L'Urbain*. Paris: Mouton, 1974.

Cheney, Charles H. "Zoning in Practice." In *Proceedings of the Eleventh National Conference on City Planning*, pp. 162-94. Cambridge, Mass.: University Press, 1919.

"Chicago Parks and their Landscape Architecture." *Architectural Record* 24 (July-December 1908): 19-30.

Child, Stephen. "Parks for Industrial Cities." *Municipal Journal and Engineer* 17 (July 1904): 1-4.

Chudacoff, Howard P. *The Evolution of American Urban Society*. Englewood Cliffs, N.J.: Prentice-Hall, 1975.

Churchill, Henry S. *The City is the People*. New York: W. W. Norton & Co., 1962.

Civic League of Saint Louis. *A City Plan for Saint Louis*. St. Louis: N.p., 1907.

Cleveland, Horace W. S. "The Influence of Parks on the Character of Children." *American Park and Outdoor Art Association* 2 (1898): 105-8.

————. *Landscape Architecture as Applied to the Wants of the West*. Edited by Roy Lubove. Pittsburgh: University of Pittsburgh Press, 1965; orig. ed. 1873.

————. "Suggestions for a System of Parks and Parkways for the City of Minneapolis." Paper read at a meeting of the Minneapolis Park Commissioners, June 2, 1883. Harvard Graduate School of Design Library.

Committee on Town Planning of the American Institute of Architects. *City Planning Progress in the United States.* Edited by George B. Ford. Washington, D.C.: American Institute of Architects, 1917.

Crawford, Andrew W. "Discussion of the Papers of Mr. Olmsted and Mr. Ford." In U.S. Congress. Senate. *City Planning* [Proceedings of the First National Conference on City Planning], pp. 81-82. 61st Cong., 2d sess., 1910. S. Doc. 422.

———. "Excess Condemnation and Public Use." *Proceedings of the Second National Conference on City Planning and Population Congestion,* pp. 155-63. Cambridge, Mass.: University Press, 1910.

———. "Recent City Planning in Philadelphia." *Charities and the Commons* 19 (February 1908): 1537-43.

Croly, Herbert. "Civic Improvements: The Case of New York." *Architectural Record* 21 (May 1907): 347-52.

———. "The Promised City of San Francisco." *Architectural Record* 19 (June 1906): 425-36.

Crook, David H. "Louis Sullivan and the Golden Doorway." *Journal of the Society of Architectural Historians* 26 (December 1967): 250-58.

Cunliff, Nelson. "Blighted Districts in St. Louis." In *Proceedings of the Tenth National Conference on City Planning,* pp. 72-73. Boston: Taylor Press, 1918.

Dahl, Robert. *Preface to Democratic Theory.* Chicago: University of Chicago Press, 1956.

———. *Who Governs?* New Haven: Yale University Press, 1961.

Dear, Michael, and Scott, Allen J., "Towards a Framework for Analysis." In *Urbanization and Urban Planning in Capitalist Society,* edited by Michael Dear and Allen J. Scott, pp. 3-18. London: Metheun, 1981.

———, eds. *Urbanization and Urban Planning in Capitalist Society.* London: Metheun, 1981.

De Forest, Robert W. "A Brief History of the Housing Movement in America." *Annals of the American Academy of Political and Social Science* 51 (January 1914): 8-16.

———. "Introduction: Tenement Reform in New York Since 1901." In *The Tenement House Problem,* edited by Robert W. de Forest and Lawrence Veiller, vol. 1, pp. ix-xxi. New York: Macmillan Co., 1903.

Diggs, Annie. "The Garden City Movement." *Arena* 28 (December 1902): 626-30.

Downing, Andrew Jackson. "Public Cemeteries and Public Gardens." *The Horticulturist* 4 (July 1849): 1-12.

———. *Rural Essays*. Edited by George W. Curtis. New York: George Putnam & Co., 1853.

———. "A Talk About Public Parks and Gardens." *Horticulturist* 3 (October 1848): 153-58.

———. *A Treatise on the Theory and Practice of Landscape Gardening*. New York: Wiley & Putnam, 1849.

Egleston, Melville. "The Land System of the New England Colonies." *Johns Hopkins University Studies in Historical and Political Science*, edited by Herbert B. Adams, 4th ser., chaps. 11-12. Baltimore: Johns Hopkins University Press, 1886.

Eliot, Charles W. *Charles Eliot, Landscape Architect*. Boston: Houghton Mifflin Co., 1902.

Elkin, Stephen. *Politics and Land Use Planning: The London Experience*. London: Cambridge University Press, 1974.

Ely, Richard T. "Pullman: A Social Study." *Harper's* (February 1885): 452-65.

Engels, Frederick. *The Condition of the Working Class in England*. Moscow: Progress Publishers, 1973; orig. German ed. 1845.

———. *The Housing Question*. Moscow: Progress Publishers, 1970; orig. German ed. 1887.

———. "Socialism: Utopian and Scientific." In *Marx & Engels: Basic Writings on Politics and Philosophy*, edited by Lewis S. Feuer, pp. 68-111. Garden City: Anchor Books, 1959.

"Farm and City and Factory," *The Survey* 25 (March 1911): 896-98.

Foner, Philip S. *History of the Labor Movement in the United States*. Vol. 1. New York: International Publishers, 1947.

Ford, Frederick. "The Scope of City Planning in the United States." In U.S. Congress. Senate. *City Planning* [Proceedings of the First National Conference on City Planning], pp. 70-73. 61st Cong., 2d sess., 1910. S. Doc. 422.

Ford, George B. "The Architectural Side of City Planning." *American Architect* 108, pt. 2 (1915): 299-300.

———. "The City Scientific." In *Proceedings of the Fifth National Conference on City Planning*, pp. 31-40. Cambridge, Mass.: University Press, 1913.

Ford, George B. "The Park System of Kansas City, Mo." *Architectural Record* 40 (December 1916): 498-504.

Ford, James. *Slums and Housing.* Vol. 1. Cambridge: Harvard University Press, 1936.

Fox, Kenneth. *Better City Government: Innovation in American Urban Politics, 1850–1937.* Philadelphia: Temple University Press, 1977.

French, Jere Stuart. "The First 'People's Park' Movement." *Landscape Architecture* 62 (October 1971): 25-29.

Friedman, Lawrence. *Government and Slum Housing: A Century of Frustration.* Chicago: Rand McNally & Co., 1968.

Fries, Sylvia Doughty. *The Urban Idea in Colonial America.* Philadelphia: Temple University Press, 1977.

"From City to Country," *The Survey* 25 (March 1911): 898-99.

Fuller, H. B. "An Industrial Utopia: Building Gary, Indiana to Order." *Harper's* 91 (October 1907): 1482-83.

"The Garden Cities Association of America." *Charities and the Commons* 17 (1906): 286.

Glaab, Charles N. *The American City: A Documentary History.* Homewood, Ill.: Dorsey Press, 1963.

Glaab, Charles N., and Brown, A. Theodore. *A History of Urban America.* 2d ed. New York: Macmillan Co., 1976.

Godelier, Maurice. "Structure and Contradiction in *Capital.*" In *Ideology and Social Science,* edited by Robin Blackburn, pp. 334-68. New York: Vintage Books, 1973.

Gordon, David. "Capitalism and the Roots of the Urban Crisis." In *The Fiscal Crisis of American Cities: Essays on the Political Economy of Urban America with Special Reference to New York,* edited by Roger E. Alcaly and David Mermelstein, pp. 86-90. New York: Vintage Books, 1977.

Gramsci, Antonio. *Selections from the Prison Notebooks.* Edited and translated by Quintin Hoare and Geoffrey N. Smith. New York: International Publishers, 1971.

Greenstone, David, and Peterson, Paul. *Race and Authority in Urban Politics.* Chicago: University of Chicago Press, 1973; Phoenix ed. 1976.

Griscom, John H. *The Sanitary Conditions of the Laboring Population of New York, with Suggestions for its Improvements.* New York: Harper & Bros., 1845.

Gross, Robert A. *The Minutemen and Their World.* American Century Series. New York: Hill and Wang, 1976.

"The Grouping of Public Buildings at Cleveland." *Inland Architect* 62 (September 1903): 13-15.

Haber, Samuel. *Efficiency and Uplift: Scientific Management in the Progressive Era, 1890–1920.* Chicago: University of Chicago Press, 1964.

Habermas, Jurgen. *Legitimation Crisis.* Boston: Beacon Press, 1973.

Haldeman, B. Antrim. "The Control of Municipal Development by the 'Zone System' and its Application in the United States." *Proceedings of the Fourth National Conference on City Planning,* pp. 173-87. Boston: N.p., 1912.

Haller, William, Jr. *The Puritan Frontier: Town Planting in New England Colonial Development, 1630–1660.* Columbia University Studies in History, Economics and Public Law, no. 568. New York: Columbia University Press, 1951.

Hansen, Willard B. "Metropolitan Planning and the New Comprehensiveness." *Journal of the American Institute of Planners* 34 (September 1968): 295-302.

Harder, J. F. "The City's Plan." *Municipal Affairs* 2 (March 1898): 25-45.

Harloe, Michael, ed. *Captive Cities: Studies of the Political Economy of Cities and Regions.* London: John Wiley & Co., 1977.

Harris, Marshall. *Origin of the Land Tenure System in the United States.* Ames: Iowa State College Press, 1953.

Harsch, Paul. "Point of View of the Real Estate Developer." In *Proceedings of the Seventh National Conference on City Planning,* pp. 71-79. Cambridge, Mass.: University Press, 1915.

Harvey, David. "Labor, Capital, and Class Struggle around the Built Environment in Advanced Capitalist Societies." *Politics & Society* 6 (1976): 265-95.

———. "The Political Economy of Urbanization in Advanced Capitalist Societies: The Case of the United States." In *The Social Economy of Cities.* Urban Affairs Annual, edited by Gary Grappert and Harold M. Rose, no. 9, pp. 119-63. Beverly Hills: Russell Sage, 1975.

———. *Social Justice and the City.* Baltimore: Johns Hopkins University Press, 1973.

Havens, Munson. "Remarks." In U.S. Congress. Senate. *City Planning* [Proceedings of the First National Conference on City Planning], pp. 82-84. 61st Cong., 2d sess., 1910. S. Doc. 422.

Hayek, Friedrich. *The Road to Serfdom.* Chicago: University of Chicago Press, 1944.

Hines, Thomas S. *Burnham of Chicago: Architect and Planner.* New York: Oxford University Press, 1974.

Hobsbawm, Eric. *The Age of Capital, 1848–1875.* New York: Scribner, 1975.

Holden, L. E. "Parks as Investments and Educators." *Report of the Park and Outdoor Art Association.* 1 (1897): 42-50.

Holme, Thomas C. "A Short Advertisement upon the Scituation and Extent of the City of Philadelphia and the Ensuing Platform thereof, by the Surveyor General" (1683). In *Narratives of Early Pennsylvania, West New Jersey and Delaware, 1630–1707,* edited by Albert C. Myers, pp. 242-44. New York: Charles Scribner's Sons, 1912.

Hooker, George B. "Congestion and its Causes in Chicago." *Proceedings of the Second National Conference on City Planning and Population Congestion,* pp. 42-57. Cambridge, Mass.: University Press, 1910.

———. "Garden Cities." *Journal of the American Institute of Architects* 2 (1914): 80-91.

Horack, Frank E., Jr., and Nolan, Val, Jr. *Land Use Controls: Supplementary Materials on Real Property.* American Casebook Series, edited by Erwin N. Griswold. St. Paul: West Publishing Co., 1955.

Howard, Ebenezer. *Garden Cities of Tomorrow.* London: Swan Sonnenschein & Co., 1902.

Howe, Frederic C. "The Cleveland Group Plan." *Charities and the Commons* 19 (February 1908): 1548.

———. "Land Values and Congestion." *The Survey* 25 (March 1911): 1067-68.

Howe, Samuel C. "Forest Hills Gardens." *American Architect* 102 (October 1912): 153-58.

Hubbard, Theodora Kimball, and Hubbard, Henry Vincent. *Our Cities To-Day and To-Morrow.* Cambridge: Harvard University Press, 1929.

Jackson, Anthony. *A Place Called Home: A History of Low-Cost Housing in Manhattan.* Cambridge: MIT Press, 1976.

"James Watt's Land Rush." *Newsweek,* 29 June 1981, p. 30.

Jameson, Franklin J. *The American Revolution Considered as a Social Movement.* Princeton: Princeton University Press, 1926.

Kantor, Harvey. "Benjamin C. Marsh and the Fight Over Population Congestion." *Journal of the American Institute of Planners* 40 (1974): 422-29.

———. "The City Beautiful in New York." *New York Historical Society Quarterly* 57 (1973): 148-71.

Karl, Barry. *Charles E. Merriam and the Study of Politics.* Chicago: University of Chicago Press, 1974.

Karlowicz, Titus. "D. H. Burnham's Role in the Selection of Architects for the World's Columbian Exposition." *Journal of the Society of Architectural Historians* 29 (1970): 247-54.

Kasson, John F. *Amusing the Million: Coney Island at the Turn of the Century.* New York: Hill & Wang, 1978.

Katznelson, Ira. *City Trenches: Urban Politics and the Patterning of Class in the United States.* New York: Pantheon, 1981.

———. "Considerations on Social Democracy in the United States." *Comparative Politics* 11 (October 1978): 77-99.

Kilham, Walter H. "Boston's New Opportunities." *American Architect* 79 (January 1903): 21-22.

Kimball, Theodora. *Manual of Information on City Planning and Zoning.* Cambridge: Harvard University Press, 1923.

Kipnis, Ira. *The American Socialist Movement, 1897–1912.* New York: Columbia University Press, 1952.

Knapp, Raymond S. "Short History of the Development of Chicago Parks." Unpublished paper, Harvard Graduate School of Design Library, June 1955. Vertical File.

Koester, Frank. "American City Planning—Part I." *American Architect* 102 (October 1912): 141-46.

Kriehn, George. "The City Beautiful." *Municipal Affairs* 3 (December 1899): 594-601.

Krueckeberg, Donald A., ed. *The American Planner: Biographies and Recollections.* New York: Metheun, 1983.

———. *Introduction to Planning History in the United States.* New Brunswick: Rutgers/Center for Urban Policy Research, 1983.

Lamarche, François. "Property Development and the Economic Foundations of the Urban Question." In *Urban Sociology: Critical Essays,* edited by Chris Pickvance, pp. 85-118. London: Tavistock Press, 1976.

Lamb, Charles R. "Civic Architecture from its Constructive Side." *Municipal Affairs* 2 (March 1898): 46-72.

Lamb, Frederick S. "Art for the People." Proceedings of the Baltimore Municipal Art Conference of 1899, as printed in *Municipal Affairs* 3 (December 1899): 711-13.

———. "New York City Improvement Report." *Charities and the Commons* 19 (February 1908): 1532-36.

Lewis, Nelson P. *The Planning of the Modern City: A Review of the Principles Governing City Planning.* New York: John Wiley & Sons, 1916.

Lindblom, Charles. *The Intelligence of Democracy.* New York: Free Press, 1965.

———. *Politics and Markets.* New York: Basic Books, 1977.

———. "The Science of Muddling Through." *Public Administration Review* 19 (Spring 1959): 79-88.

Lindblom, Charles, and Braybrooke, David. *A Strategy of Decision: Policy Evaluation as a Social Process.* New York: Free Press of Glencoe, 1963.

Lockridge, Kenneth A. *A New England Town: The First Hundred Years, Dedham, Massachusetts, 1636–1736.* New York: W. W. Norton, 1970.

Lowi, Theodore. *The End of Liberalism.* New York: W. W. Norton, 1969.

Lubove, Roy. "Lawrence Veiller and the New York State Tenement House Commission of 1900." *Mississippi Valley Historical Review* 47 (March 1961): 659-67.

———. "The New York Association for Improving the Condition of the Poor: The Formative Years." *New York Historical Society Quarterly* 43 (January 1959): 307-27.

———. *The Progressives and the Slums.* N.p.: University of Pittsburgh Press, 1963.

———. "The Roots of Urban Planning." In *The Urbanization of America: An Historical Anthology,* edited by Allen Wakstein, pp. 315-29. Boston: Houghton Mifflin Co., 1970.

MacFadyen, Dugald. *Sir Ebenezer Howard and the Town Planning Movement.* Cambridge: MIT Press, 1970.

McFarland, Henry B. F. "The Rebuilding of the National Capital." *American City* 1 (1909): 3-13.

McFarland, J. Horace. "The Relation of City Planning to Business." In *Proceedings of the Ninth National Conference on City Planning,* pp. 155-67. New York: N.p., 1917.

Magee, William A. "The Organization and Functions of a City Plan Commission." In *Proceedings of the Fifth National Con-*

ference on City Planning, pp. 73-84. Cambridge, Mass.: University Press, 1913.

Marcuse, Peter. "Housing in Early City Planning." *Journal of Urban History* 6 (February 1980): 153-76.

———. "Housing Policy and the Myth of the Benevolent State." *Social Policy* (January-February 1978): 21-26.

Marsh, Benjamin C. "City Planning in Justice to the Working Population." *Survey* 19 (February 1908): 1514-18.

———. "The Congestion Exhibit in Brooklyn." *Charities and the Commons* 20 (May 1908): 209-11.

———. "Economic Aspects of City Planning." In U.S. Congress. Senate. *City Planning* [Proceedings of the First National Conference on City Planning], pp. 104-5. 61st Cong., 2d sess., 1910. S. Doc. 422.

———. *An Introduction to City Planning: Democracy's Challenge to the American City*. New York: N.p., 1909.

———. *Lobbyist for the People: A Record of Fifty Years*. Washington: Public Affairs Press, 1953.

———. "Statement of Mr. Benjamin Clarke Marsh." *Hearing before the Senate Committee on the District of Columbia*. In U.S. Congress. Senate. *City Planning*, p. 10. 61st Cong., 2d sess., 1910. S. Doc. 422.

———. "Taxation and the Improvement of Living Conditions in American Cities." *The Survey* 24 (July 1910): 605-9.

———. *Taxation of Land Values in American Cities: The Next Step in Eliminating Poverty*. New York: N.p., 1911.

Martin, John. "The Exhibit of Congestion Interpreted." *Charities and the Commons* 20 (April 1908): 27-39.

Marx, Karl. *Capital: A Critique of Political Economy*. Vol. 1. Edited by Frederick Engels. Translated by Samuel Moore and Edward Aveling. New York: International Publishers, 1967; orig. German ed. 1867.

Marx, Karl, and Engels, Frederick. "Manifesto of the Communist Party." In *Marx & Engels: Basic Writings on Politics and Philosophy*, edited by Lewis S. Feuer, pp. 1-41. Garden City: Anchor Books, 1959.

Meakin, Budgett. *Model Factories and Villages: Ideal Conditions of Labour and Housing*. London: T. Fisher Unwin, 1905.

Melville, Ralph. "Garden Cities." *American Architect* 83 (February 1904): 67-68.

Merriam, Charles E. "The National Resources Planning Board; A Chapter in the American Planning Experience." *American Political Science Review* 38 (December 1944): 1075-88.

Meyeison, Martin, and Banfield, Edward. *Politics, Planning and the Public Interest.* New York: Free Press, 1955.

Miliband, Ralph. *The State in Capitalist Society.* New York: Basic Books, 1969.

Miller, Wilhelm. "What England Can Teach Us About Garden Cities." *Country Life* 17 (March 1910): 531-34.

Mogulof, Melvin B. *Governing Metropolitan Areas: A Critical Review of Council of Governments and the Federal Role.* Washington, D.C.: Urban Institute, 1971.

Mohl, Raymond A., and Betten, Neil. "The Failure of Industrial City Planning: Gary, Indiana, 1906–1910." *Journal of the American Institute of Planners* 38 (July 1972): 203-15.

Mollenkopf, John H. "The Postwar Politics of Urban Development." In *Marxism and the Metropolis,* edited by William K. Tabb and Larry Sawers, pp. 117-52. New York: Oxford University Press, 1978.

Moody, Walter D. *Wacker's Manual of the Plan of Chicago.* N.p.: N.p., 1909.

Moore, Charles. *Daniel H. Burnham, Architect: Planner of Cities.* 2 vols. in one. Boston: Houghton Mifflin Co., 1921. Reprint. New York: Da Capo Press, 1968.

———. "The Improvement of Washington." *American Architect* 78 (December 1902): 101-2.

Morgenthau, Henry. "A National Constructive Programme for City Planning." In U.S. Congress. Senate. *City Planning* [Proceedings of the First National Conference on City Planning], pp. 59-62. 61st Cong., 2d sess., 1910. S. Doc. 422.

Moses, Robert. "What Happened to Haussmann?" *Architectural Forum* 77 (July 1942): 57-66.

"The Movement in America." *The Garden City* 1 (December 1906): 252.

Mulford, F. L. "Recent Park Reports." *National Municipal Review* 4 (July 1915): 398-405.

Mullin, John R. "American Perceptions of German City Planning at the Turn of the Century." *Urbanism Past and Present* 3 (1976-1977): 5-15.

Mumford, Lewis. *The Brown Decades: A Study of the Arts in*

America, 1865–1895. New York: Harcourt, Brace and Co., 1931.

———. *Sticks and Stones: A Study of American Architecture and Civilization.* New York: Dover Publications, 1924.

Myers, Albert C., ed. *Narratives of Early Pennsylvania, West New Jersey and Delaware, 1630–1707.* New York: Charles Scribner's Sons, 1912.

Nash, Gary B. "City Planning and Political Tension in the Seventeenth Century: The Case of Philadelphia." In *American Philosophical Society Proceedings* 112 (February 1968): 54-73.

———. *The Urban Crucible: Social Change, Political Consciousness and the Origins of the American Revolution.* Cambridge: Harvard University Press, 1979.

National Capital Planning Commission. *Worthy of the Nation: The History of Planning for the National Capital.* Frederick Gutheim, consultant. Washington, D.C.: Smithsonian Institute, 1977.

National Housing Association. *Constitution and By-Laws.* January 1910.

Nevins, Allan. *The Evening Post: A Century of Journalism.* New York: Russell & Russell, 1922.

Nolen, John. "Types of City Plans." *American Architect* 117 (February 1920): 213-15.

O'Connor, James. *The Fiscal Crisis of the State.* New York: St. Martin's Press, 1973.

O'Donnell, Patrick. "Industrial Capitalism and the Rise of Modern American Cities." *Kapitalistate*, no. 6 (1977): 91-128.

Offe, Claus. "The Abolition of Market Control and the Problem of Legitimacy (I)." *Kapitalistate*, no. 1 (1973): 109-16.

———. "Modes of Class Struggle and the Capitalist State." *Kapitalistate*, nos. 4-5 (1976): 186-220.

———. "Structural Problems of the Capitalist State." *German Political Studies* 1 (1974): 31-57.

———. "The Theory of the Capitalist State and the Problem of Policy Formation." In *Stress and Contradiction in Modern Capitalism: Public Policy and the Theory of the State*, edited by Leon Lindberg et al., pp. 125-44. Lexington, Mass.: Lexington Books, D. C. Heath & Co., 1975.

Olmsted, Frederick Law, Jr. "A City Planning Program." In *Proceedings of the Fifth National Conference on City Planning*, pp. 1-16. Cambridge, Mass.: University Press, 1913.

Olmsted, Frederick Law, Jr. "Introductory Address on City Planning." In *Proceedings of the Second National Conference on City Planning and the Problems of Congestion*, pp. 15-32. Cambridge, Mass.: University Press, 1910.

————. "Reply on Behalf of the City Planning Conference." In *Proceedings of the Third National Conference on City Planning*, pp. 3-13. Cambridge, Mass.: University Press, 1911.

————. "The Scope and Results of City Planning in Europe." In U.S. Congress. Senate. *City Planning* [Proceedings of the First National Conference on City Planning], pp. 63-70. 61st Cong., 2d sess., 1910. S. Doc. 422.

————. "The Town-Planning Movement in America." *Annals of the American Academy of Political and Social Science* 51 (January 1914): 172-81.

Olmsted, Frederick Law, Jr., and Kimball, Theodora, eds. *Frederick Law Olmsted, Landscape Architect, 1822–1903*. 2 vols. in one. New York: Benjamin Blom, 1970; orig. ed. 1922.

Olmsted, Frederick Law, Sr. "A Consideration of the Justifying Value of a Public Park." Paper prepared for the meeting of the American Social Science Association, 1880. Boston: Tolman & White, 1881.

————. *The Cotton Kingdom; A Traveller's Observations on Cotton and Slavery in the American Slave States*. 2 vols. New York: Mason Brothers, 1861.

————. *Notes on the Plan of Franklin Park* (1886). In *City Planning* 1 (April 1925): 32.

————. *The Park for Detroit*. Boston: Rand, Avery & Co. 1882.

————. "Passages in the Life of an Unpractical Man." *Landscape Architecture* 2 (July 1912): 149-62.

————. "Public Parks and the Enlargement of Towns." *Journal of Social Science*, no. 3 (1871): 1-36.

————. "The Spoils of the Park: With a Few Leaves from the Deep-Laden Notebooks of 'A Wholly Unpractical Man.'" (1882). Reprinted in *Landscape into Cityscape: Frederick Law Olmsted's Plans for a Greater New York City*, edited by Albert Fein, pp. 422-23. Cornell Reprints in Urban Studies. Ithaca, N.Y.: Cornell University Press, 1967.

————. *Walks and Talks of an American Farmer in England*. New York: G. P. Putnam & Co., 1852.

Olmsted, John C. "The Boston Park System." *Transactions of the American Society of Landscape Architects, 1899–1908* (1908): 42-55.

————. "The True Purpose of a Large Public Park." *Report of the Park and Outdoor Art Association* 1 (1897): 11-17.

Olmsted, Vaux & Co. "Observations on the Progress of Improvements in Street Plans, with Special Reference to the Parkway Proposed to Be Laid Out in Brooklyn" (1868). In *Civilizing American Cities: A Selection of Frederick Law Olmsted's Writings on City Landscapes*, edited by S. B. Sutton. Cambridge: MIT Press, 1971.

————. "Preliminary Report Upon the Proposed Suburban Village at Riverside, Near Chicago." Reprinted, with an Introduction by Theodora Kimball Hubbard, in *Landscape Architecture* 31 (July 1931): 257-77.

"Organized Labor and the World's Fair." *Inland Architect and News Record* 17 (June 1891): 54.

Osborn, F. J. "The Garden City Movement: Reaffirmation of the Validity of Ebenezer Howard's Idea." *Landscape Architecture* 36 (January 1946): 43-54.

Palmer, Alice Freeman. "Some Lasting Results of the World's Fair." *The Forum* 16 (December 1893): 517-23.

Penn, William C. "A Further Account of the Province of Pennsylvania." Letter to the Free Society of Traders, 1685. In *Narratives of Early Pennsylvania, West New Jersey and Delaware, 1630–1707*, edited by Albert C. Myers, pp. 259-78. New York: Charles Scribner's Sons, 1912.

Petersen, William. "The Ideological Origins of Britain's New Towns." *Journal of the American Institute of Planners* 34 (May 1968): 160-70.

Peterson, Jon A. "The City Beautiful Movement: Forgotten Origins and Lost Meanings." *Journal of Urban History* 2 (August 1976): 415-34.

————. "The Impact of Sanitary Reform upon American Urban Planning, 1840–1890." In *Introduction to Planning History in the United States*, edited by Donald A. Krueckeberg, pp. 13-39. New Brunswick: Rutgers/Center for Urban Policy Research, 1983.

Pickvance, Chris, ed. *Urban Sociology: Critical Essays*. London: Tavistock Press, 1976.

Pierce, Bessie Louise. *A History of Chicago*. Vol. 3, *The Rise of a Modern City, 1871–1893*. New York: Alfred A. Knopf, 1957.

Pope, Robert A. "What is Needed in City Planning?" In U.S. Congress. Senate. *City Planning* [Proceedings of the First National

Conference on City Planning], pp. 75-79. 61st Cong. 2d sess., 1910. S. Doc. 422.

Poulantzas, Nicos. *Political Power and Social Classes.* London: New Left Books and Sheed and Ward, 1973.

Powell, Sumner Chilton. *Puritan Village: The Formation of a New England Town.* Middletown, Conn.: Wesleyan University Press, 1963.

Pratt, Edwin E. "Garden Cities in Europe." *American City* 7 (1912): 503-10.

Preteceille, Edmond. "Urban Planning: The Contradictions of Capitalist Urbanization." *Antipode* 8 (March 1976): 69-76.

Preteceille, Edmond et al. *Equipment Collectif, Structures Urbaines et Consommation Sociale.* Paris: Centre de Sociologie Urbaine, 1976.

Purdy, Lawson. "Districting and Zoning of Cities." In *Proceedings of the Ninth National Conference on City Planning,* pp. 170-82. New York: N.p., 1917.

Rabinovitz, Francine. *City Politics and Planning.* New York: Atherton Press, 1969.

Ravenel, Mazyck P. "The American Public Health Association: Past, Present, Future." In *A Half Century of Public Health,* edited by Mazyck Ravenal. New York: American Public Health Association, 1921.

Report of the Board of Park and Boulevard Commissioners of Kansas City, Missouri, 1893. In *The Urban Community: Housing and Planning in the Progressive Era,* edited by Roy Lubove. Englewood Cliffs: Prentice-Hall, 1967.

Report of the Committee on Municipal Improvements to the American Institute of Architects. In *Proceedings of the Thirty-Eighth Annual Convention of the AIA.* Washington: Gibson Bros., 1905.

Reps, John. *The Making of Urban America.* Princeton: Princeton University Press, 1965.

Riis, Jacob. *How the Other Half Lives.* New York: Charles Scribner's Sons, 1890.

Roach, Hannah B. "The Planting of Philadelphia: A Seventeenth-Century Real Estate Development." Part I. *The Pennsylvania Magazine of History and Biography* 92 (January 1968): 3-47.

Robinson, Charles M. "Ambitions of Three Cities." *Architectural Record* 21 (May 1907): 337-46.

———. "The City Plan Exhibition." *The Survey* 22 (October 1909): 313-19.

————. "Improvement in City Life III: Aesthetic Progress." *Atlantic Monthly* 83 (June 1899): 771-78.

————. *The Improvement of Towns and Cities or the Practical Bases of Civic Aesthetics*. New York: G. P. Putnam's Sons, Knickerbocker Press, 1901.

————. *Modern Civic Art or the City Made Beautiful*. New York: G. P. Putnam's Sons, Knickerbocker Press, 1903.

————. "New Dream for Cities." *Architectural Record* 17 (May 1905): 410-21.

————. "The Street Plan of a City's Business District." *Architectural Record* 13 (March 1903): 233-47.

Roper, Laura. *FLO: A Biography of Frederick Law Olmsted*. Baltimore: Johns Hopkins University Press, 1973.

Roweis, Shoukry. "Urban Planning in Early and Late Capitalist Societies." In *Urbanization and Urban Planning in Capitalist Society*, edited by Michael Dear and Allen Scott, pp. 159-78. London: Metheun, 1981.

Scheffauer, Herman. "The City Beautiful—San Francisco Rebuilt—I." *Architectural Review* 20 (July 1906): 3-8.

Schuyler, Montgomery. "The Art of City-Making." *Architectural Record* 12 (May 1902): 1-26.

————. "Last Words About the World's Fair." *Architectural Record* 3 (January-March 1894): 291-301.

Scofield, Edna. "The Origin of Settlement Patterns in Rural New England." *Geographical Review* 28 (October 1938): 652-63.

Scott, Mel. *American City Planning Since 1890*. Berkeley: University of California Press, 1969.

"The Shaping of Towns." *American Architect and Building News* 2 (23 June 1877): 195.

Shefter, Martin. "The Emergence of the Political Machine: An Alternative View." In *Theoretical Perspectives on Urban Politics*, edited by Willis D. Hawley et al., pp. 14-44. Englewood Cliffs: Prentice-Hall, 1976.

Shurcliff, Sidney N. "Progress in Park Design During the Last Fifty Years." *Parks and Recreation* 31 (November 1948): 621-27.

Shurtleff, Arthur A. "The Practice of Replanning: Suggestions from Boston." *Charities and the Commons* 19 (February 1908): 1529-33.

Shurtleff, Flavel. "City and Regional Planning Since 1876." *American Architect* 129 (January 1926): 57-60.

————. "The Progress of City Planning." In *Proceedings of the Fifth National Conference on City Planning*, pp. 17-23. Cambridge, Mass.: University Press, 1913.

Shurtleff, Flavel. "Six Years of City Planning in the United States." In *Proceedings of the Seventh National Conference on City Planning*, pp. 33-41. Cambridge, Mass.: University Press, 1915.

Simutis, Leonard J. "Frederick Law Olmsted, Sr.: A Reassessment." *Journal of the American Institute of Planners* 38 (September 1972): 276-84.

Sternberg, George M. "Housing Conditions in Washington." In U.S. Congress. Senate. *City Planning*, pp. 62-63. 61st Cong., 2d sess., 1910. S. Doc. 422.

Stevenson, Frederick R., and Feiss, Carl. "Charleston and Savannah." *Journal of the Society of Architectural Historians* 10 (December 1951): 3-9.

Sullivan, Louis H. *The Autobiography of an Idea*. New York: Dover Publications, 1956.

Sutcliffe, Anthony. *Toward the Planned City: Germany, Britain, the United States and France, 1780–1914*. New York: St. Martin's Press, 1981.

Sutcliffe, Anthony, ed. *The Rise of Modern Urban Planning, 1800–1914*. New York: St. Martin's Press, 1980.

Taylor, Frederick Winslow. *The Principles of Scientific Management*. New York: Harper & Brothers, 1911.

Taylor, Graham R. "The New Chicago." *Charities and the Commons* 19 (February 1908): 1551-57.

———. *Satellite Cities: A Study of Industrial Suburbs*. National Municipal League Series. New York: D. Appleton & Co., 1915.

"The Tenement House Problem," Report of the New York State Tenement House Commission of 1900. In *The Tenement House Problem*, edited by Robert W. de Forest and Lawrence Veiller, vol. 1, p. 7. New York: Macmillan Co., 1903.

Thirty-First and Thirty-Second Annual Reports of the City Park Association of Philadelphia. 1 vol. Philadelphia: N.p., 1919–1920.

Thompson, E. P. "The Poverty of Theory." In E. P. Thompson, *The Poverty of Theory and Other Essays*. New York: Monthly Review Press, 1978.

Toll, Seymour I. *Zoned America*. New York: Grossman, 1969.

Trueblood, Lyra Dale. "The Bournville Village Experiment: A Twentieth Century Attempt at Housing the Workers." *Arena* 34 (November 1905): 449-58.

Tselos, Dimitri. "The Chicago Fair and the Myth of the 'Lost Cause.'" *Journal of the Society of Architectural Historians* 26 (December 1967): 259-68.

Tunnard, Christopher. "A City Called Beautiful." *Journal of the Society of Architectural Historians* 9 (March–May 1950): 31-35.

Ulmer, W. L. "Zoning from the Viewpoint of the Lender on Real Estate Mortgages." *Proceedings of the Twelfth National Conference on City Planning*, pp. 133-38. N.p.: N.p., 1917.

U.S. Congress. Senate. Committee on the District of Columbia. "Statement of Mr. Benjamin Clarke Marsh." *City Planning*, pp. 5-19. 61st Cong., 2d sess., 1910. S. Doc. 422.

U.S. Department of Commerce. *A Standard City Planning Enabling Act*. Washington, D.C.: GPO, 1928.

U.S. Department of Commerce. *A Standard State Zoning Enabling Act*. Rev. ed. Washington, D.C.: GPO, 1926.

U.S. Department of Commerce. Bureau of the Census. *Historical Statistics of the United States, 1789–1945*. Washington, D.C.: GPO, 1949.

U.S. National Resources Committee. Committee on Urbanism. *Our Cities: Their Role in the National Economy*. Washington, D.C.: GPO, 1937.

Valentine, David T. *History of the City of New York*. New York: G. P. Putnam & Co., 1853.

Veiller, Lawrence. "Are Great Cities a Menace? The Garden City as a Way Out." *Architectural Record* 51 (1922): 175-84.

————. "Buildings in Relation to Street and Site." In *Proceedings of the Third National Conference on City Planning*, pp. 80-96. Cambridge, Mass.: University Press, 1911.

————. "The Housing Problem in American Cities." *Annals of the American Academy of Political and Social Science* 25 (March 1905): 248-72.

————. *Housing Reform*. New York: Charities Publication Committee/Russell Sage Foundation, 1911.

————. *A Model Housing Law*. Rev. ed. New York: Russell Sage Foundation, 1920.

————. "Slumless America." In *Proceedings of the Twelfth National Conference on City Planning*, pp. 154-61. N.p. 1920.

————. "The Speculative Building of Tenement Houses." In *The Tenement House Problem*, edited by Robert W. de Forest and Lawrence Veiller, vol. 1, pp. 367-82. New York: Macmillan Co., 1903.

————. "Tenement House Reform in New York City, 1834–1900." In *The Tenement House Problem*, edited by Robert W. de Forest and Lawrence Veiller, vol. 1, pp. 69-118. New York: Macmillan Co., 1903.

Vinton, Warren J. "Has Physical Planning Been Over-Emphasized?" In *Proceedings of the Twenty-Eighth National Conference on City Planning*, pp. 94-101. Chicago: American Society of Planning Officials, 1936.

Vogel, David. "Why Businessmen Distrust Their State: The Political Consciousness of American Corporate Executives." *British Journal of Political Science* 8 (July 1978): 45-78.

Wacker, Charles H. "Gaining Public Support for a City Planning Movement." In *Proceedings of the Fifth National Conference on City Planning*, pp. 222-46. Cambridge, Mass.: University Press, 1913.

Wade, Richard C. *Urban Frontier: The Rise of Western Cities, 1780–1830.* Chicago: University of Chicago Press, 1964.

Wahl, Christian. "The Duties of Park Commissioners." *Report of the American Park and Outdoor Art Association* 2 (1898): 132-34.

Walker, C. Howard. "The Grouping of Public Buildings in a Great City." *American Architect* 71 (January 12, 1901): 11-13.

Walker, Richard A. "The Suburban Solution: Urban Geography and Urban Reform in the Capitalist Development of the United States." Ph.D. diss., Department of Geography and Environmental Engineering, Johns Hopkins University, 1976.

Walker, Robert A. *The Planning Function in Urban Government.* 2d ed., enl. Chicago: University of Chicago Press, 1950.

Ward, David. *Cities and Immigrants: A Geography of Change in Nineteenth-Century America.* New York: Oxford University Press, 1971.

Ward, John William. "The Politics of Design." In *Who Designs America?* edited by Laurence B. Holland, pp. 51-85. Garden City, N.Y.: Doubleday & Co., Anchor Books, 1964.

Warner, Sam Bass, Jr. *The Private City: Philadelphia in Three Periods of Growth.* Philadelphia: University of Pennsylvania Press, 1968.

————. *The Urban Wilderness: A History of the American City.* New York: Harper & Row, 1972.

"Washington: The Development and Improvement of the Park System, I & II." *American Architect* 75 (February 1902 and March 1902): 35-36 and 75-77.

Watson, Frank D. *The Charity Organization Movement in the United States.* New York: Macmillan Co., 1922.

Wheeler, Candace. "A Dream City." *Harper's* 86 (May 1893): 830-46.

Wheelwright, Robert. "The Appointment and Powers of Park Commissioners." *Landscape Architecture* 3 (October 1912): 25-29.

Whitten, Robert H. "The Constitution and Powers of a City Planning Authority." In *Proceedings of the Seventh National Conference on City Planning*, pp. 134-43. Cambridge, Mass.: University Press, 1915.

————. "Zoning and Living Conditions." In *Proceedings of the Thirteenth National Conference on City Planning*, pp. 22-30. Pittsburgh: N.p., 1921.

Williams, Raymond. *The Country and the City*. London: Chatto & Windus, 1973.

Wilson, William H. *The City Beautiful Movement in Kansas City*. University of Missouri Studies, vol. 40. Columbia: University of Missouri Press, 1964.

————. "J. Horace McFarland and the City Beautiful Movement." *Journal of Urban History* 7 (May 1981): 315-34.

Wirth, Louis. "Urbanism as a Way of Life." *American Journal of Sociology* 44 (July 1938): 1-24.

Wollner, Edward. "Daniel Burnham and the Tradition of the City Builder in Chicago: Technique, Ambition and City Planning." Ph.D. diss., Department of Public Administration, New York University, 1977.

Wood, Edith E. *The Housing of the Unskilled Wage Earner*. New York: Macmillan Co., 1919.

Wright, Erik Olin. *Class, Crisis and the State*. London: New Left Books, 1978.

X, Malcolm, and Haley, Alex. *The Autobiography of Malcolm X*. New York: Grove Press, 1966.

LIBRARY OF CONGRESS CATALOGING-IN-PUBLICATION DATA

Foglesong, Richard E., 1948–
Planning the capitalist city.

Bibliography: p.   Includes index.
1. City planning—United States—History. I. Title.
HT167.F64 1986   307.1′2′0973   85–43278
ISBN 0–691–07705–3 (alk. paper)